LONG WALK TO VALHALLA™

ADAM SMITH   MATTHEW FOX

Published by
ARCHAIA™

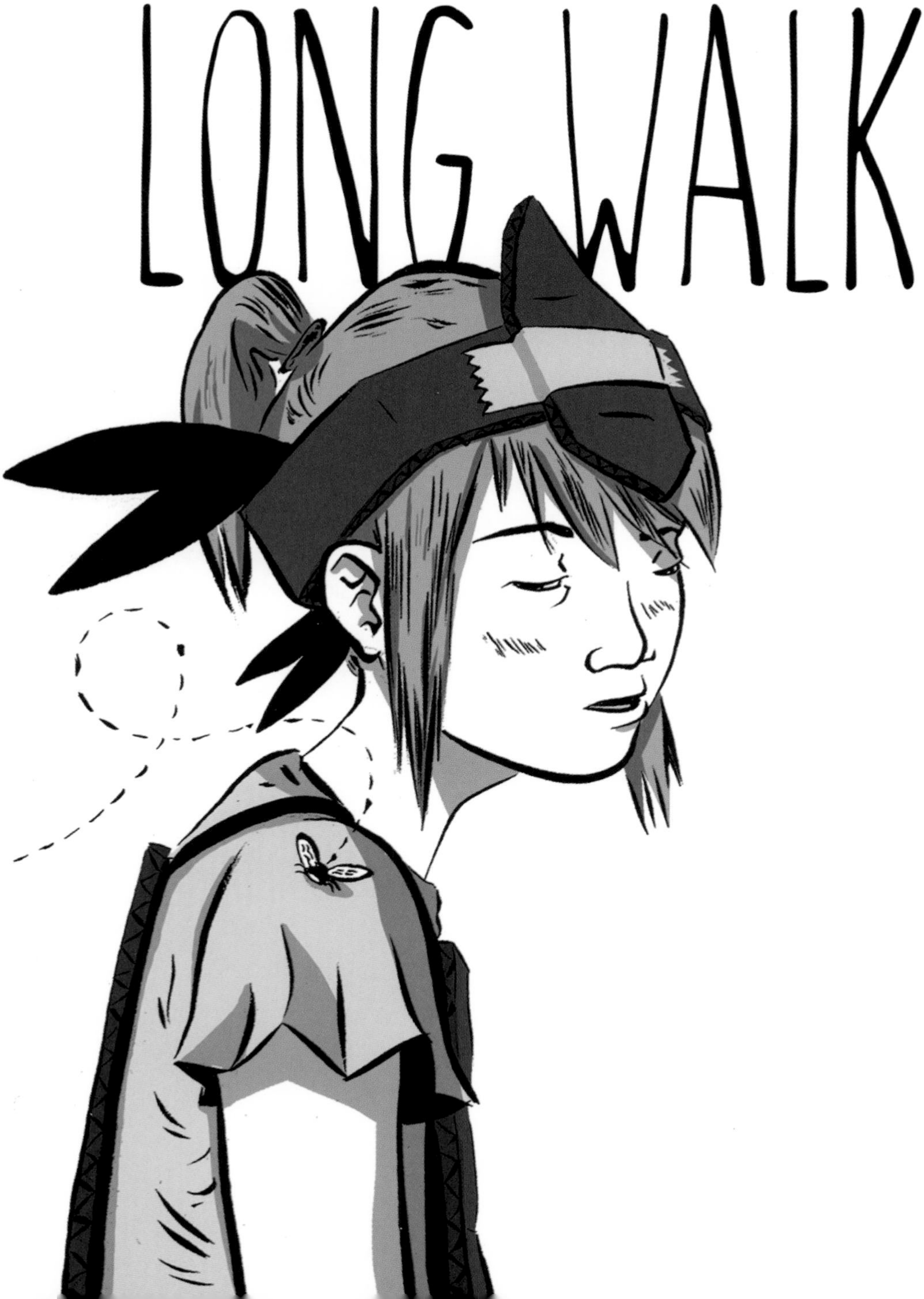
LONG WALK

TO VALHALLA™

AN ORIGINAL GRAPHIC NOVEL

ROSS RICHIE .... CEO & Founder
MARK SMYLIE .... Founder of Archaia
MATT GAGNON .... Editor-in-Chief
FILIP SABLIK .... President of Publishing & Marketing
STEPHEN CHRISTY .... President of Development
LANCE KREITER .... VP of Licensing & Merchandising
PHIL BARBARO .... VP of Finance
BRYCE CARLSON .... Managing Editor
MEL CAYLO .... Marketing Manager
SCOTT NEWMAN .... Production Design Manager
IRENE BRADISH .... Operations Manager
CHRISTINE DINH .... Brand Communications Manager
DAFNA PLEBAN .... Editor
SHANNON WATTERS .... Editor
ERIC HARBURN .... Editor
REBECCA TAYLOR .... Editor
IAN BRILL .... Editor
WHITNEY LEOPARD .... Associate Editor
JASMINE AMIRI .... Associate Editor
CHRIS ROSA .... Assistant Editor
ALEX GALER .... Assistant Editor
CAMERON CHITTOCK .... Assistant Editor
MARY GUMPORT .... Assistant Editor
KELSEY DIETERICH .... Production Designer
JILLIAN CRAB .... Production Designer
KARA LEOPARD .... Production Designer
DEVIN FUNCHES .... E-Commerce & Inventory Coordinator
AARON FERRARA .... Operations Coordinator
JOSÉ MEZA .... Sales Assistant
MICHELLE ANKLEY .... Sales Assistant
ELIZABETH LOUGHRIDGE .... Accounting Assistant
STEPHANIE HOCUTT .... PR Assistant

ARCHAIA™

LONG WALK TO VALHALLA, July 2015. Published by Archaia, a division of Boom Entertainment, Inc. Long Walk to Valhalla is ™ and © 2015 Adam Smith & Matthew Fox. All Rights Reserved. Archaia™ and the Archaia logo are trademarks of Boom Entertainment, Inc., registered in various countries and categories. All characters, events, and institutions depicted herein are fictional. Any similarity between any of the names, characters, persons, events, and/or institutions in this publication to actual names, characters, and persons, whether living or dead, events, and/or institutions is unintended and purely coincidental.

BOOM! Studios, 5670 Wilshire Boulevard, Suite 450, Los Angeles, CA 90036-5679.
Printed in China. First Printing. ISBN: 978-1-60886-692-2, eISBN: 978-1-61398-363-8

CREATED BY
ADAM SMITH & MATTHEW FOX

WRITTEN BY
ADAM SMITH

ILLUSTRATED AND LETTERED BY
MATTHEW FOX
WITH COLOR ASSISTS BY FRED STRESING

DESIGNED BY
KELSEY DIETERICH

EDITED BY
REBECCA TAYLOR

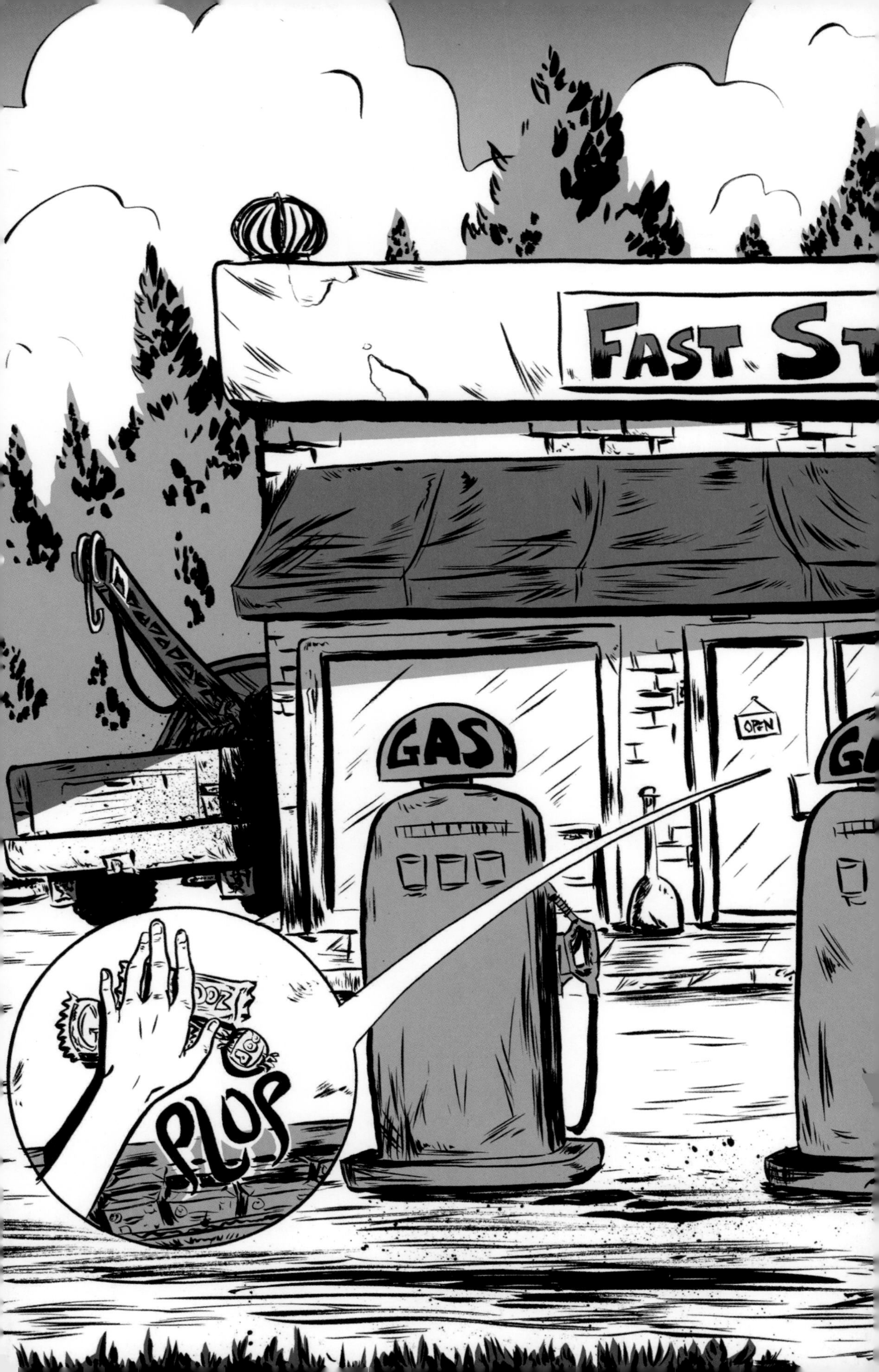
FAST
GAS
OPEN
PLUP

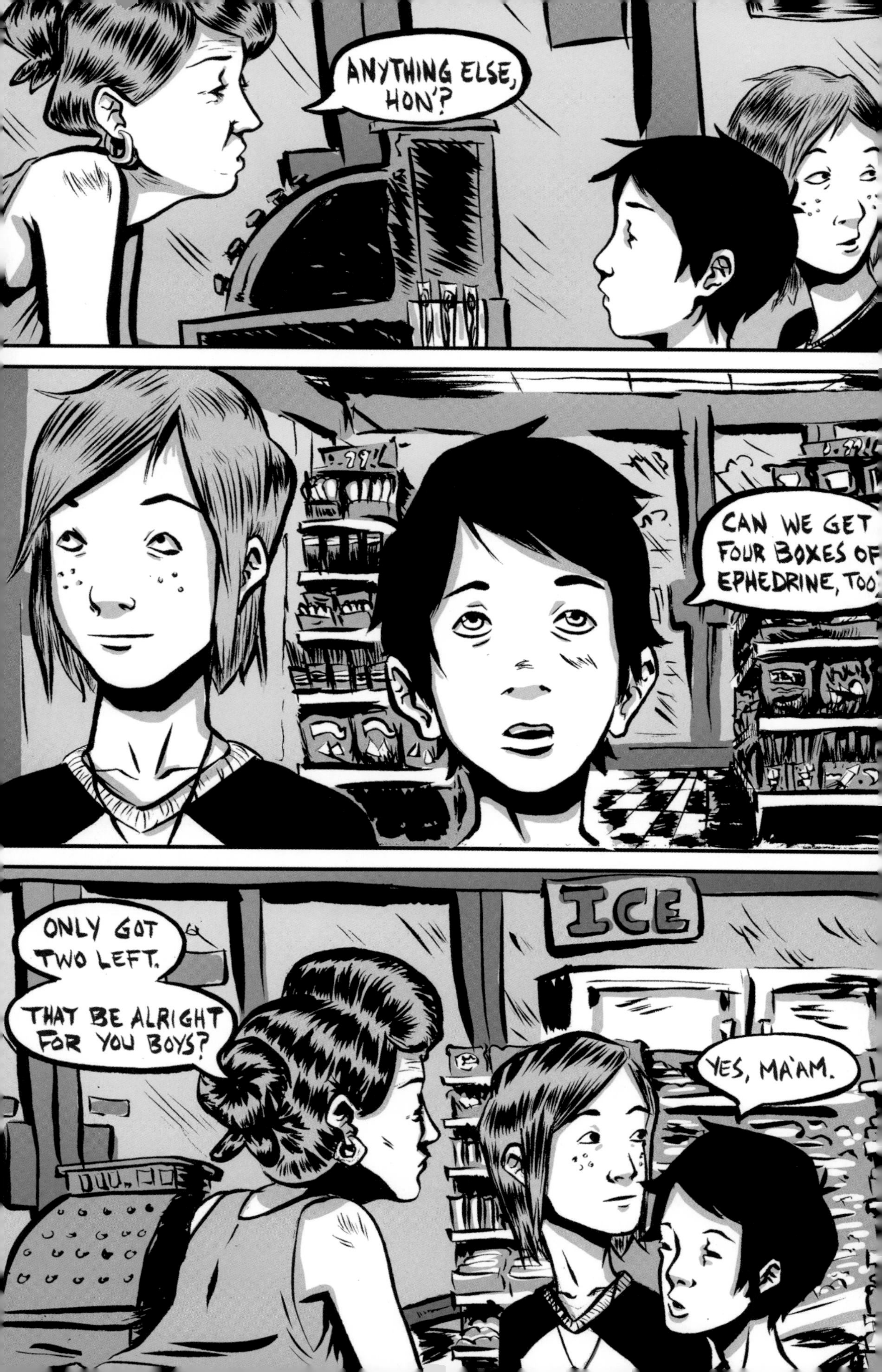
ANYTHING ELSE, HON'?
CAN WE GET FOUR BOXES OF EPHEDRINE, TOO
ICE
ONLY GOT TWO LEFT.
THAT BE ALRIGHT FOR YOU BOYS?
YES, MA'AM.

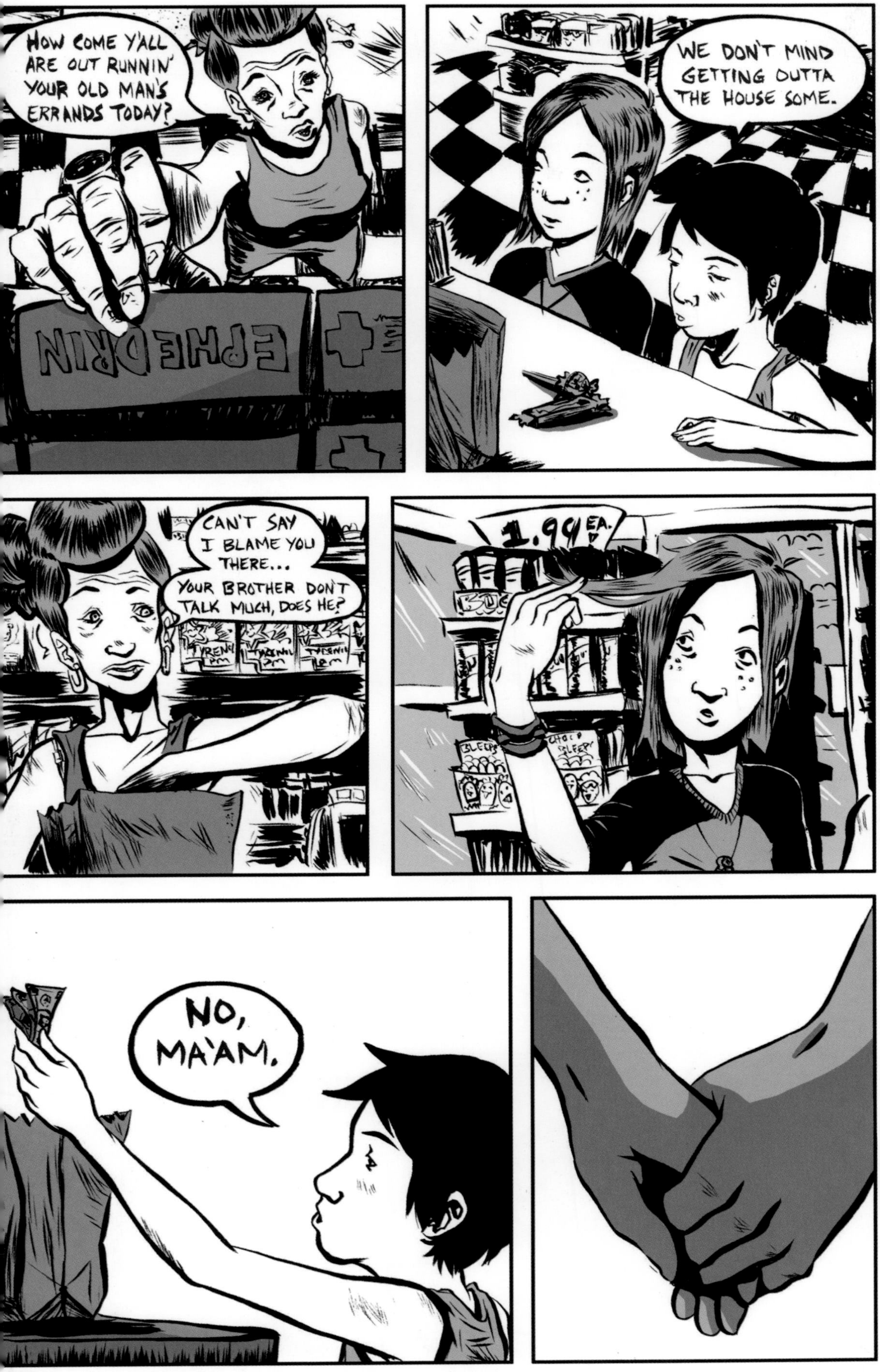
HOW COME Y'ALL ARE OUT RUNNIN' YOUR OLD MAN'S ERRANDS TODAY?
WE DON'T MIND GETTING OUTTA THE HOUSE SOME.
CAN'T SAY I BLAME YOU THERE...
YOUR BROTHER DON'T TALK MUCH, DOES HE?
1.99 EA.
NO, MA'AM.

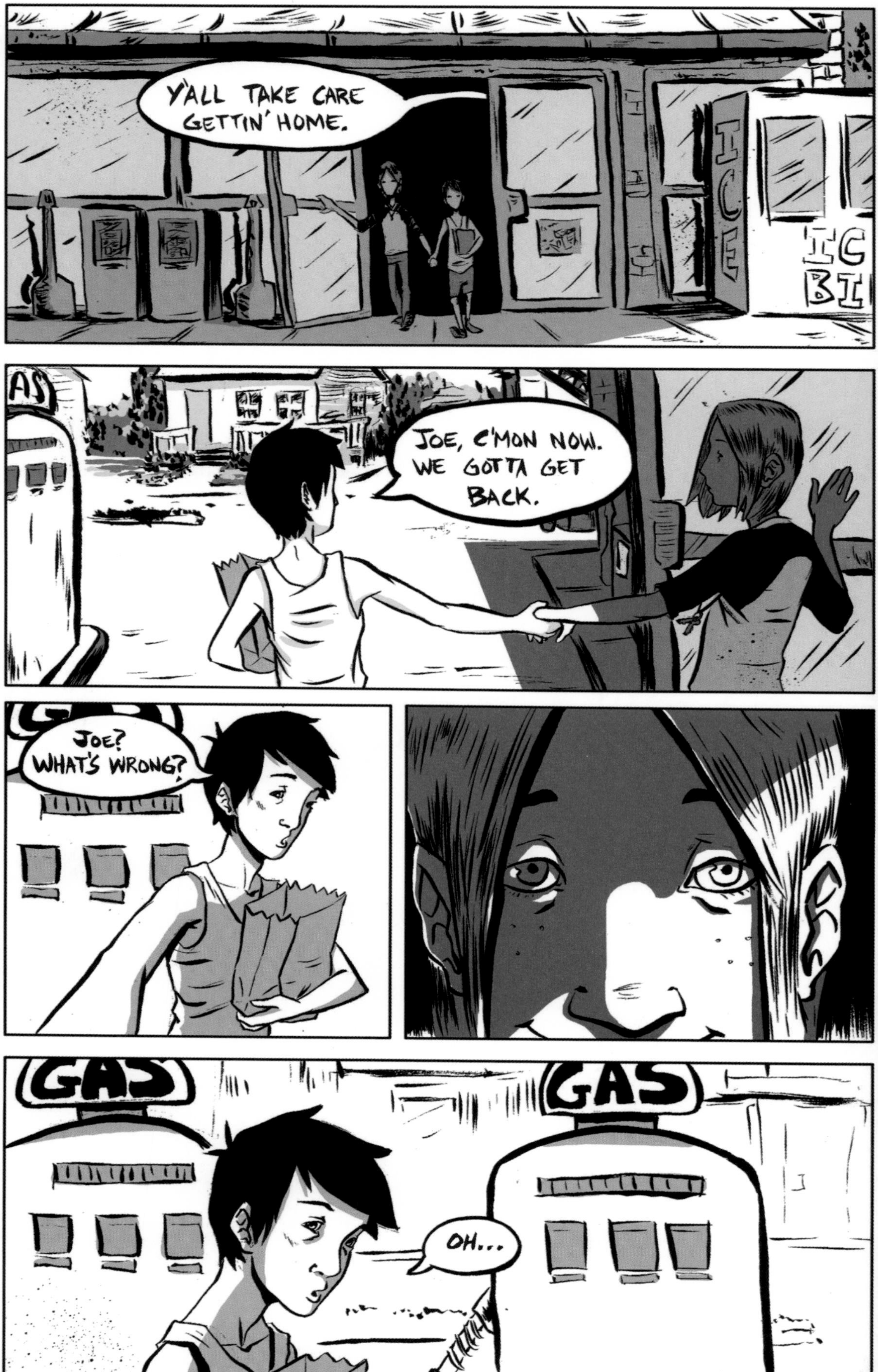
Y'ALL TAKE CARE GETTIN' HOME.
ICE
IC BI
AS
JOE, C'MON NOW. WE GOTTA GET BACK.
JOE? WHAT'S WRONG?
GAS
GAS
OH...

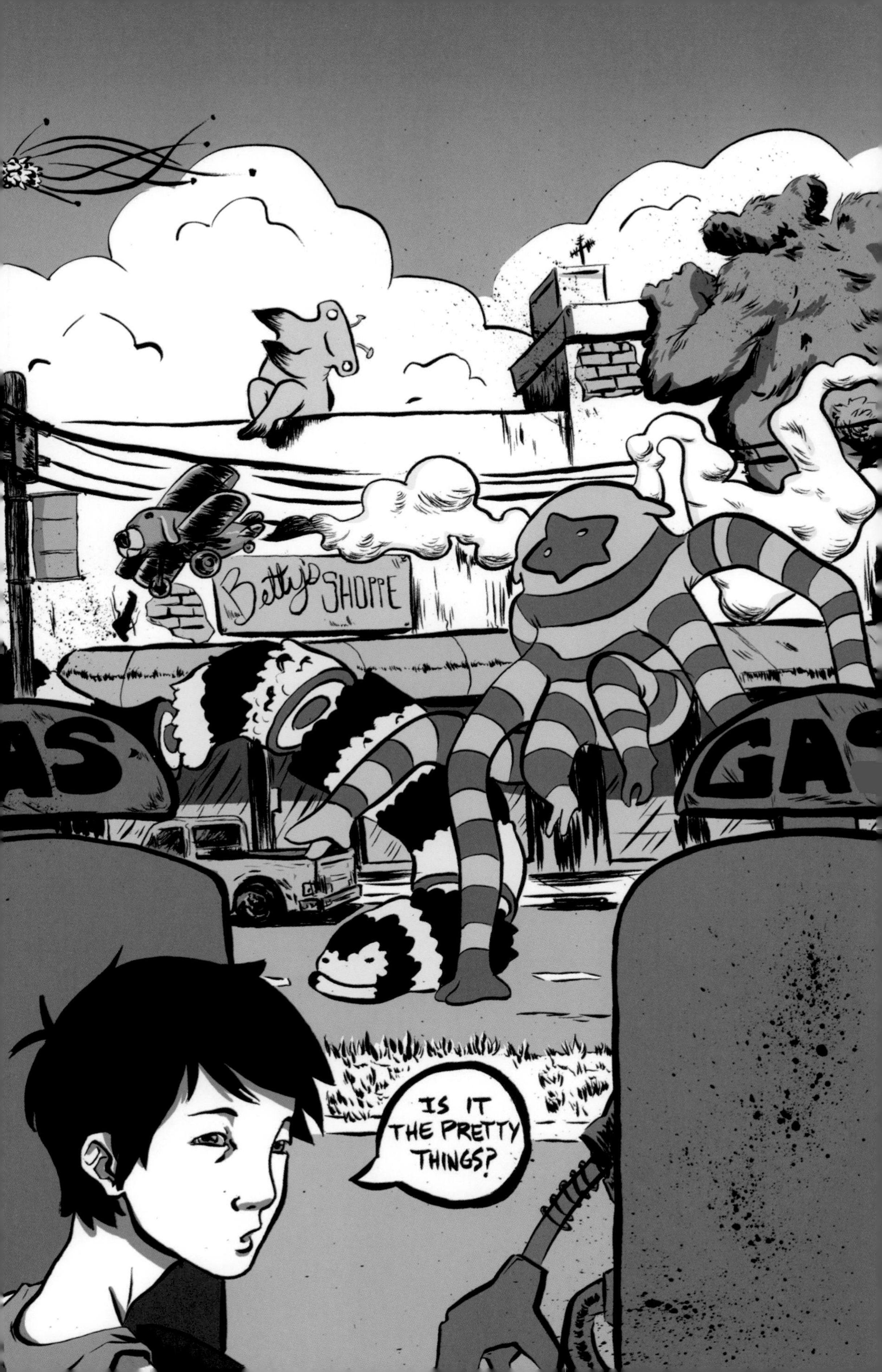
Betty's SHOPPE
GAS
GAS
IS IT THE PRETTY THINGS?

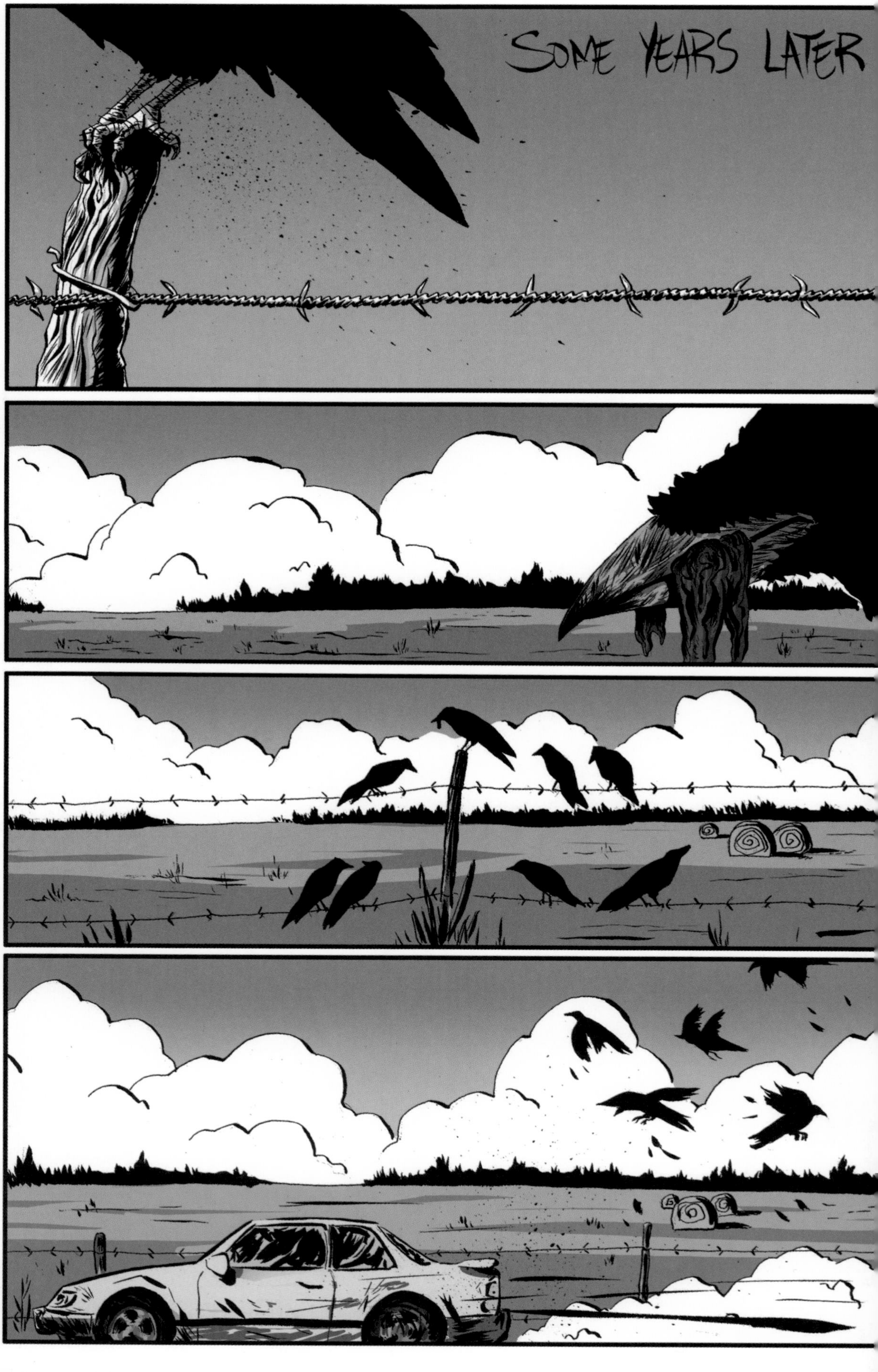
SOME YEARS LATER

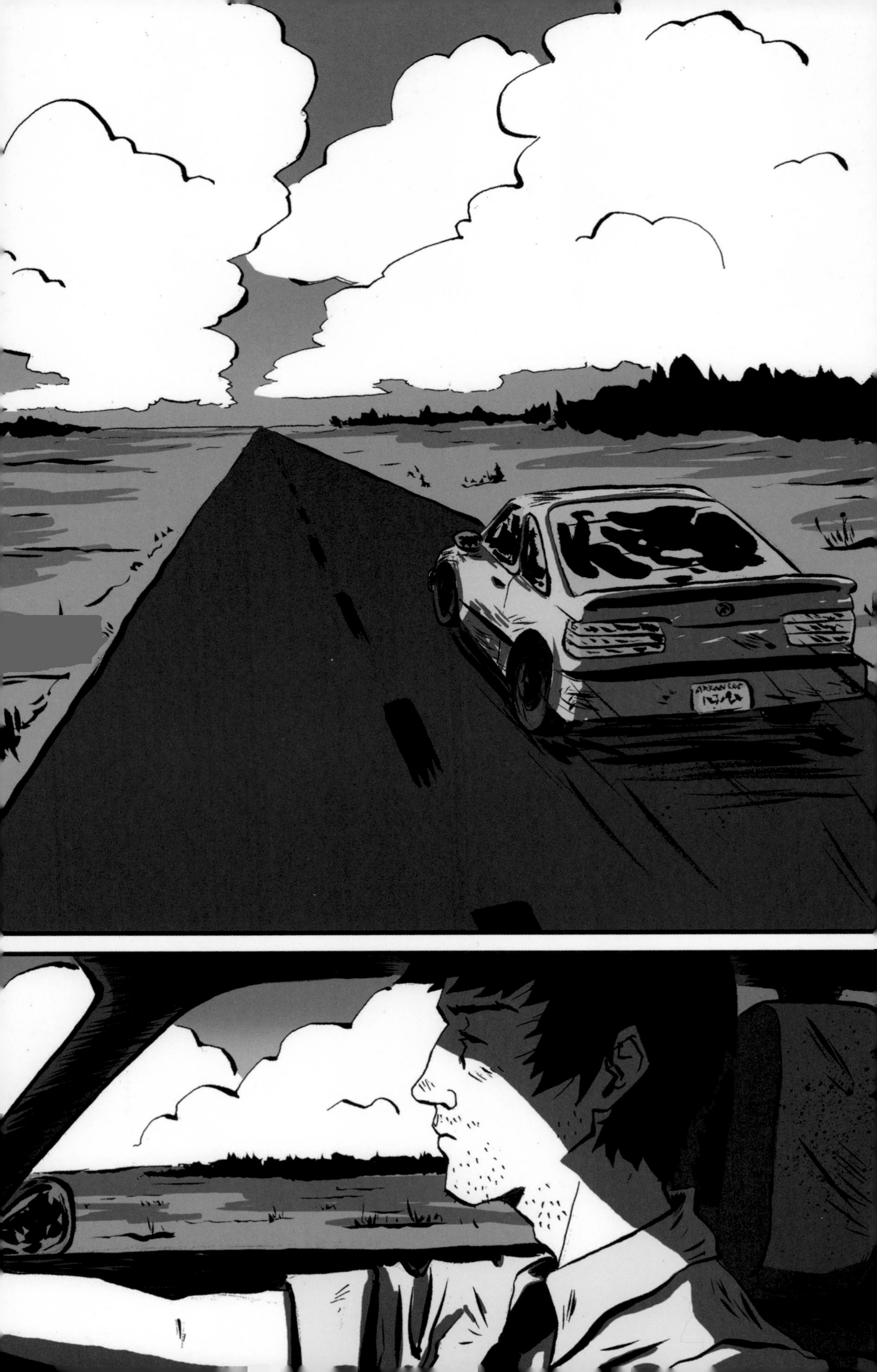

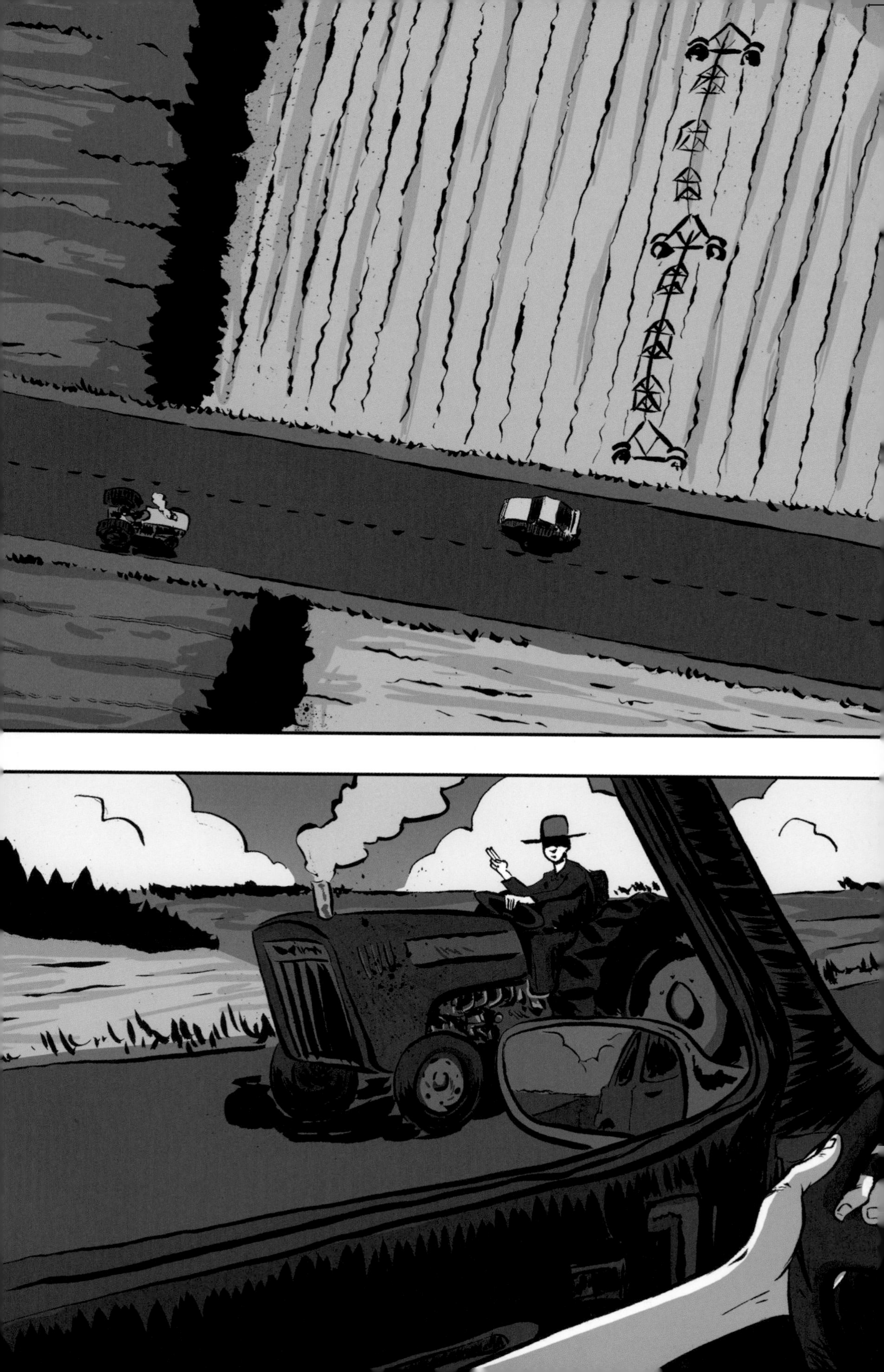

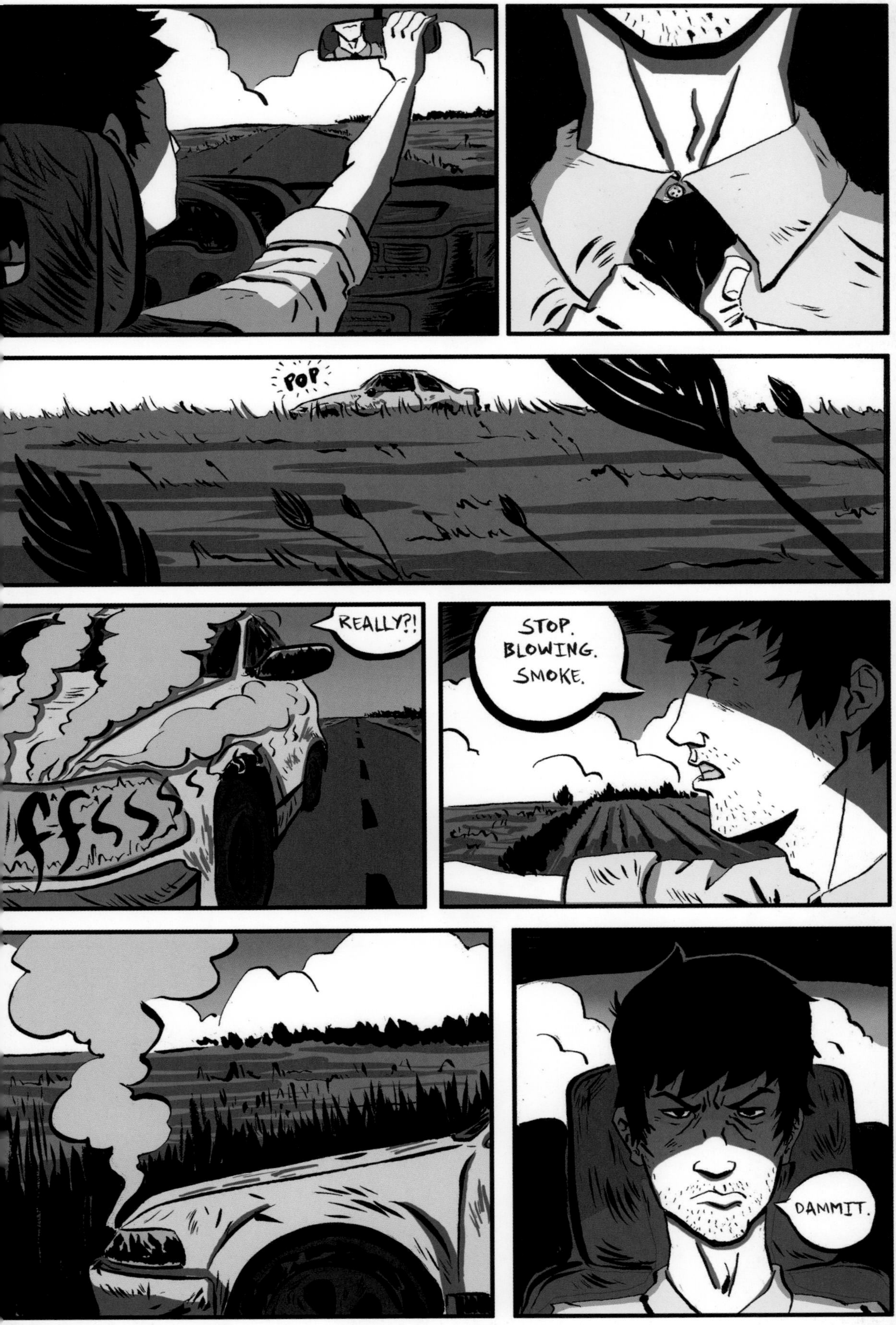
POP
REALLY?!
ffsss
STOP. BLOWING. SMOKE.
DAMMIT.

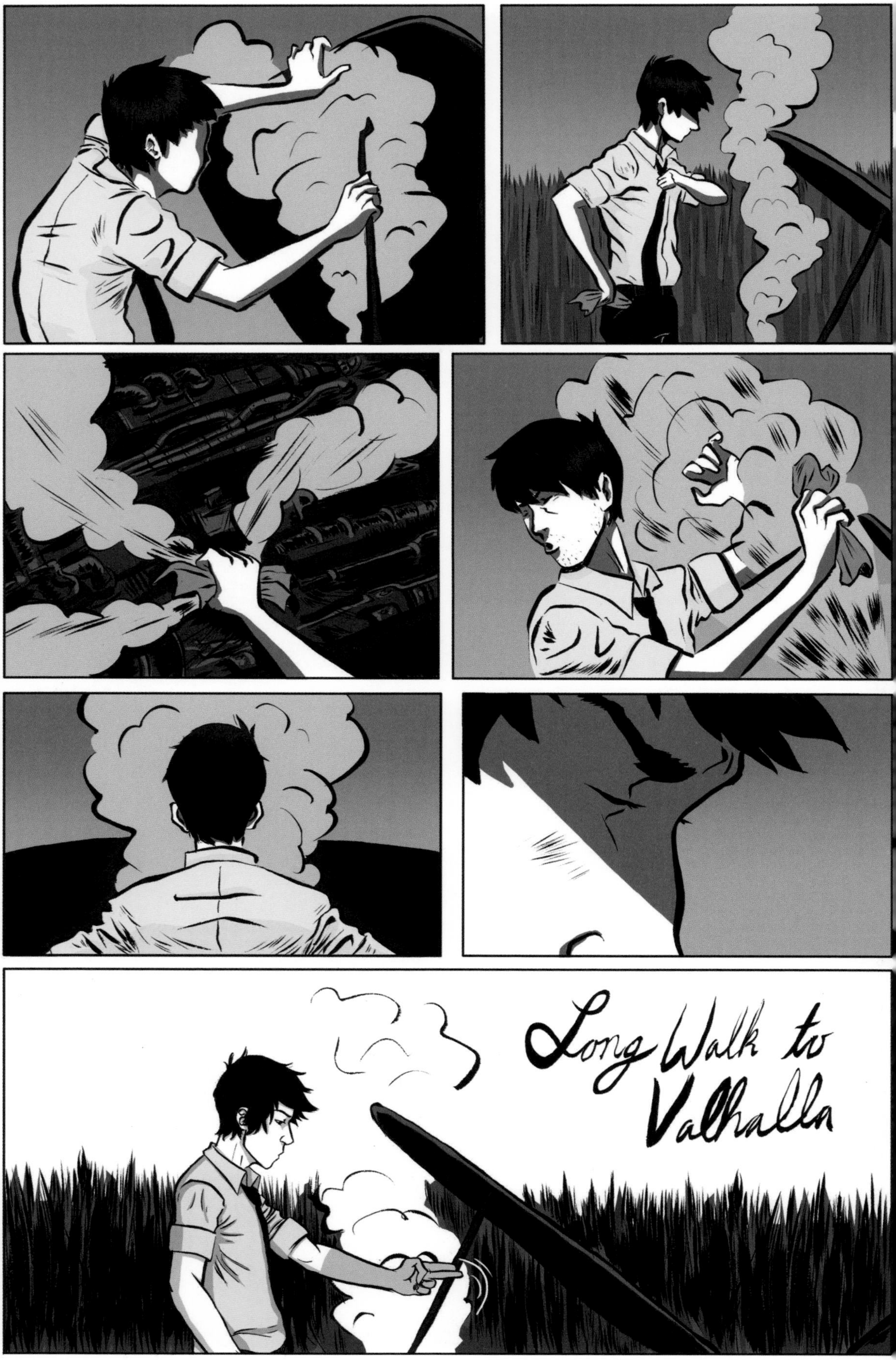
Long Walk to Valhalla

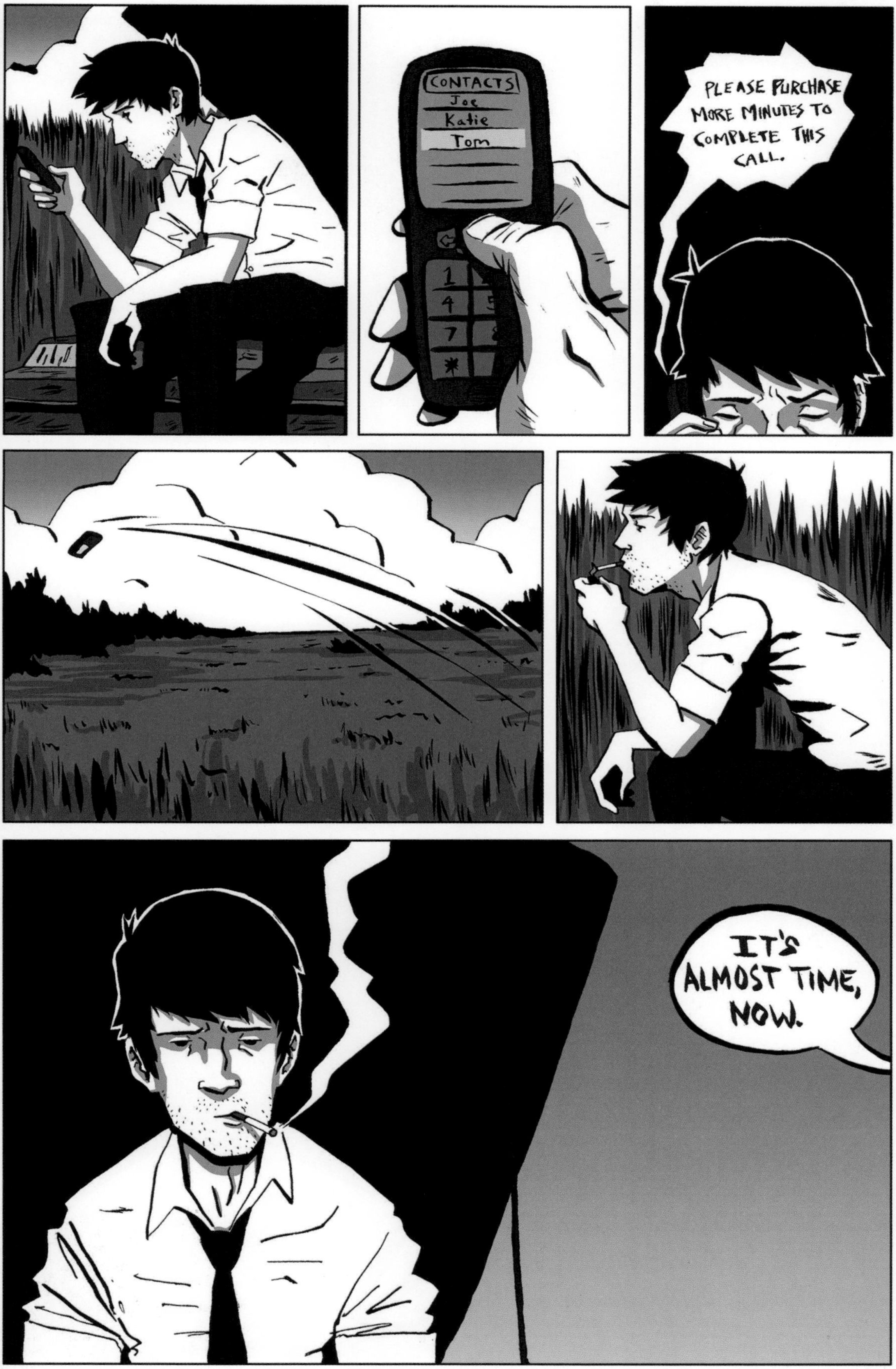
CONTACTS
Joe
Katie
Tom
PLEASE PURCHASE MORE MINUTES TO COMPLETE THIS CALL.
IT'S ALMOST TIME, NOW.

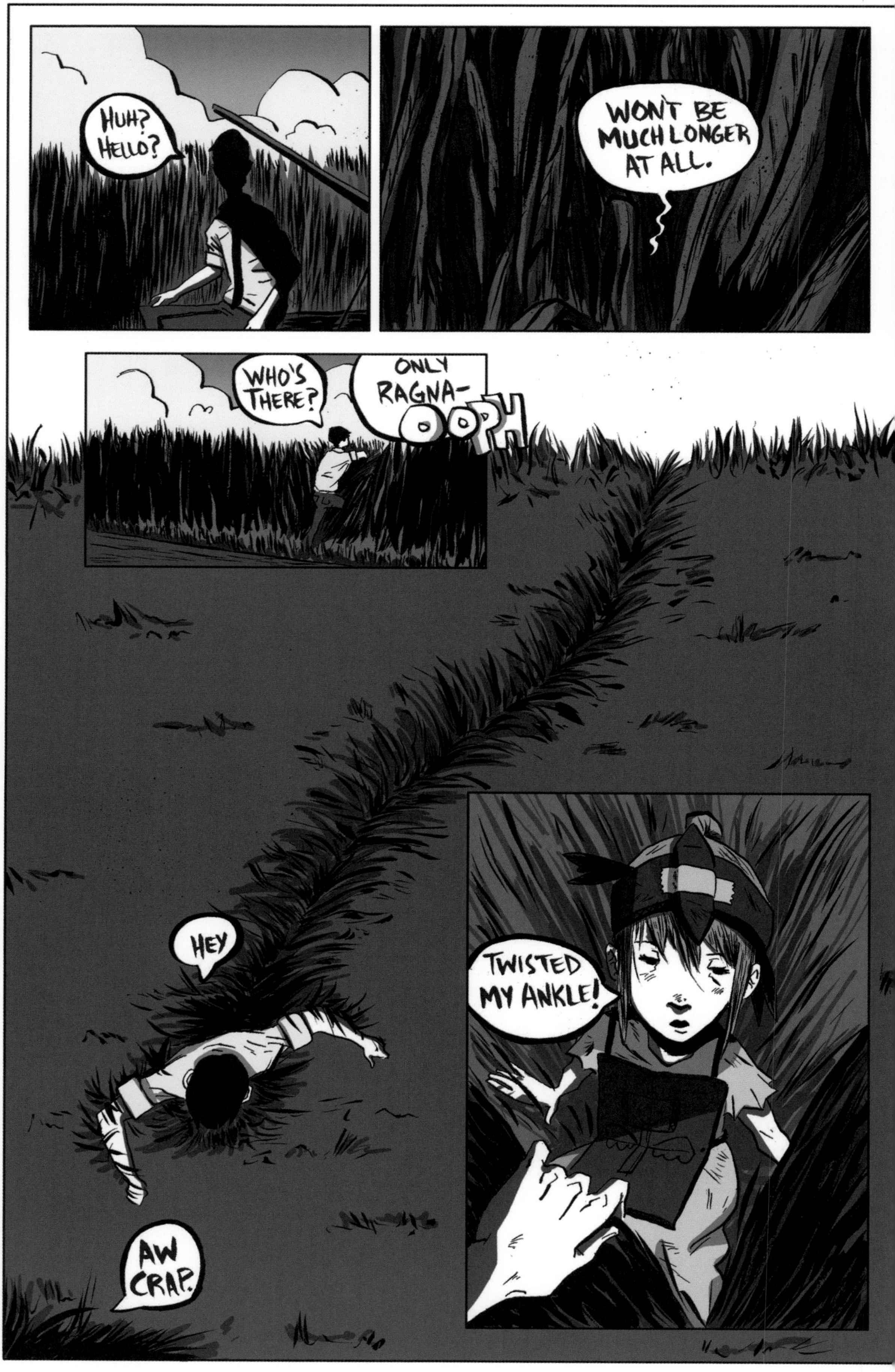
HUH? HELLO?
WON'T BE MUCH LONGER AT ALL.
WHO'S THERE?
ONLY RAGNA-
OOOPH
HEY
AW CRAP.
TWISTED MY ANKLE!

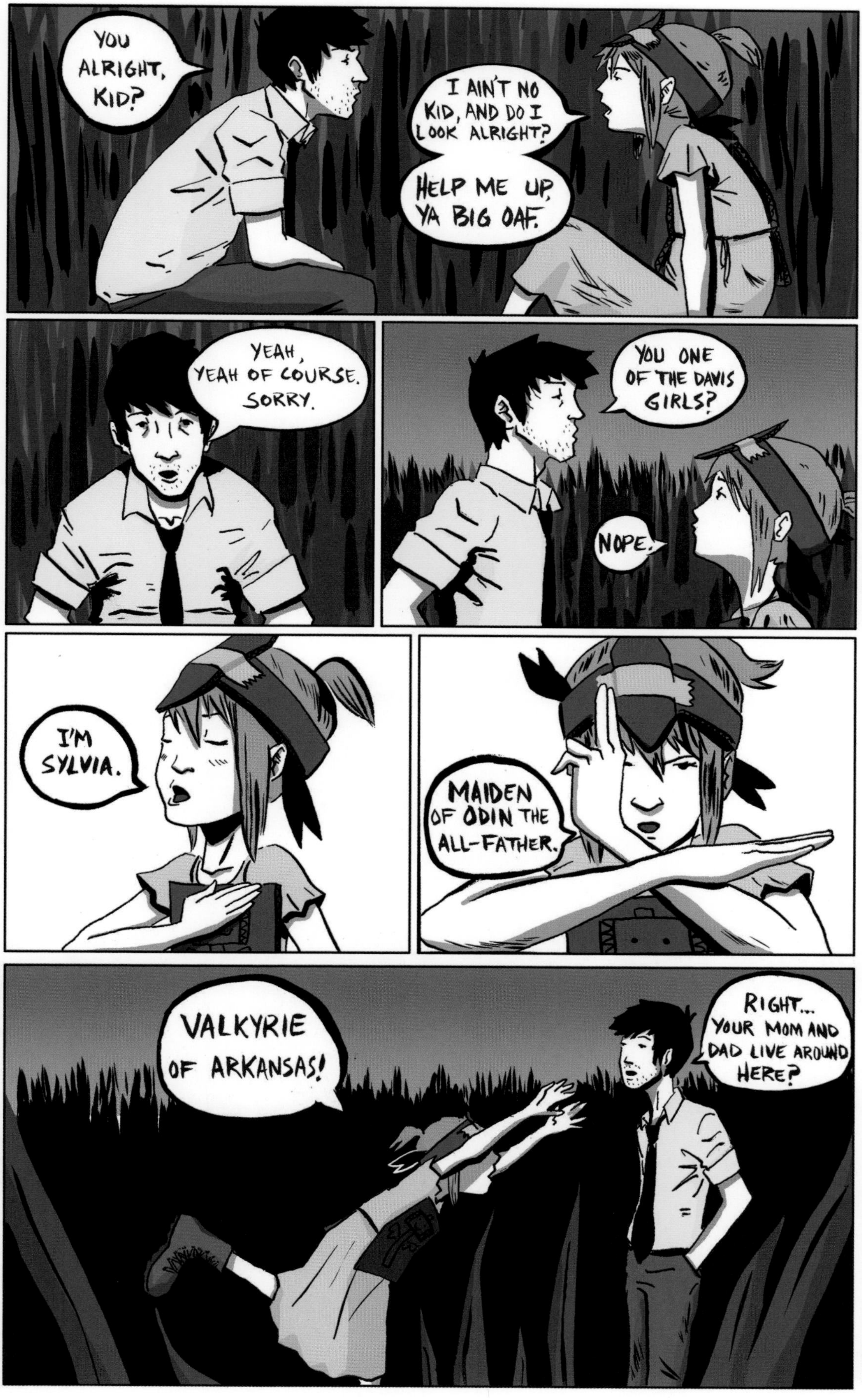
YOU ALRIGHT, KID?
I AIN'T NO KID, AND DO I LOOK ALRIGHT?
HELP ME UP, YA BIG OAF.
YEAH, YEAH OF COURSE. SORRY.
YOU ONE OF THE DAVIS GIRLS?
NOPE.
I'M SYLVIA.
MAIDEN OF ODIN THE ALL-FATHER.
VALKYRIE OF ARKANSAS!
RIGHT... YOUR MOM AND DAD LIVE AROUND HERE?

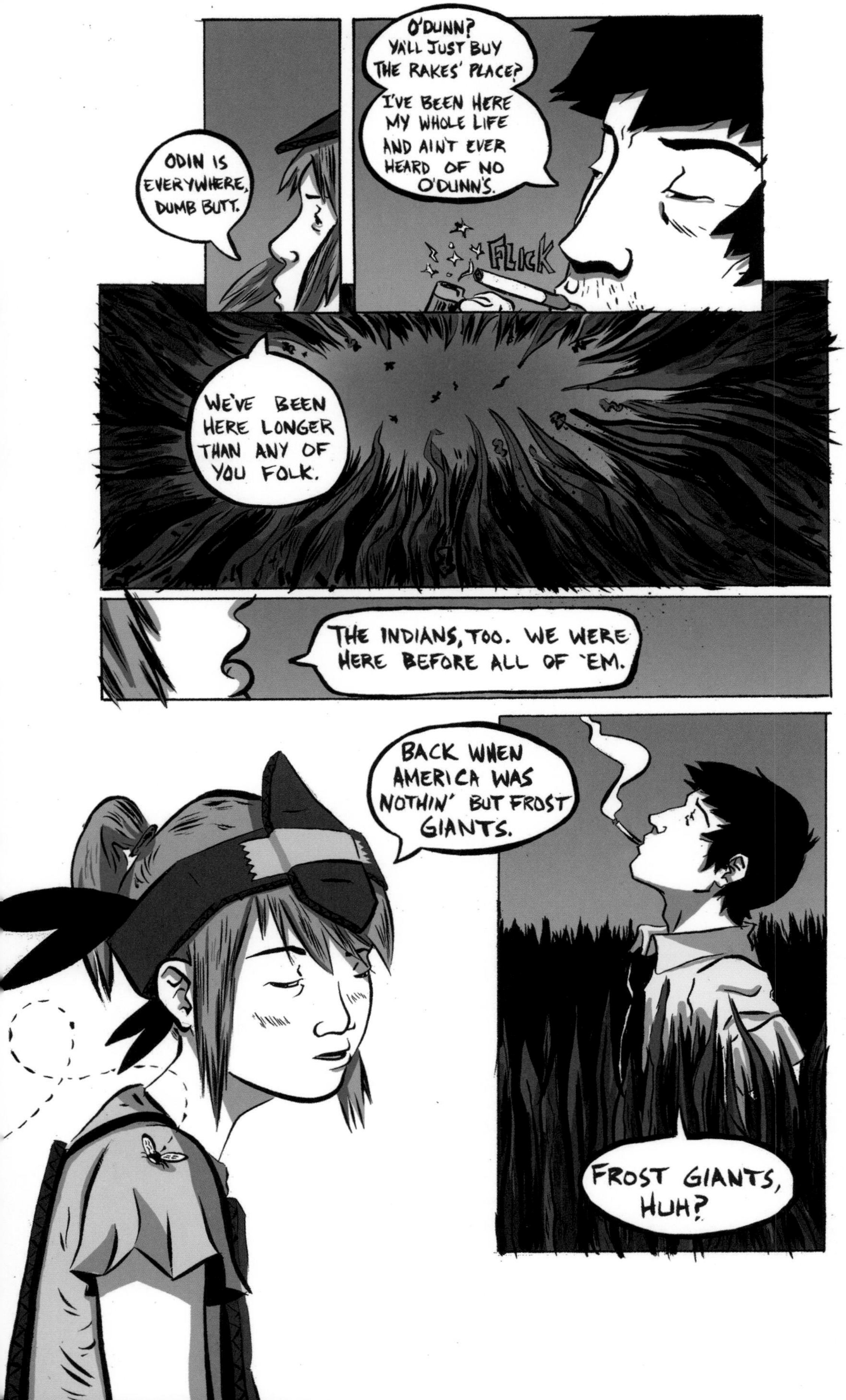
ODIN IS EVERYWHERE, DUMB BUTT.
O'DUNN? YA'LL JUST BUY THE RAKES' PLACE?
I'VE BEEN HERE MY WHOLE LIFE AND AIN'T EVER HEARD OF NO O'DUNN'S.
FLICK
WE'VE BEEN HERE LONGER THAN ANY OF YOU FOLK.
THE INDIANS, TOO. WE WERE HERE BEFORE ALL OF 'EM.
BACK WHEN AMERICA WAS NOTHIN' BUT FROST GIANTS.
FROST GIANTS, HUH?

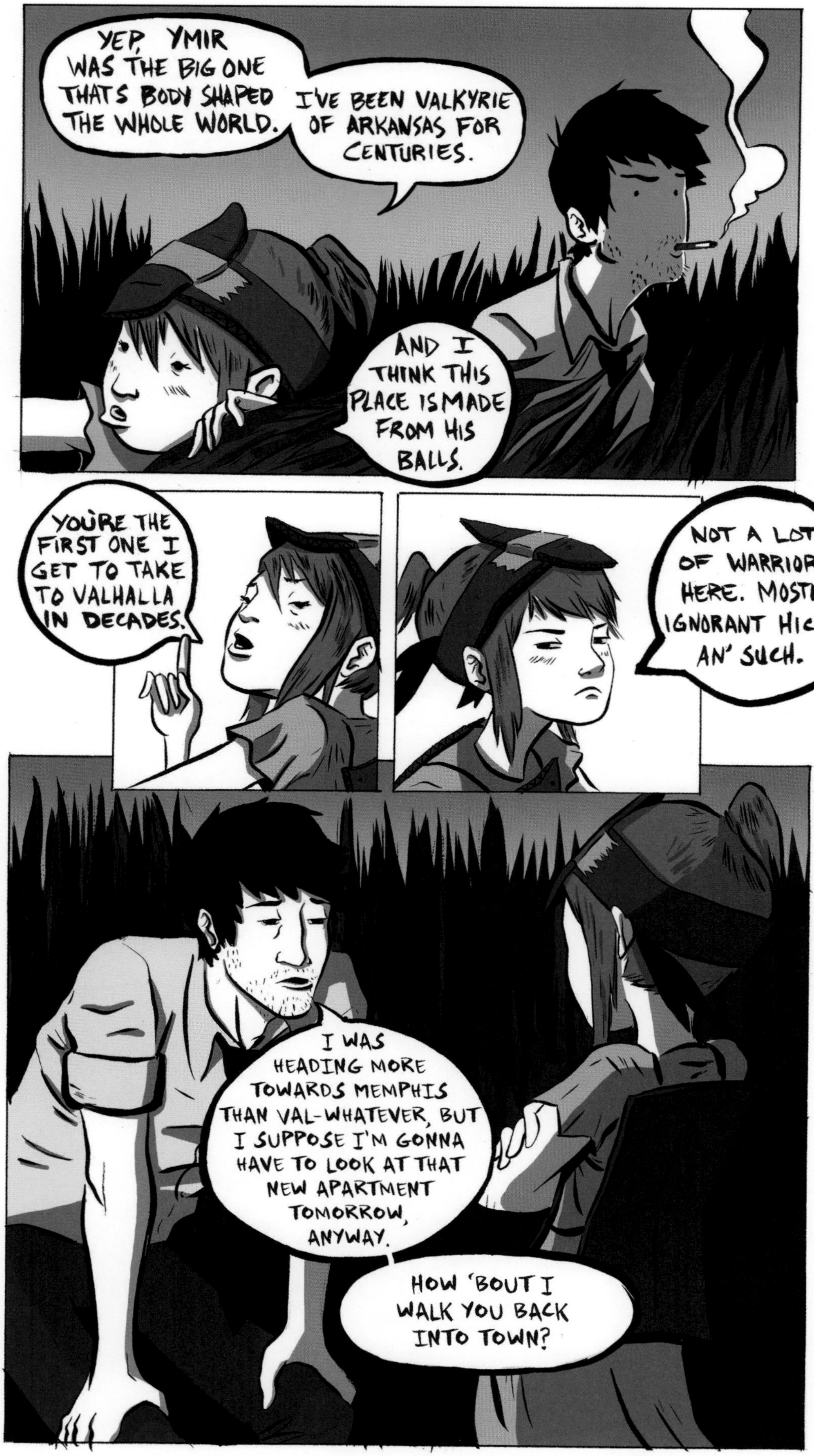
YEP, YMIR WAS THE BIG ONE THATS BODY SHAPED THE WHOLE WORLD.
I'VE BEEN VALKYRIE OF ARKANSAS FOR CENTURIES.
AND I THINK THIS PLACE IS MADE FROM HIS BALLS.
YOU'RE THE FIRST ONE I GET TO TAKE TO VALHALLA IN DECADES.
NOT A LOT OF WARRIORS HERE. MOSTLY IGNORANT HICKS AN' SUCH.
I WAS HEADING MORE TOWARDS MEMPHIS THAN VAL-WHATEVER, BUT I SUPPOSE I'M GONNA HAVE TO LOOK AT THAT NEW APARTMENT TOMORROW, ANYWAY.
HOW 'BOUT I WALK YOU BACK INTO TOWN?

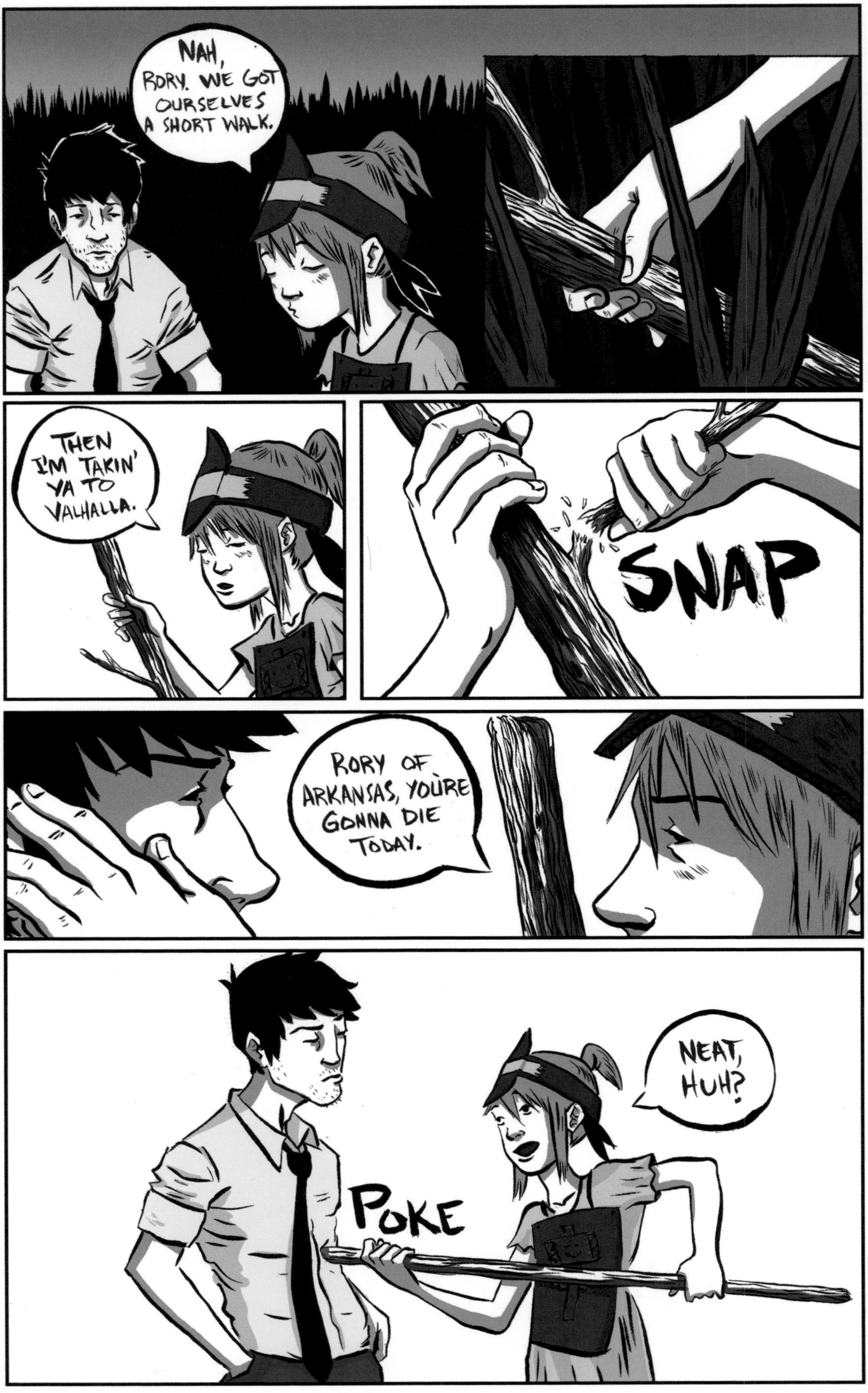
NAH, RORY. WE GOT OURSELVES A SHORT WALK.
THEN I'M TAKIN' YA TO VALHALLA.
SNAP
RORY OF ARKANSAS, YOU'RE GONNA DIE TODAY.
NEAT, HUH?
POKE

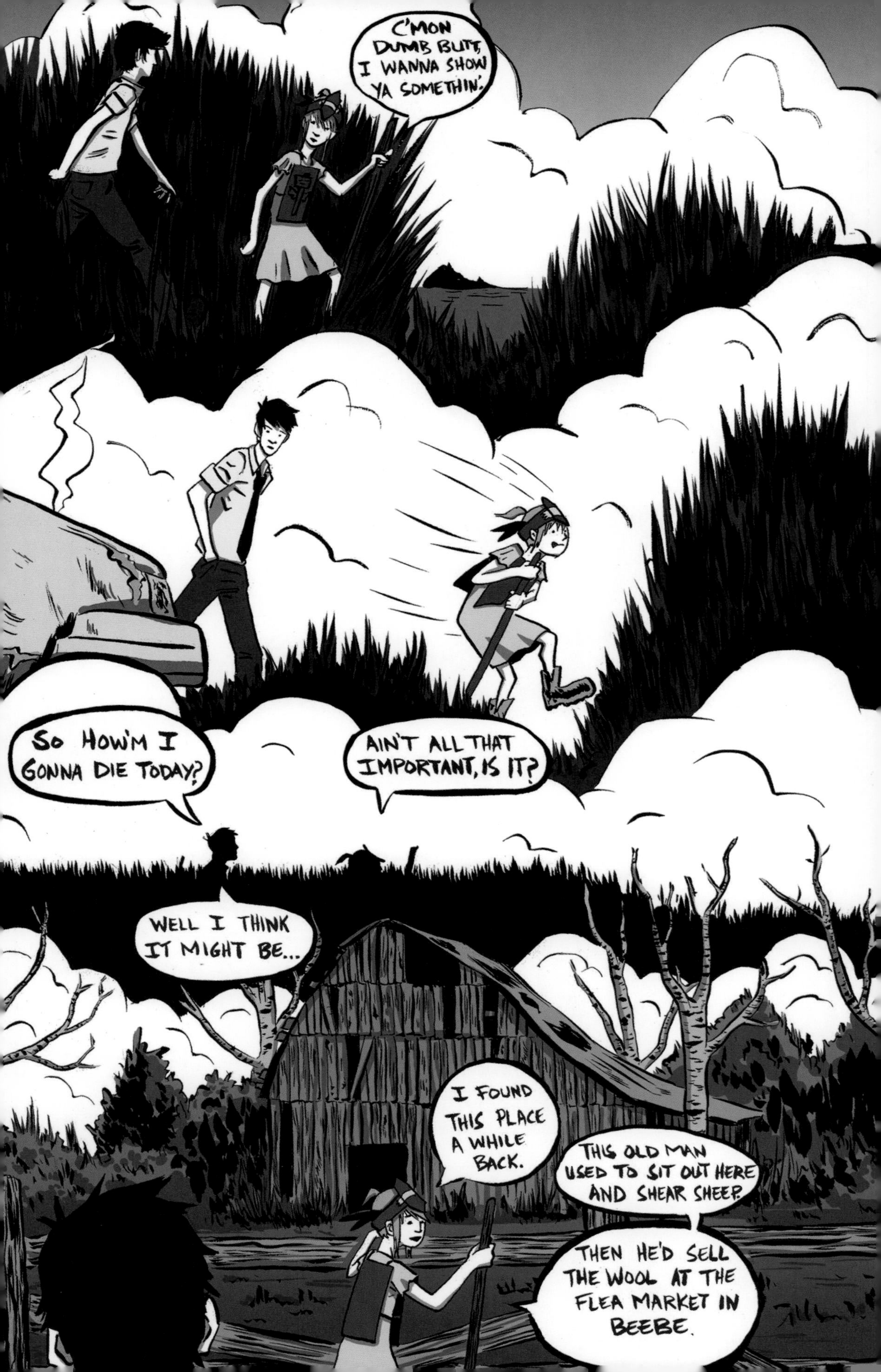
C'MON DUMB BUTT, I WANNA SHOW YA SOMETHIN'.
SO HOW'M I GONNA DIE TODAY?
AIN'T ALL THAT IMPORTANT, IS IT?
WELL I THINK IT MIGHT BE...
I FOUND THIS PLACE A WHILE BACK.
THIS OLD MAN USED TO SIT OUT HERE AND SHEAR SHEEP.
THEN HE'D SELL THE WOOL AT THE FLEA MARKET IN BEEBE.

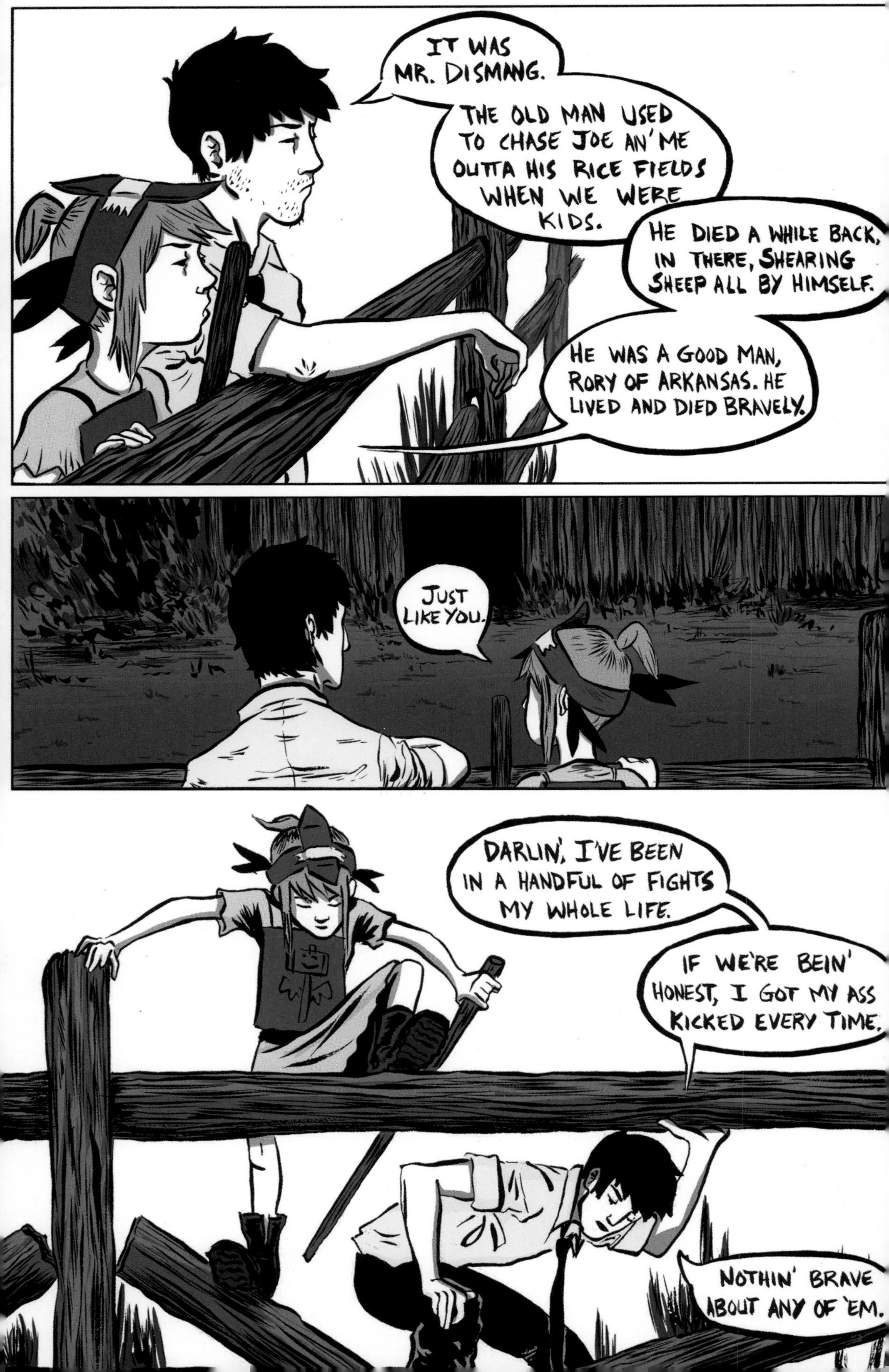
IT WAS MR. DISMANG.
THE OLD MAN USED TO CHASE JOE AN' ME OUTTA HIS RICE FIELDS WHEN WE WERE KIDS.
HE DIED A WHILE BACK, IN THERE, SHEARING SHEEP ALL BY HIMSELF.
HE WAS A GOOD MAN, RORY OF ARKANSAS. HE LIVED AND DIED BRAVELY.
JUST LIKE YOU.
DARLIN', I'VE BEEN IN A HANDFUL OF FIGHTS MY WHOLE LIFE.
IF WE'RE BEIN' HONEST, I GOT MY ASS KICKED EVERY TIME.
NOTHIN' BRAVE ABOUT ANY OF 'EM.

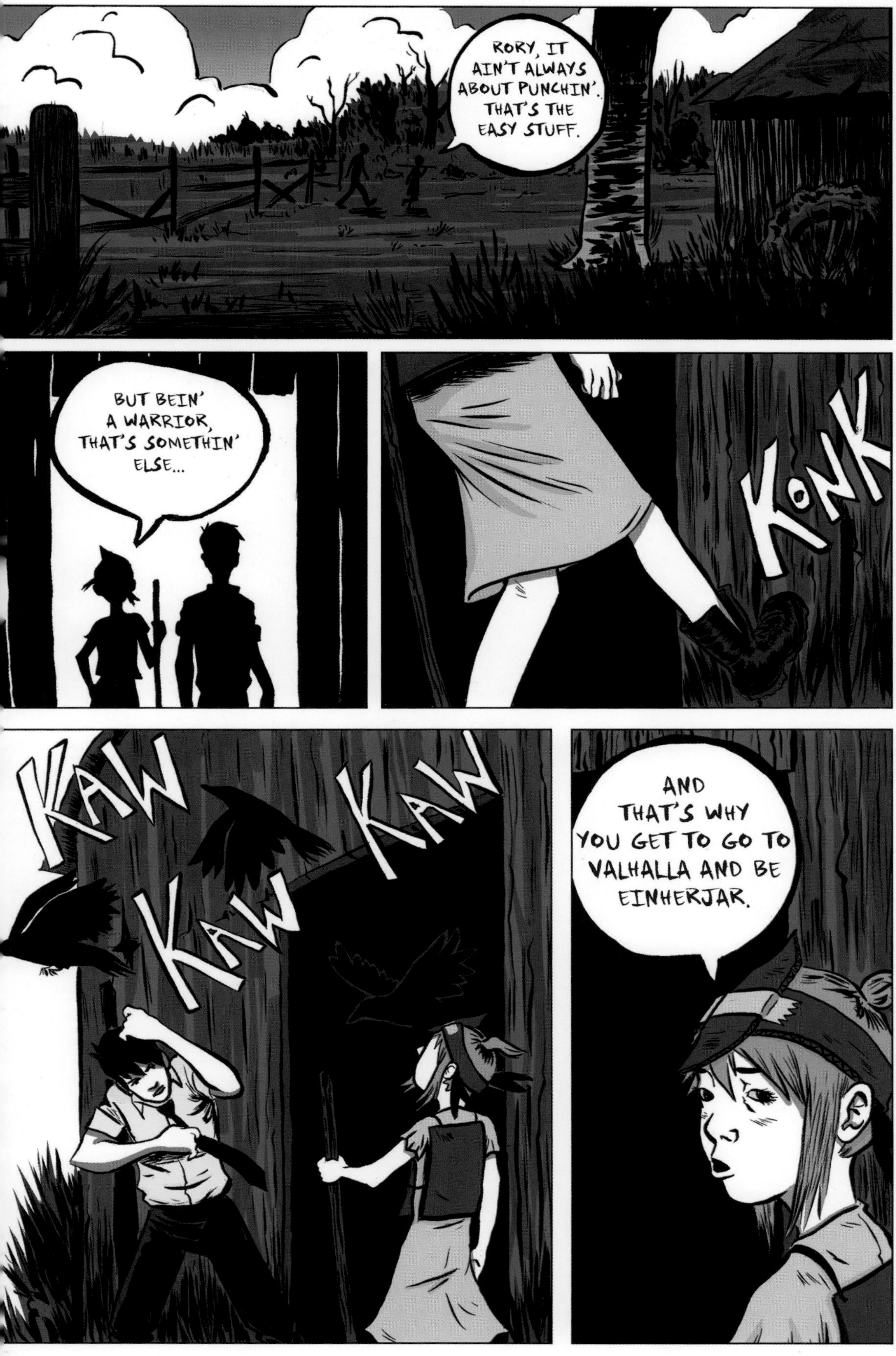
RORY, IT AIN'T ALWAYS ABOUT PUNCHIN'. THAT'S THE EASY STUFF.
BUT BEIN' A WARRIOR, THAT'S SOMETHIN' ELSE...
KONK
KAW
KAW
KAW
AND THAT'S WHY YOU GET TO GO TO VALHALLA AND BE EINHERJAR.

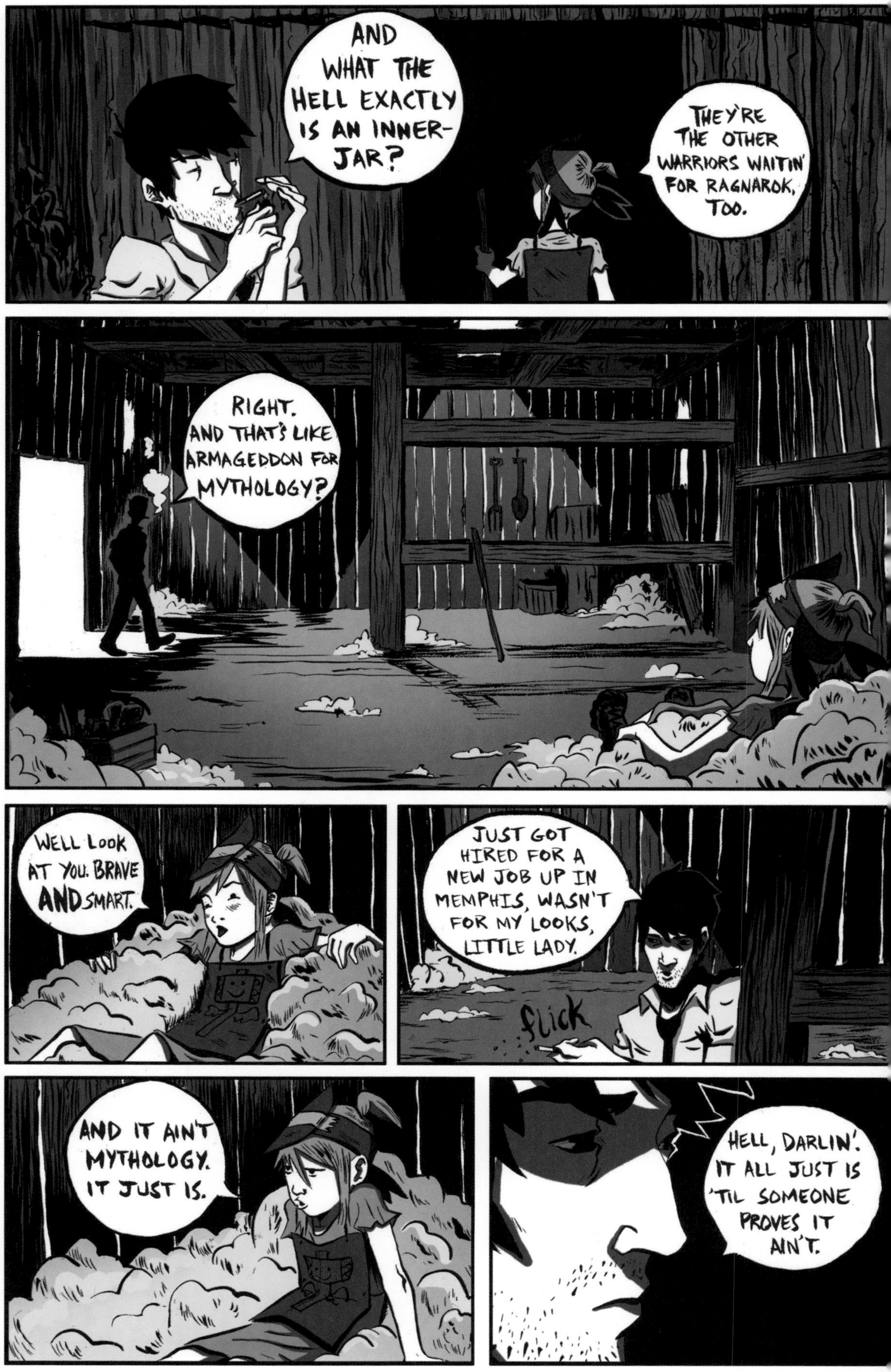
AND WHAT THE HELL EXACTLY IS AN INNER-JAR?
THEY'RE THE OTHER WARRIORS WAITIN' FOR RAGNAROK, TOO.
RIGHT. AND THAT'S LIKE ARMAGEDDON FOR MYTHOLOGY?
WELL LOOK AT YOU. BRAVE AND SMART.
JUST GOT HIRED FOR A NEW JOB UP IN MEMPHIS, WASN'T FOR MY LOOKS, LITTLE LADY.
flick
AND IT AIN'T MYTHOLOGY. IT JUST IS.
HELL, DARLIN'. IT ALL JUST IS 'TIL SOMEONE PROVES IT AIN'T.

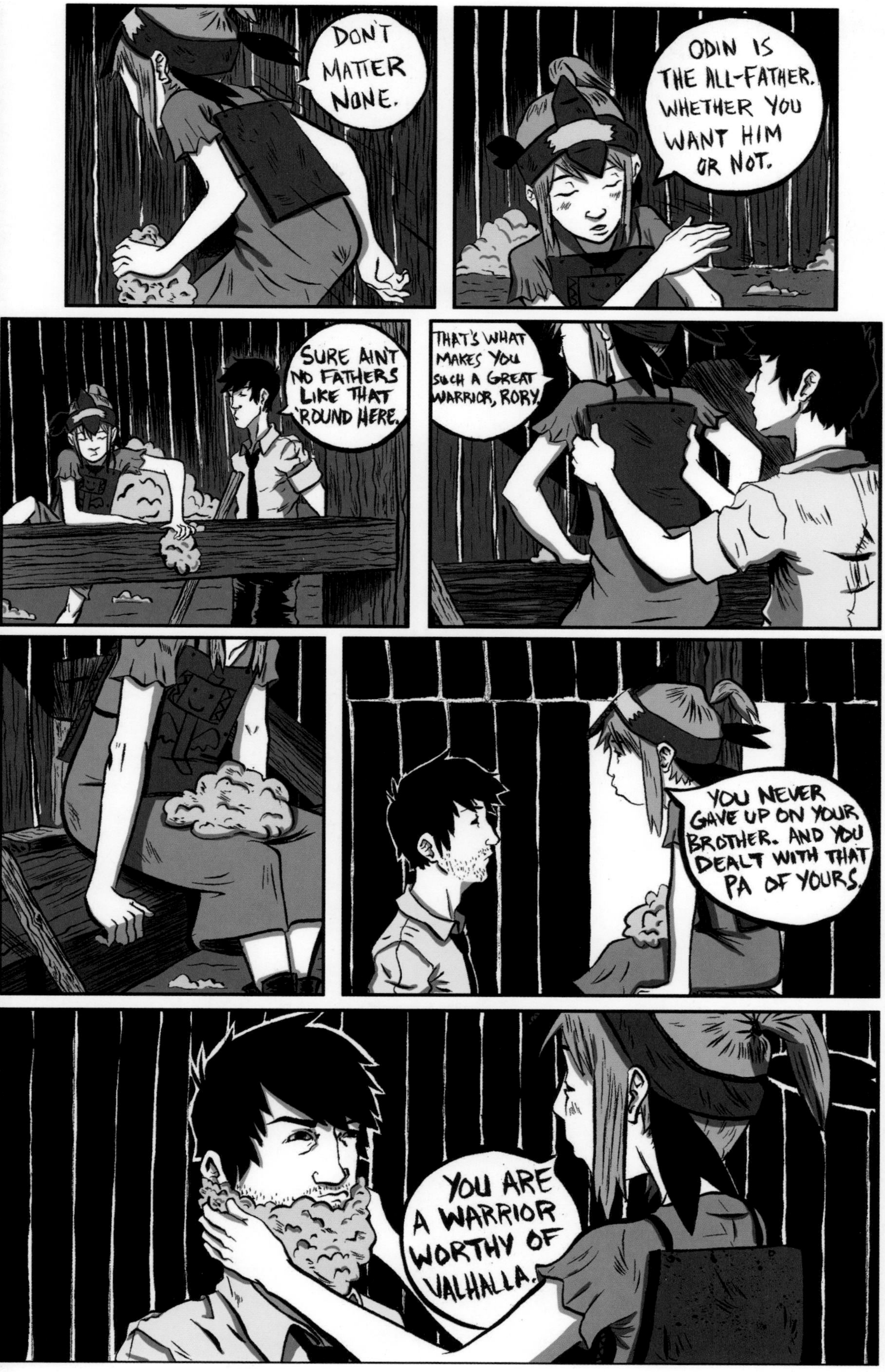
DON'T MATTER NONE.
ODIN IS THE ALL-FATHER. WHETHER YOU WANT HIM OR NOT.
SURE AIN'T NO FATHERS LIKE THAT 'ROUND HERE.
THAT'S WHAT MAKES YOU SUCH A GREAT WARRIOR, RORY.
YOU NEVER GAVE UP ON YOUR BROTHER. AND YOU DEALT WITH THAT PA OF YOURS.
YOU ARE A WARRIOR WORTHY OF VALHALLA.

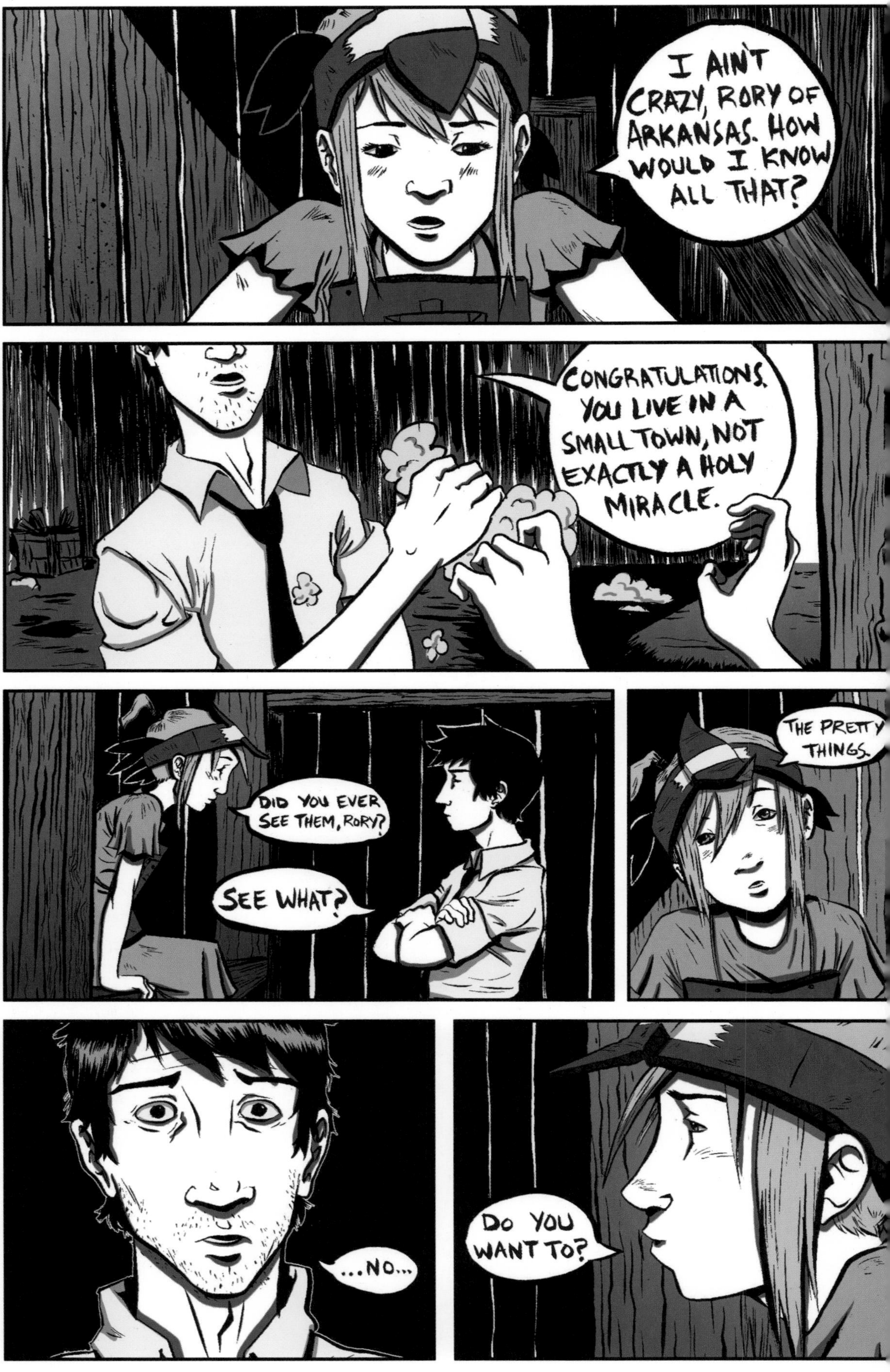
I AIN'T CRAZY, RORY OF ARKANSAS. HOW WOULD I KNOW ALL THAT?
CONGRATULATIONS. YOU LIVE IN A SMALL TOWN, NOT EXACTLY A HOLY MIRACLE.
DID YOU EVER SEE THEM, RORY?
SEE WHAT?
THE PRETTY THINGS.
...NO...
DO YOU WANT TO?

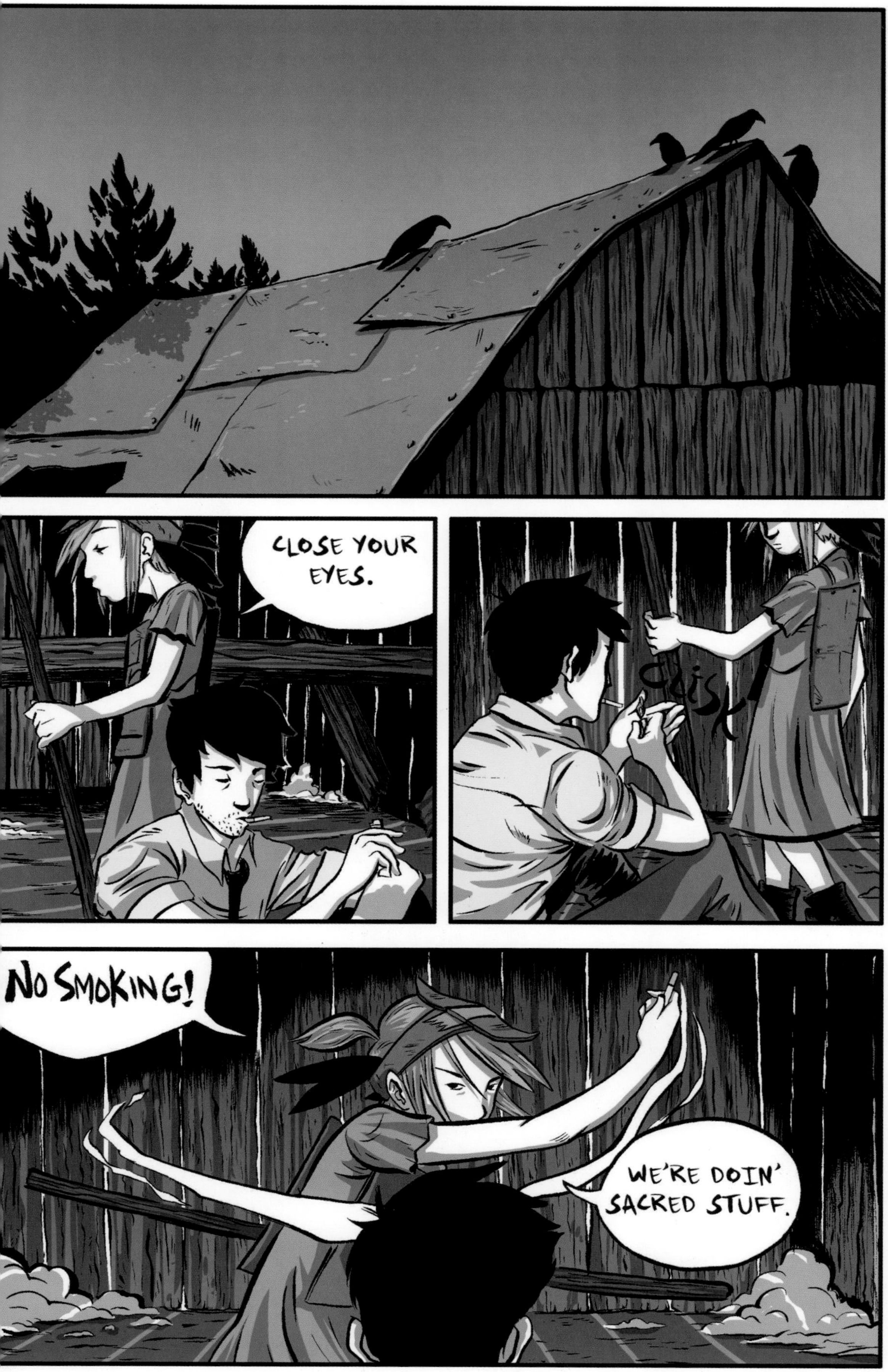
CLOSE YOUR EYES.
Crisk
NO SMOKING!
WE'RE DOIN' SACRED STUFF.

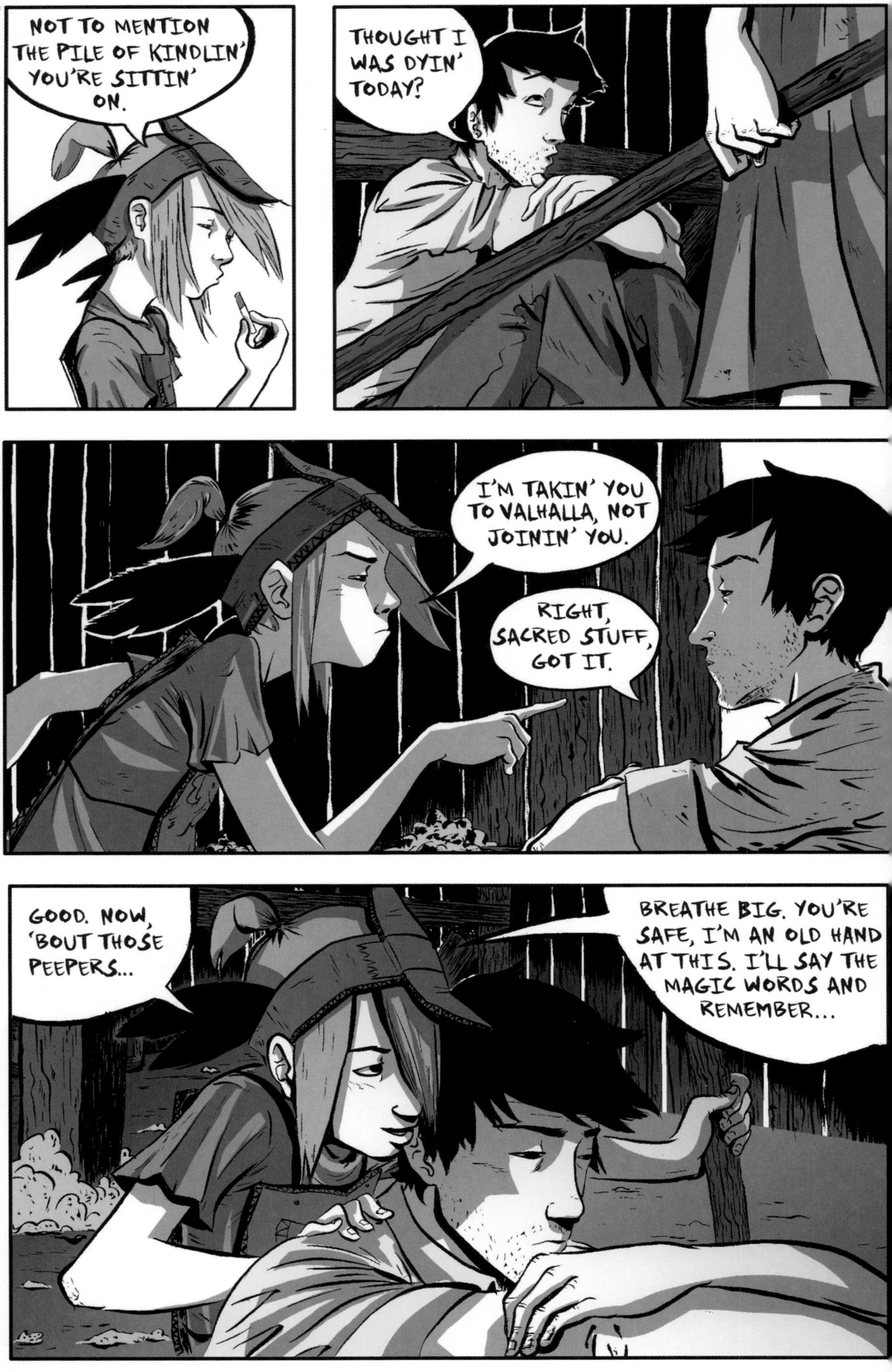
NOT TO MENTION THE PILE OF KINDLIN' YOU'RE SITTIN' ON.
THOUGHT I WAS DYIN' TODAY?
I'M TAKIN' YOU TO VALHALLA, NOT JOININ' YOU.
RIGHT, SACRED STUFF, GOT IT.
GOOD. NOW, 'BOUT THOSE PEEPERS...
BREATHE BIG. YOU'RE SAFE, I'M AN OLD HAND AT THIS. I'LL SAY THE MAGIC WORDS AND REMEMBER...

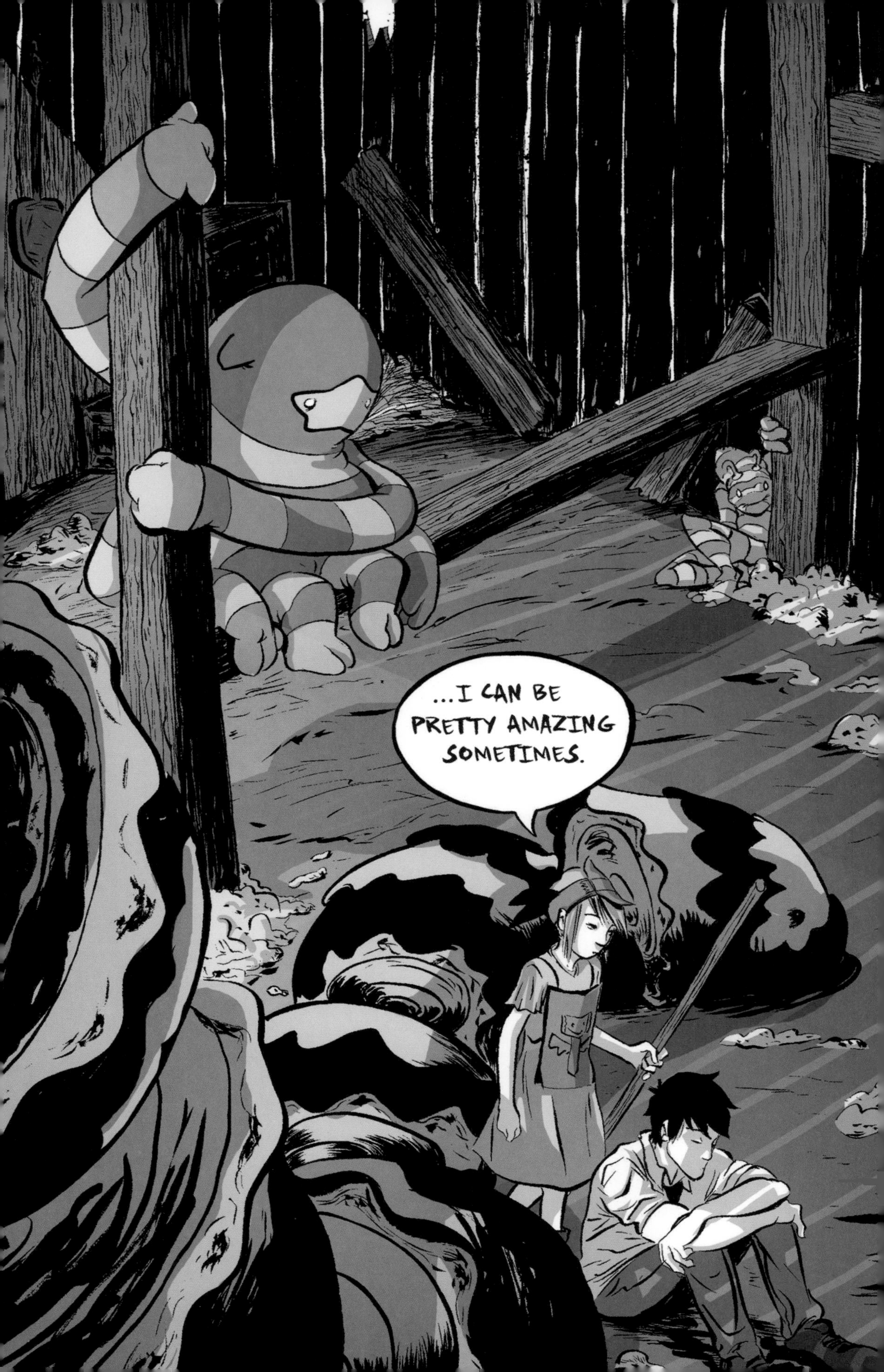
...I CAN BE PRETTY AMAZING SOMETIMES.

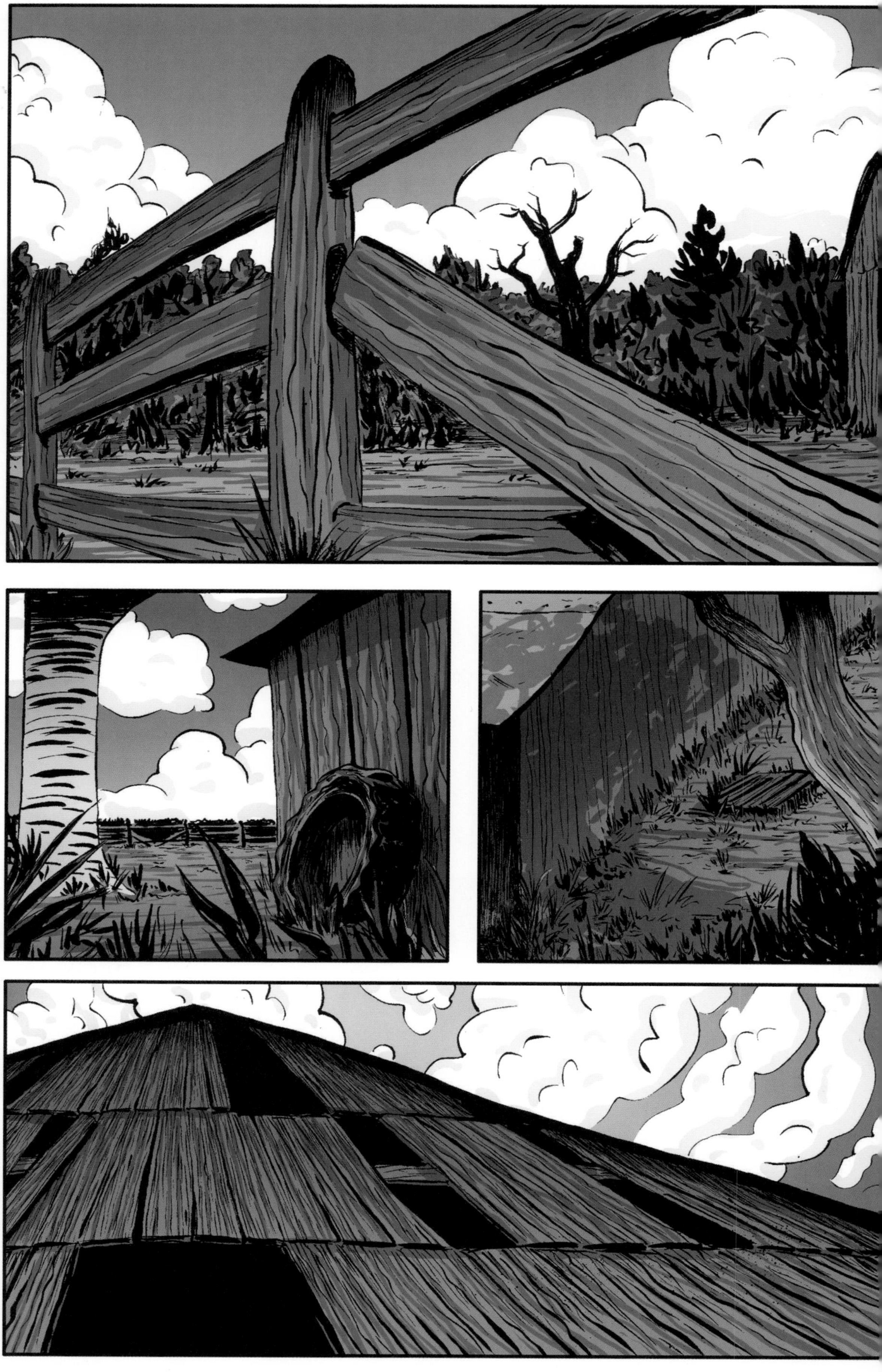

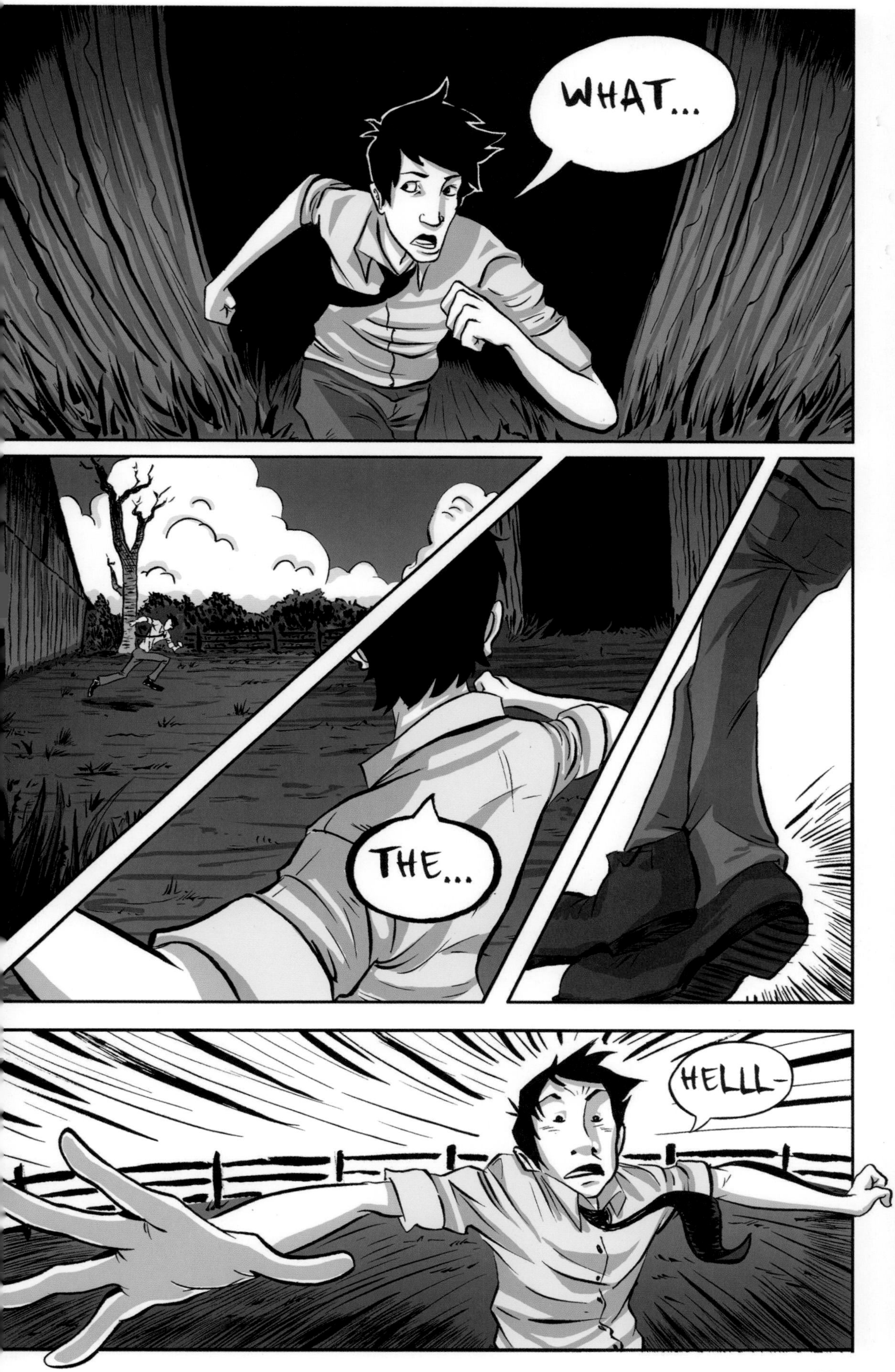
WHAT...
THE...
HELLL-

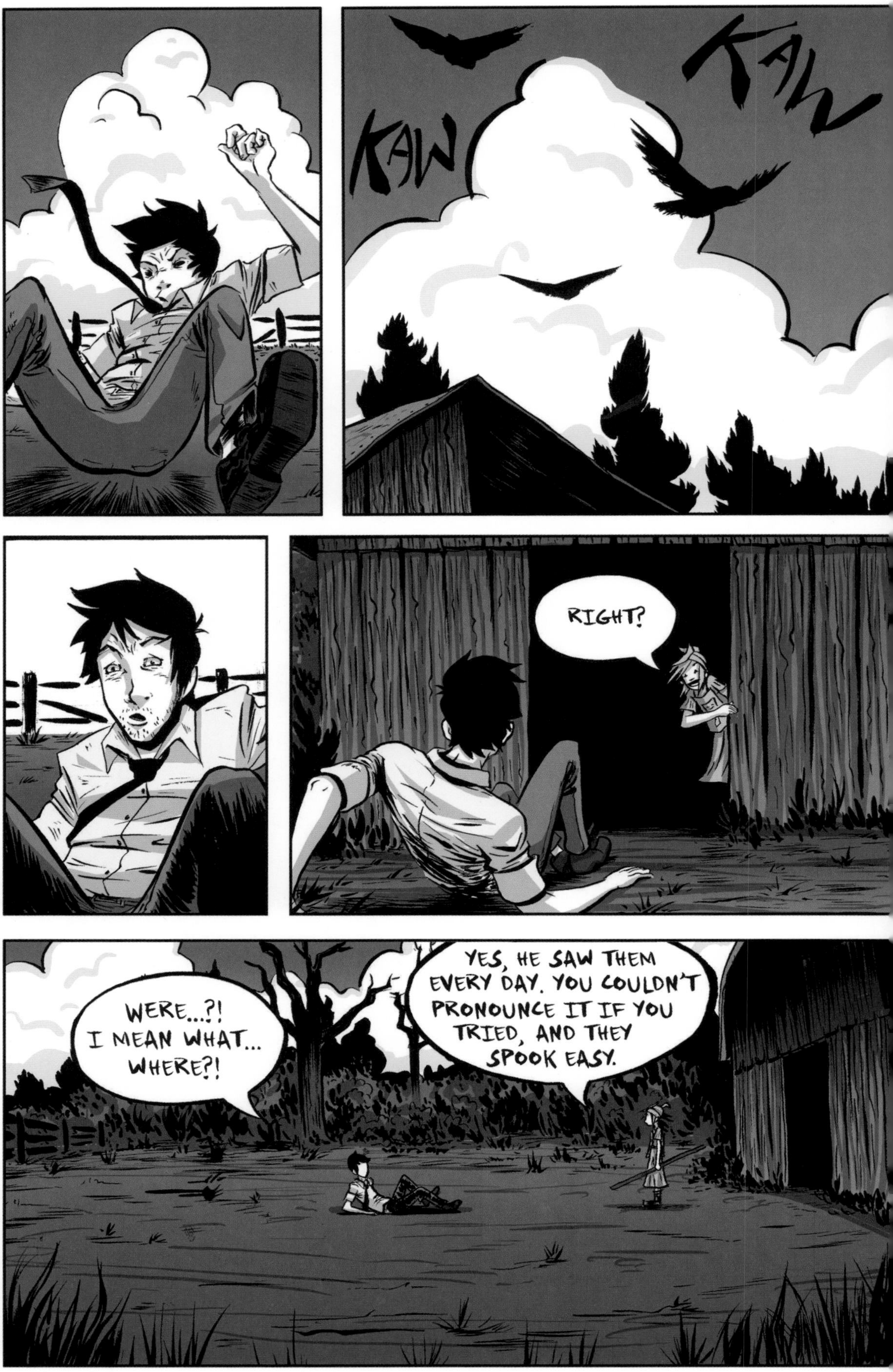
KAW
KAW
RIGHT?
WERE...?! I MEAN WHAT... WHERE?!
YES, HE SAW THEM EVERY DAY. YOU COULDN'T PRONOUNCE IT IF YOU TRIED, AND THEY SPOOK EASY.

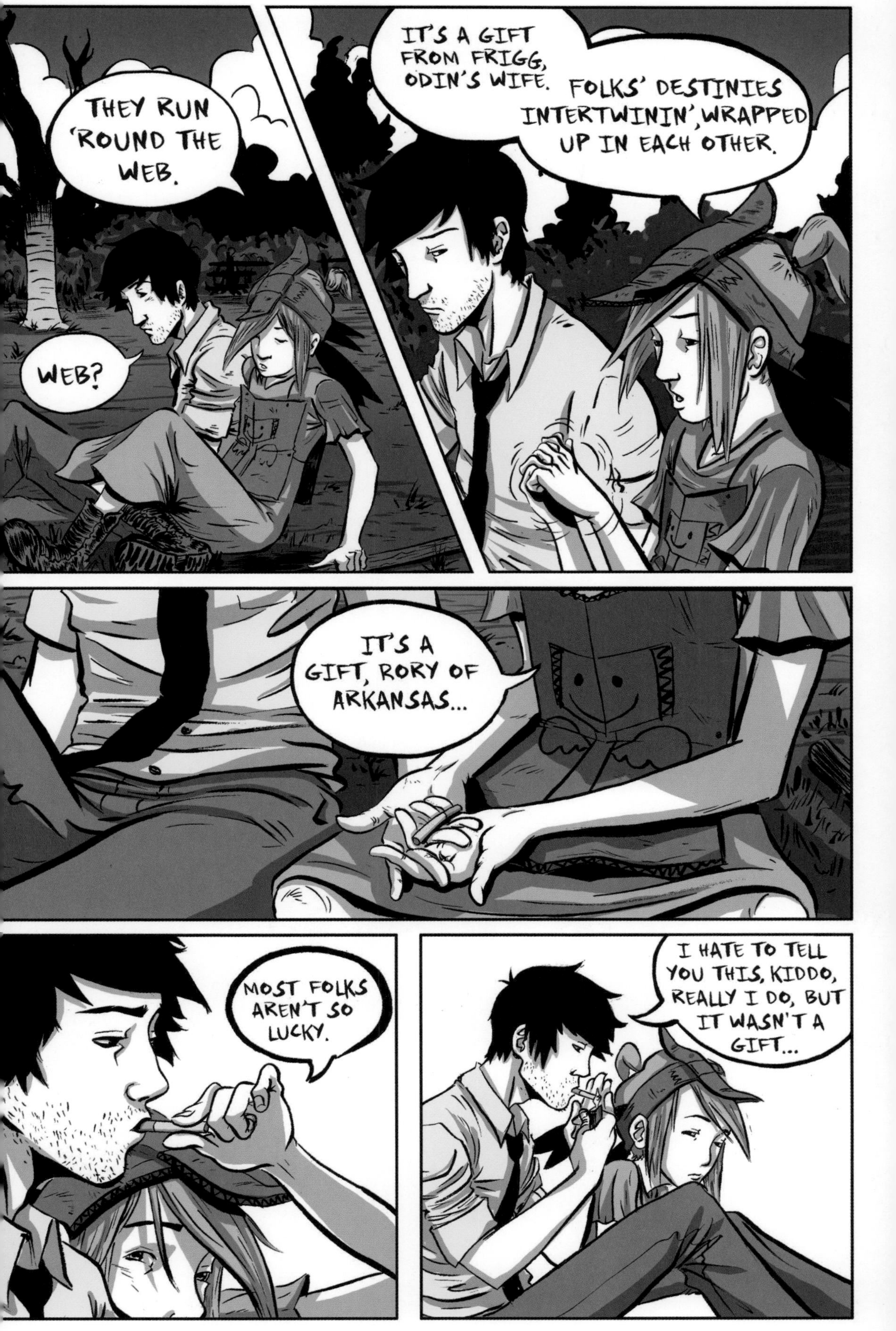
THEY RUN 'ROUND THE WEB.
WEB?
IT'S A GIFT FROM FRIGG, ODIN'S WIFE.
FOLKS' DESTINIES INTERTWININ', WRAPPED UP IN EACH OTHER.
IT'S A GIFT, RORY OF ARKANSAS...
MOST FOLKS AREN'T SO LUCKY.
I HATE TO TELL YOU THIS, KIDDO, REALLY I DO, BUT IT WASN'T A GIFT...

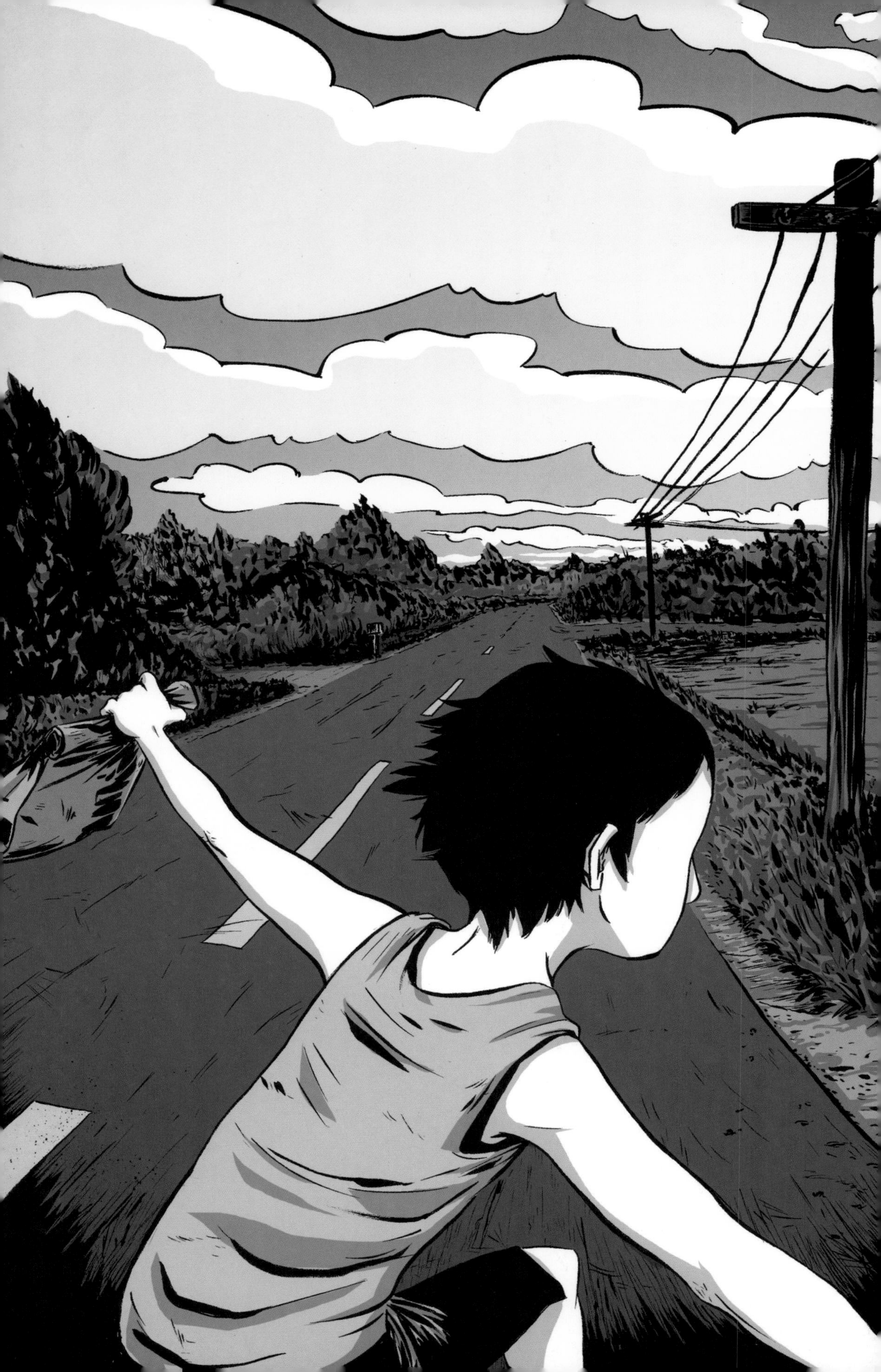

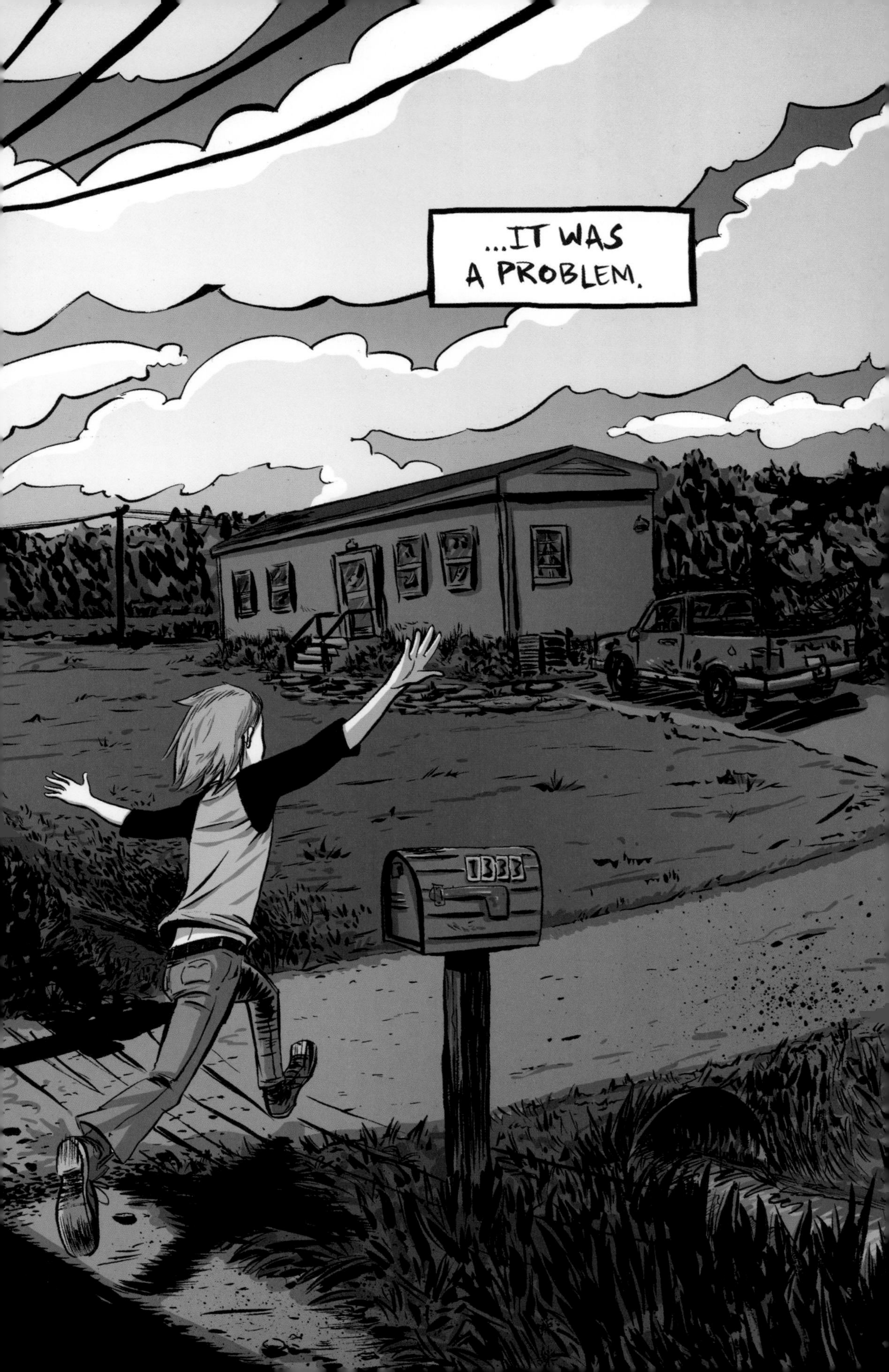
...IT WAS A PROBLEM.
1333

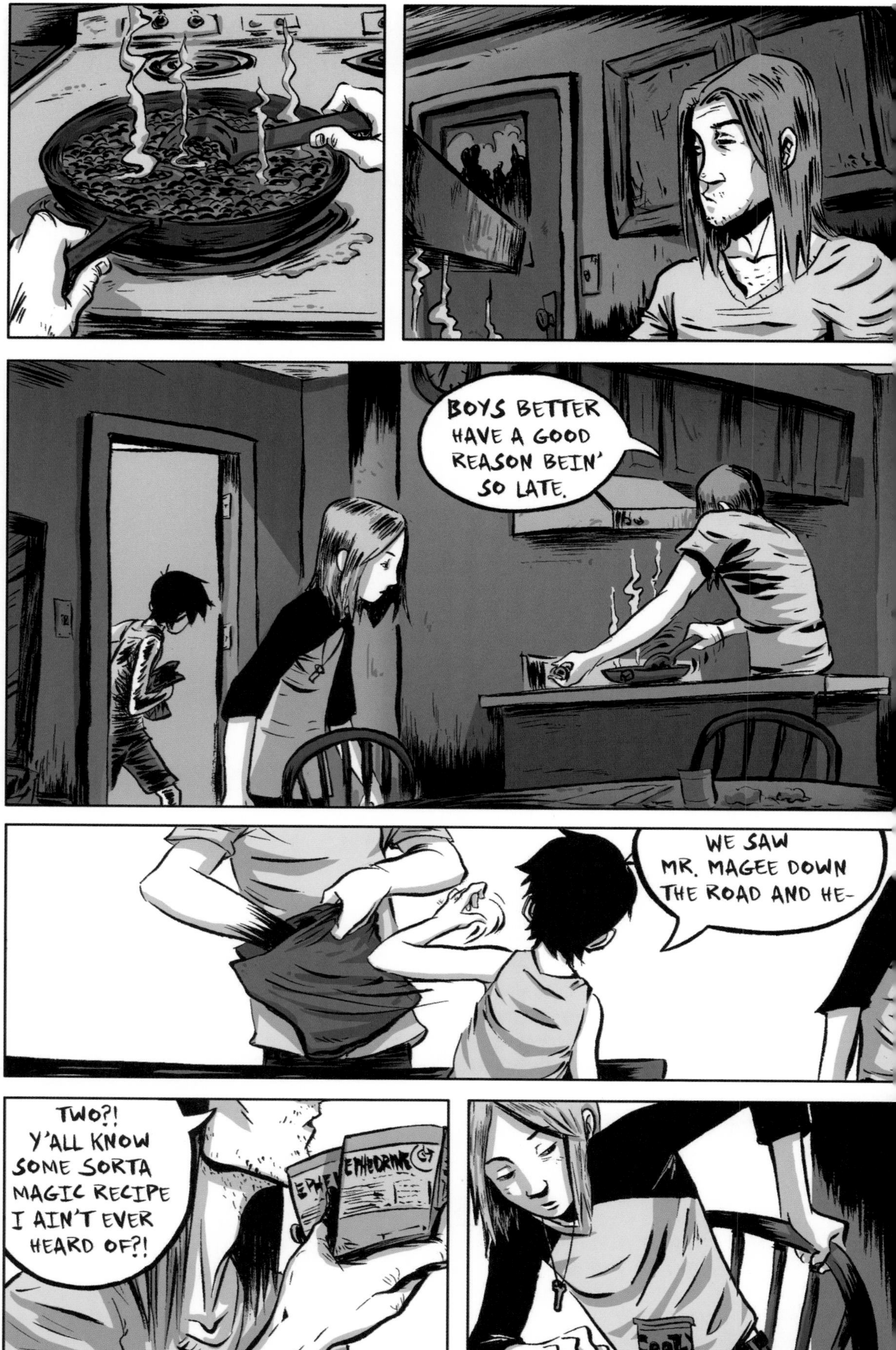
BOYS BETTER HAVE A GOOD REASON BEIN' SO LATE.
WE SAW MR. MAGEE DOWN THE ROAD AND HE-
TWO?! Y'ALL KNOW SOME SORTA MAGIC RECIPE I AIN'T EVER HEARD OF?!

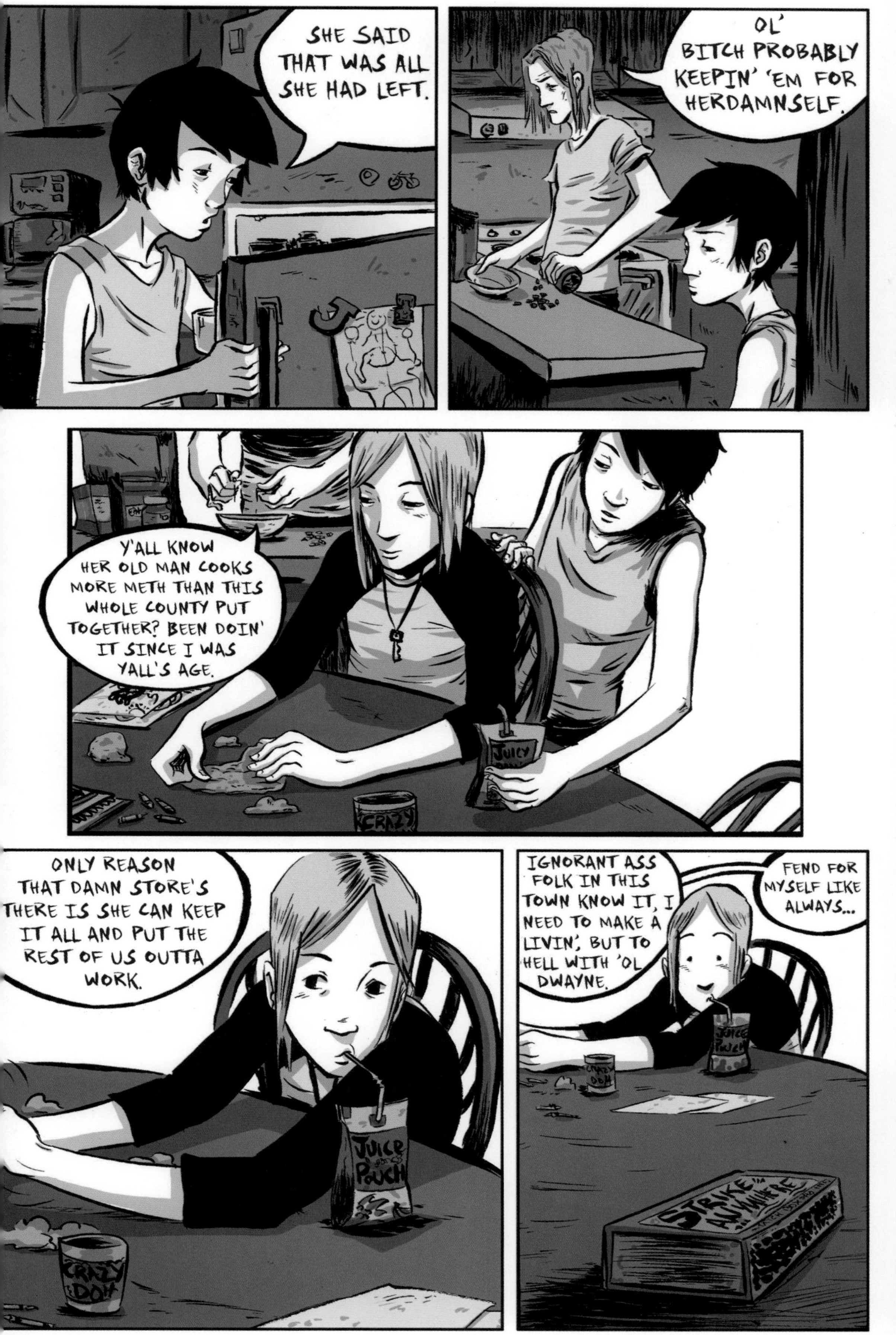
SHE SAID THAT WAS ALL SHE HAD LEFT.
OL' BITCH PROBABLY KEEPIN' 'EM FOR HERDAMNSELF.
Y'ALL KNOW HER OLD MAN COOKS MORE METH THAN THIS WHOLE COUNTY PUT TOGETHER? BEEN DOIN' IT SINCE I WAS YALL'S AGE.
JUICY POUCH
CRAZY
ONLY REASON THAT DAMN STORE'S THERE IS SHE CAN KEEP IT ALL AND PUT THE REST OF US OUTTA WORK.
JUICE POUCH
CRAZY DOH
IGNORANT ASS FOLK IN THIS TOWN KNOW IT, I NEED TO MAKE A LIVIN', BUT TO HELL WITH 'OL DWAYNE.
FEND FOR MYSELF LIKE ALWAYS...
STRIKE ANYWHERE

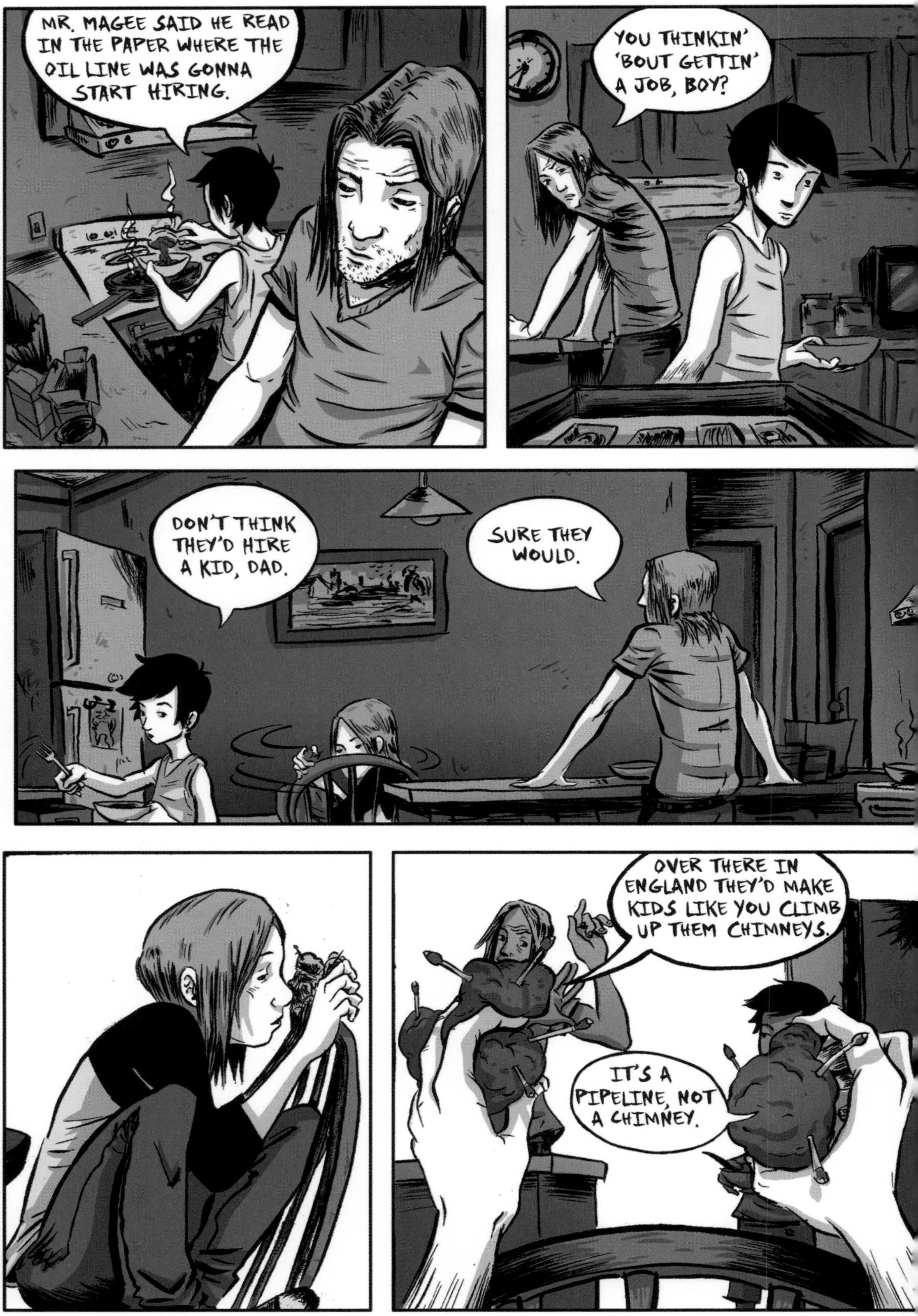
MR. MAGEE SAID HE READ IN THE PAPER WHERE THE OIL LINE WAS GONNA START HIRING.
YOU THINKIN' 'BOUT GETTIN' A JOB, BOY?
DON'T THINK THEY'D HIRE A KID, DAD.
SURE THEY WOULD.
OVER THERE IN ENGLAND THEY'D MAKE KIDS LIKE YOU CLIMB UP THEM CHIMNEYS.
IT'S A PIPELINE, NOT A CHIMNEY.

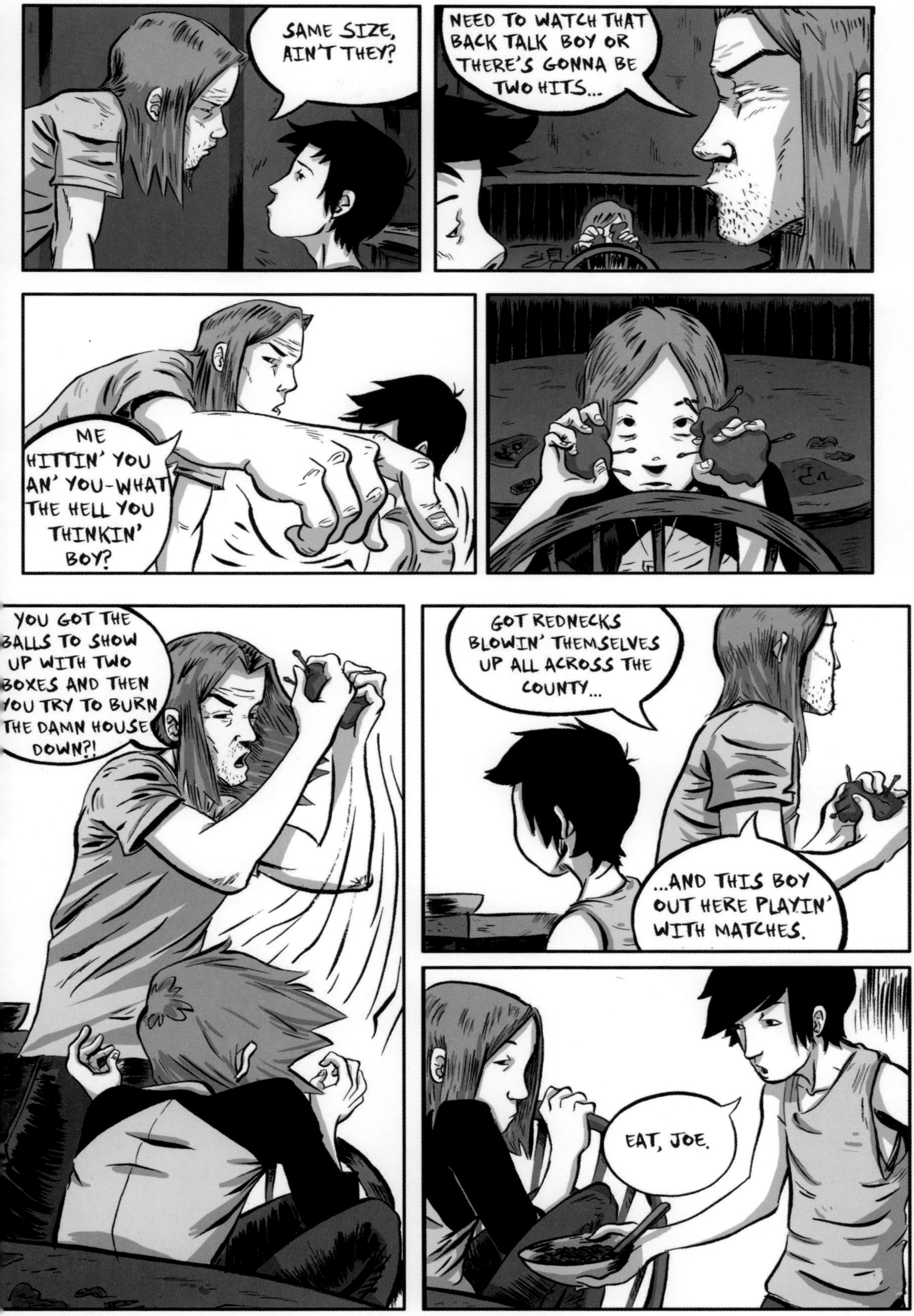
SAME SIZE, AIN'T THEY?
NEED TO WATCH THAT BACK TALK BOY OR THERE'S GONNA BE TWO HITS...
ME HITTIN' YOU AN' YOU-WHAT THE HELL YOU THINKIN' BOY?
YOU GOT THE BALLS TO SHOW UP WITH TWO BOXES AND THEN YOU TRY TO BURN THE DAMN HOUSE DOWN?!
GOT REDNECKS BLOWIN' THEMSELVES UP ALL ACROSS THE COUNTY...
...AND THIS BOY OUT HERE PLAYIN' WITH MATCHES.
EAT, JOE.

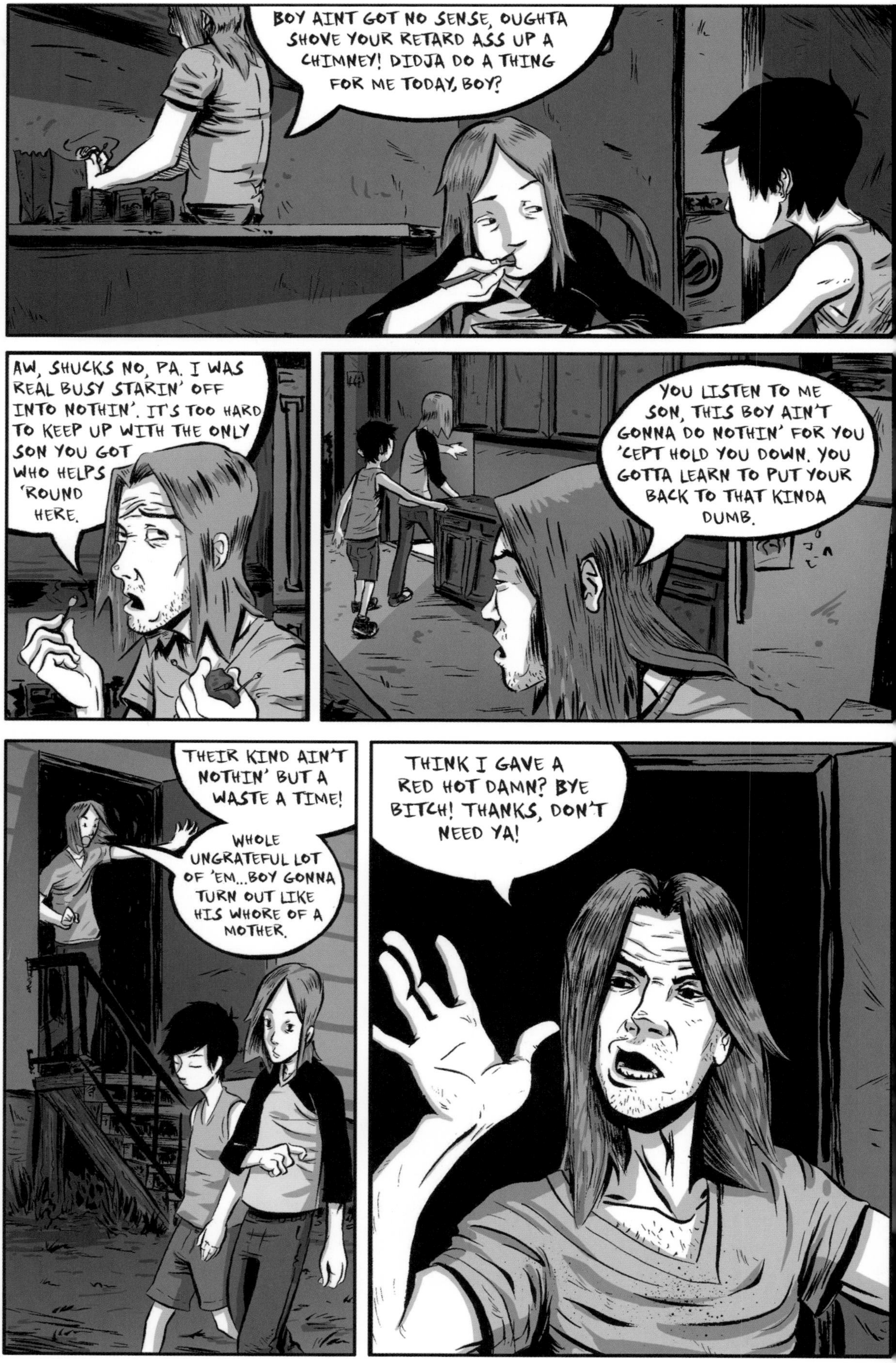
BOY AINT GOT NO SENSE, OUGHTA SHOVE YOUR RETARD ASS UP A CHIMNEY! DIDJA DO A THING FOR ME TODAY, BOY?
AW, SHUCKS NO, PA. I WAS REAL BUSY STARIN' OFF INTO NOTHIN'. IT'S TOO HARD TO KEEP UP WITH THE ONLY SON YOU GOT WHO HELPS 'ROUND HERE.
YOU LISTEN TO ME SON, THIS BOY AIN'T GONNA DO NOTHIN' FOR YOU 'CEPT HOLD YOU DOWN. YOU GOTTA LEARN TO PUT YOUR BACK TO THAT KINDA DUMB.
THEIR KIND AIN'T NOTHIN' BUT A WASTE A TIME!
WHOLE UNGRATEFUL LOT OF 'EM...BOY GONNA TURN OUT LIKE HIS WHORE OF A MOTHER.
THINK I GAVE A RED HOT DAMN? BYE BITCH! THANKS, DON'T NEED YA!

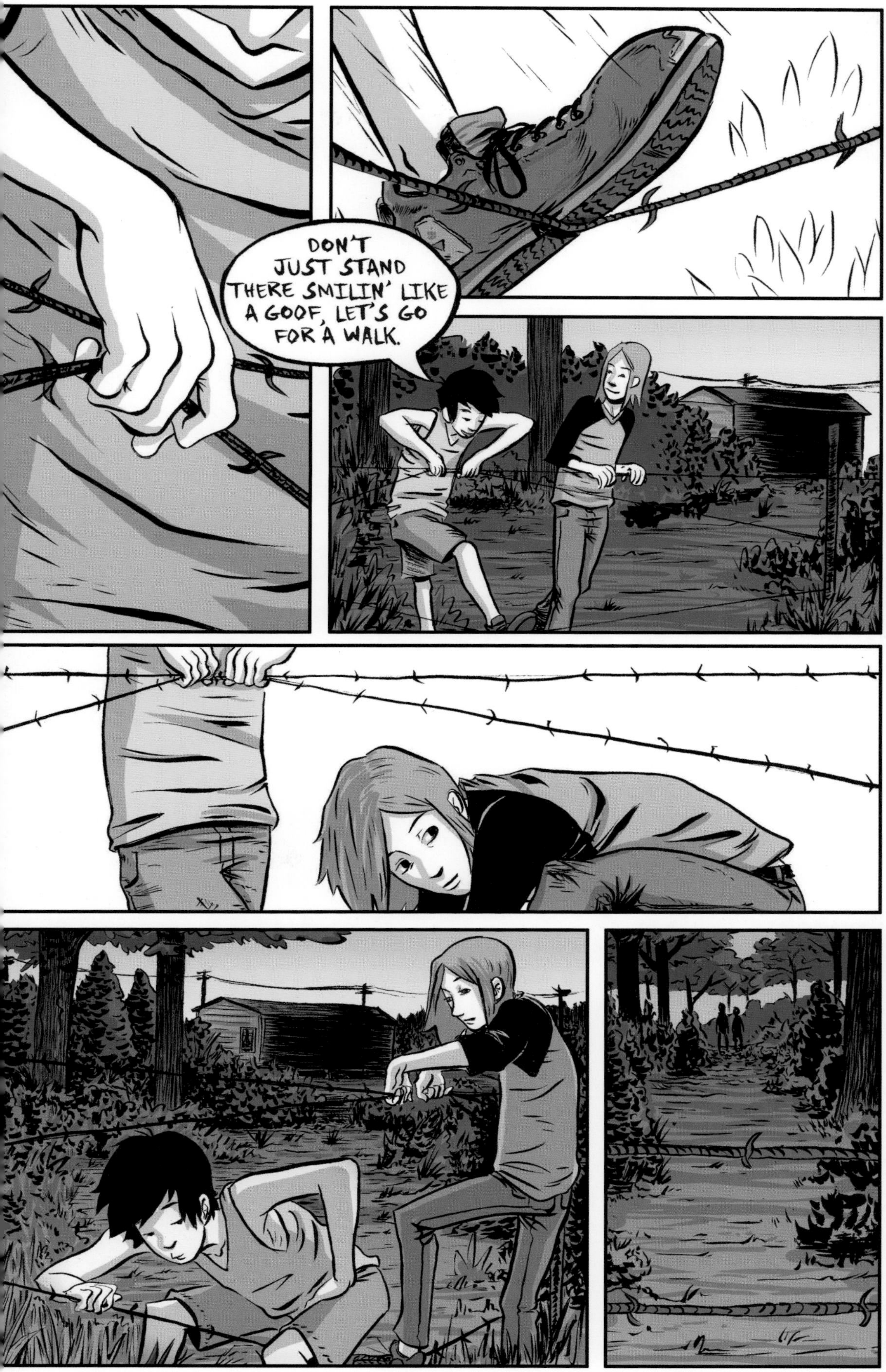
DON'T JUST STAND THERE SMILIN' LIKE A GOOF, LET'S GO FOR A WALK.

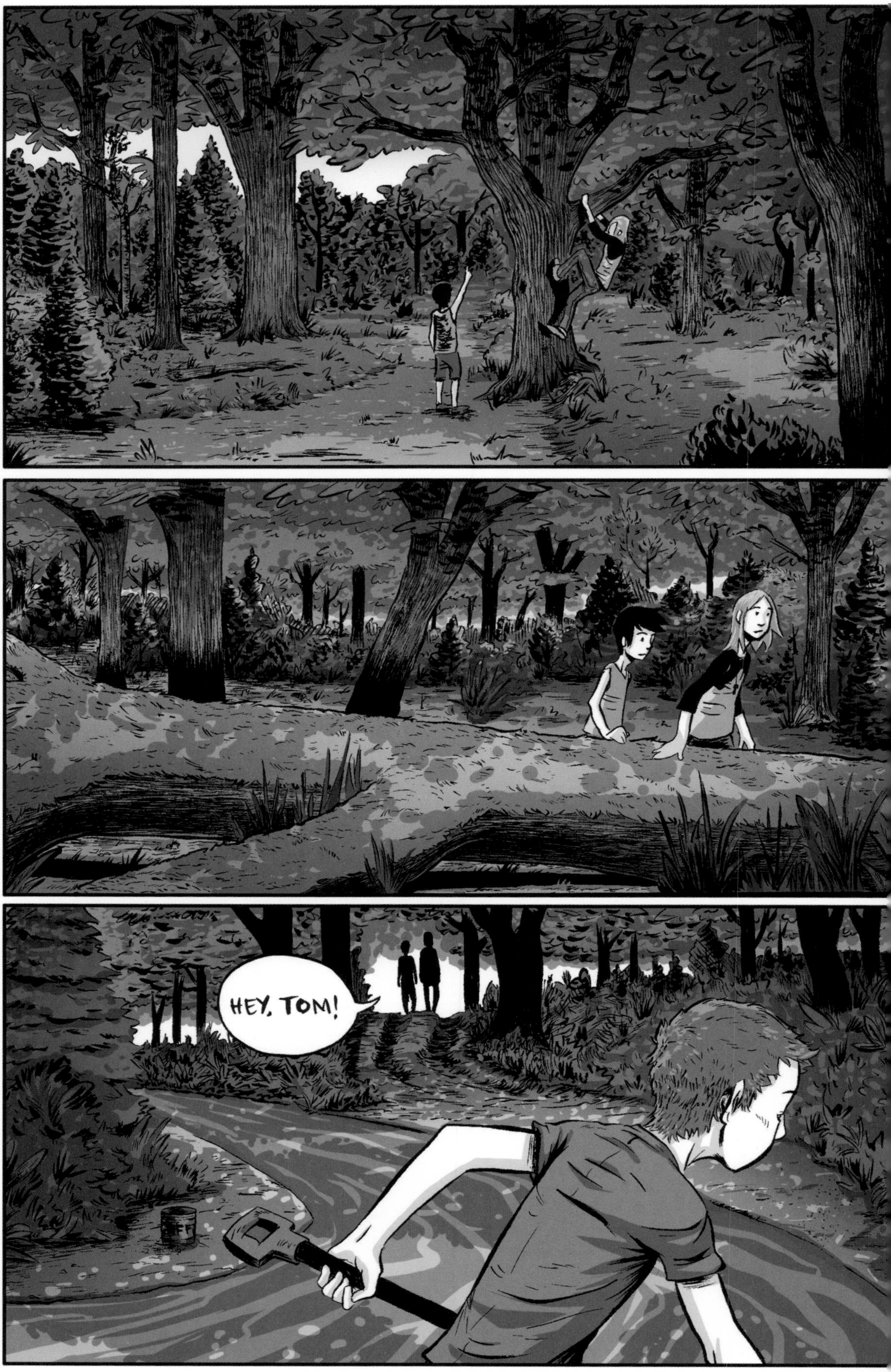
HEY, TOM!

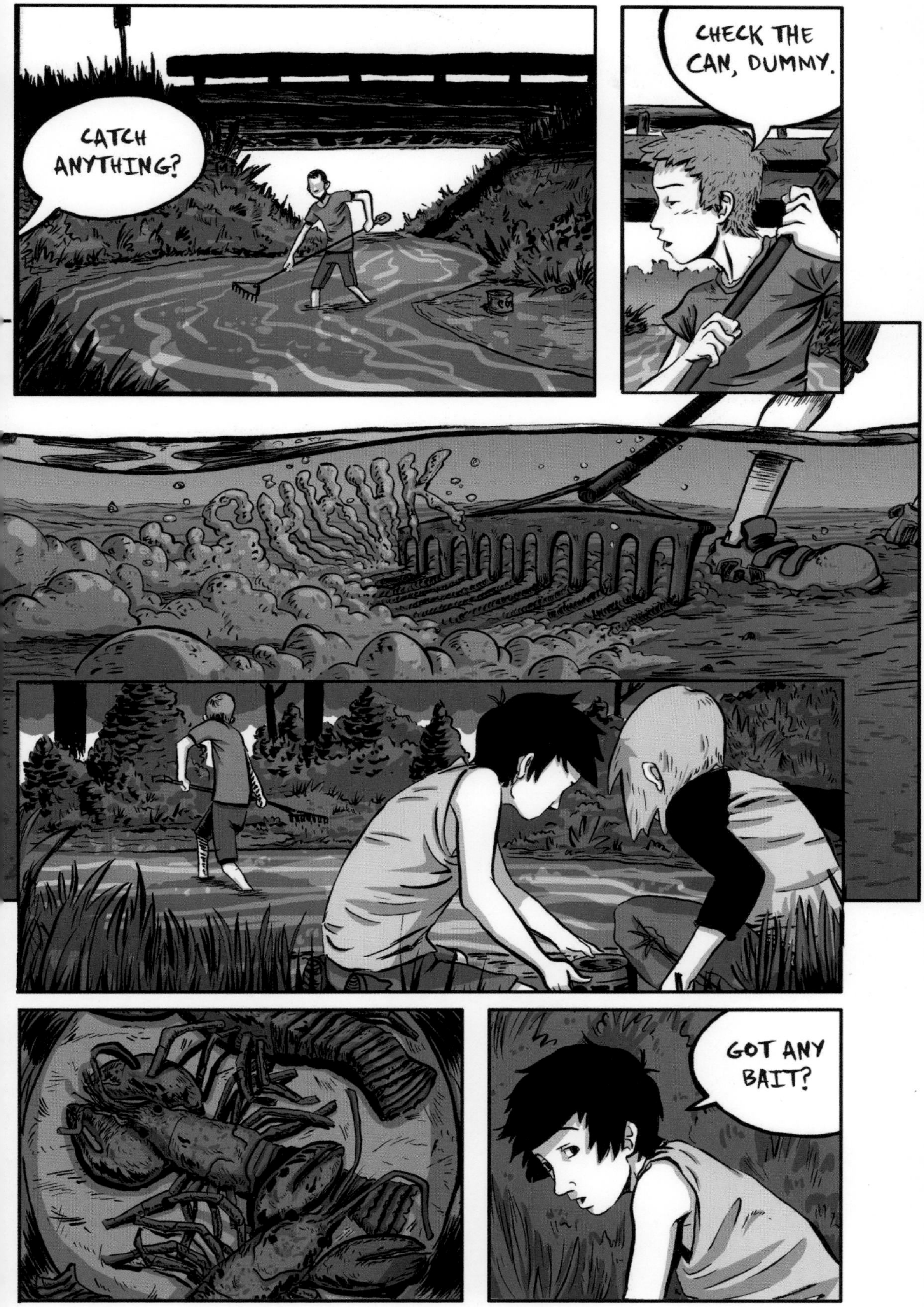
CATCH ANYTHING?
CHECK THE CAN, DUMMY.
SHHUK
GOT ANY BAIT?

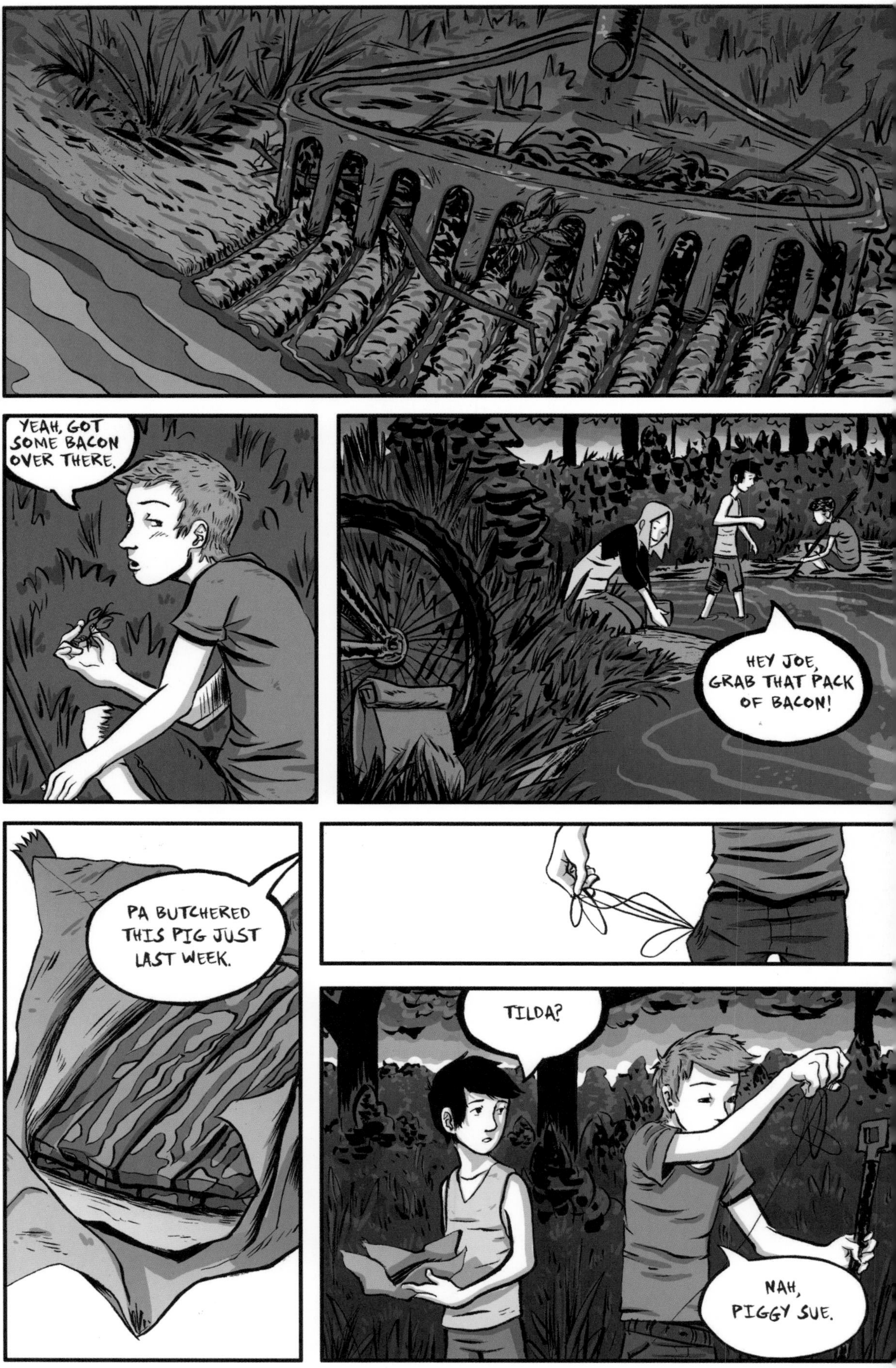
YEAH, GOT SOME BACON OVER THERE.
HEY JOE, GRAB THAT PACK OF BACON!
PA BUTCHERED THIS PIG JUST LAST WEEK.
TILDA?
NAH, PIGGY SUE.

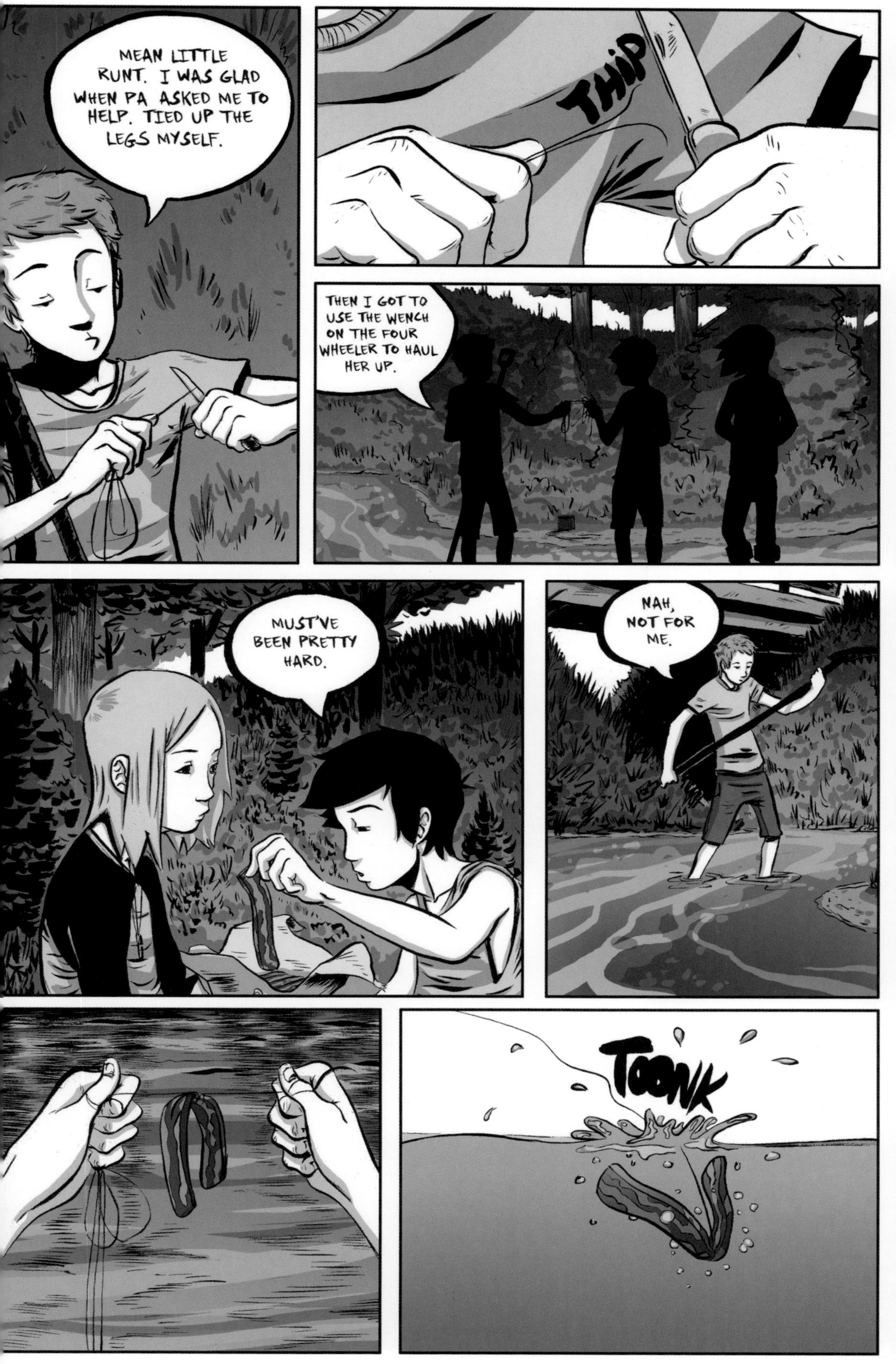
MEAN LITTLE RUNT. I WAS GLAD WHEN PA ASKED ME TO HELP. TIED UP THE LEGS MYSELF.
THIP
THEN I GOT TO USE THE WENCH ON THE FOUR WHEELER TO HAUL HER UP.
MUST'VE BEEN PRETTY HARD.
NAH, NOT FOR ME.
TOONK

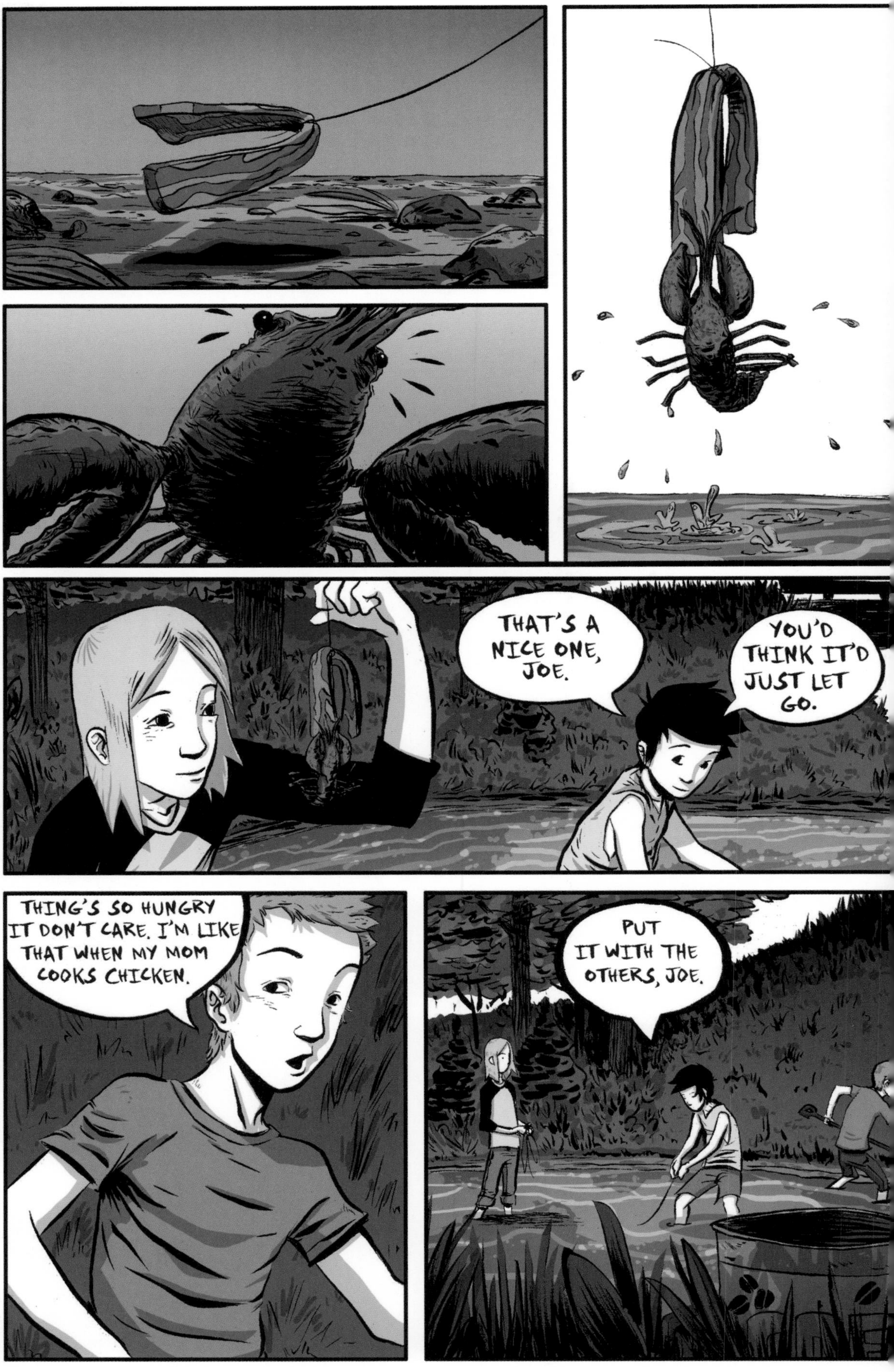
THAT'S A NICE ONE, JOE.
YOU'D THINK IT'D JUST LET GO.
THING'S SO HUNGRY IT DON'T CARE. I'M LIKE THAT WHEN MY MOM COOKS CHICKEN.
PUT IT WITH THE OTHERS, JOE.

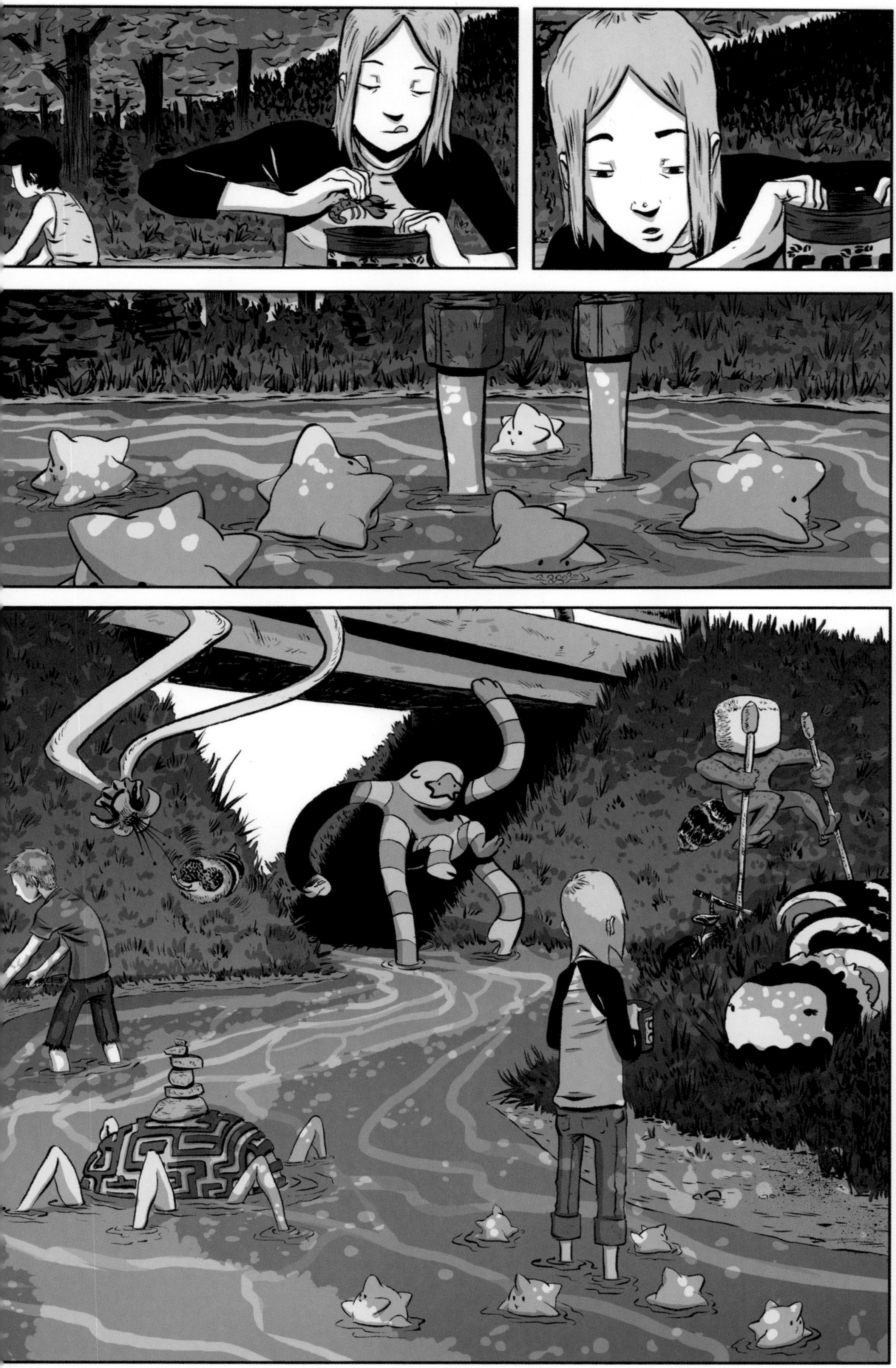

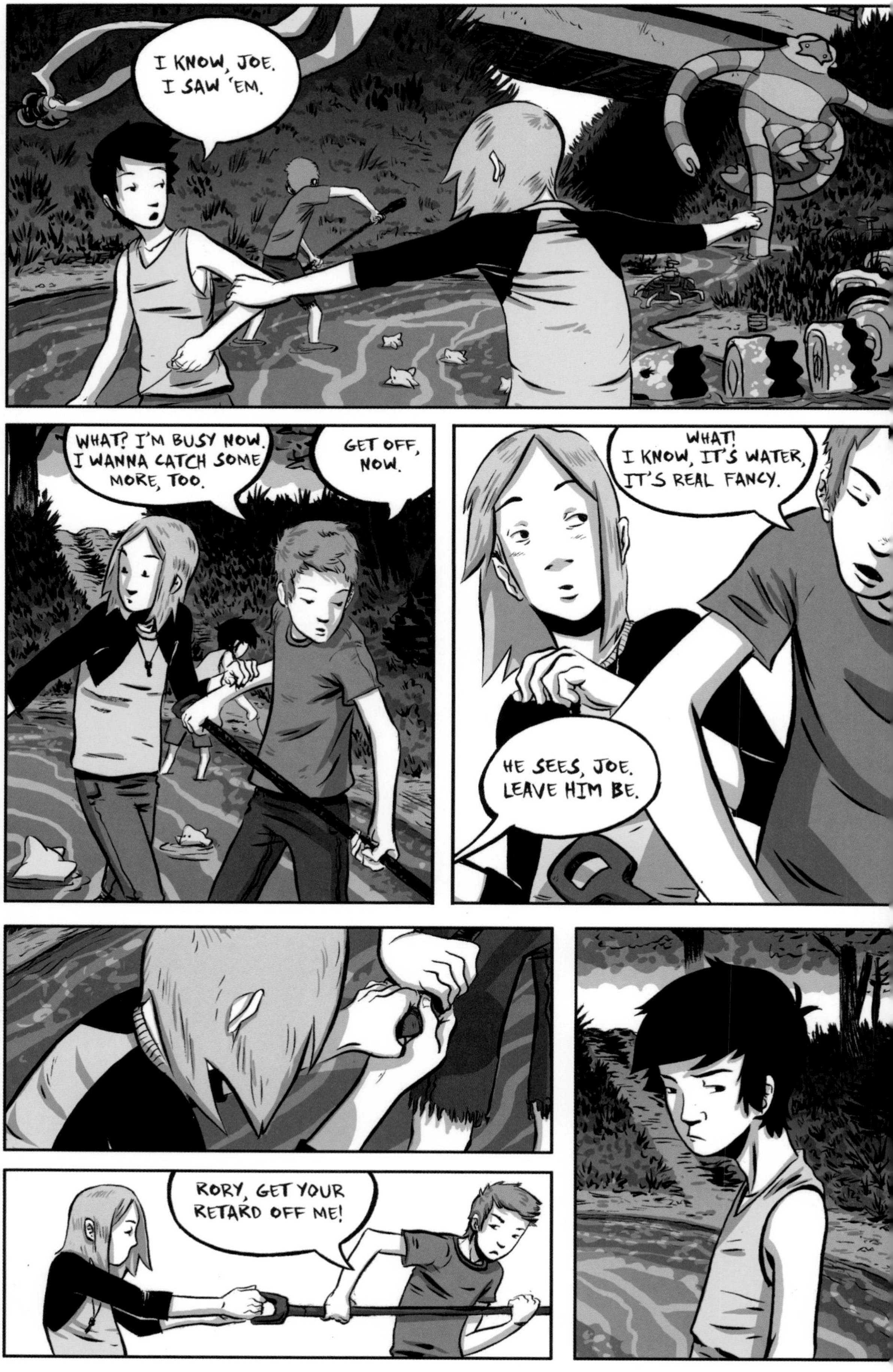
I KNOW, JOE. I SAW 'EM.
WHAT? I'M BUSY NOW. I WANNA CATCH SOME MORE, TOO.
GET OFF, NOW.
WHAT! I KNOW, IT'S WATER, IT'S REAL FANCY.
HE SEES, JOE. LEAVE HIM BE.
RORY, GET YOUR RETARD OFF ME!

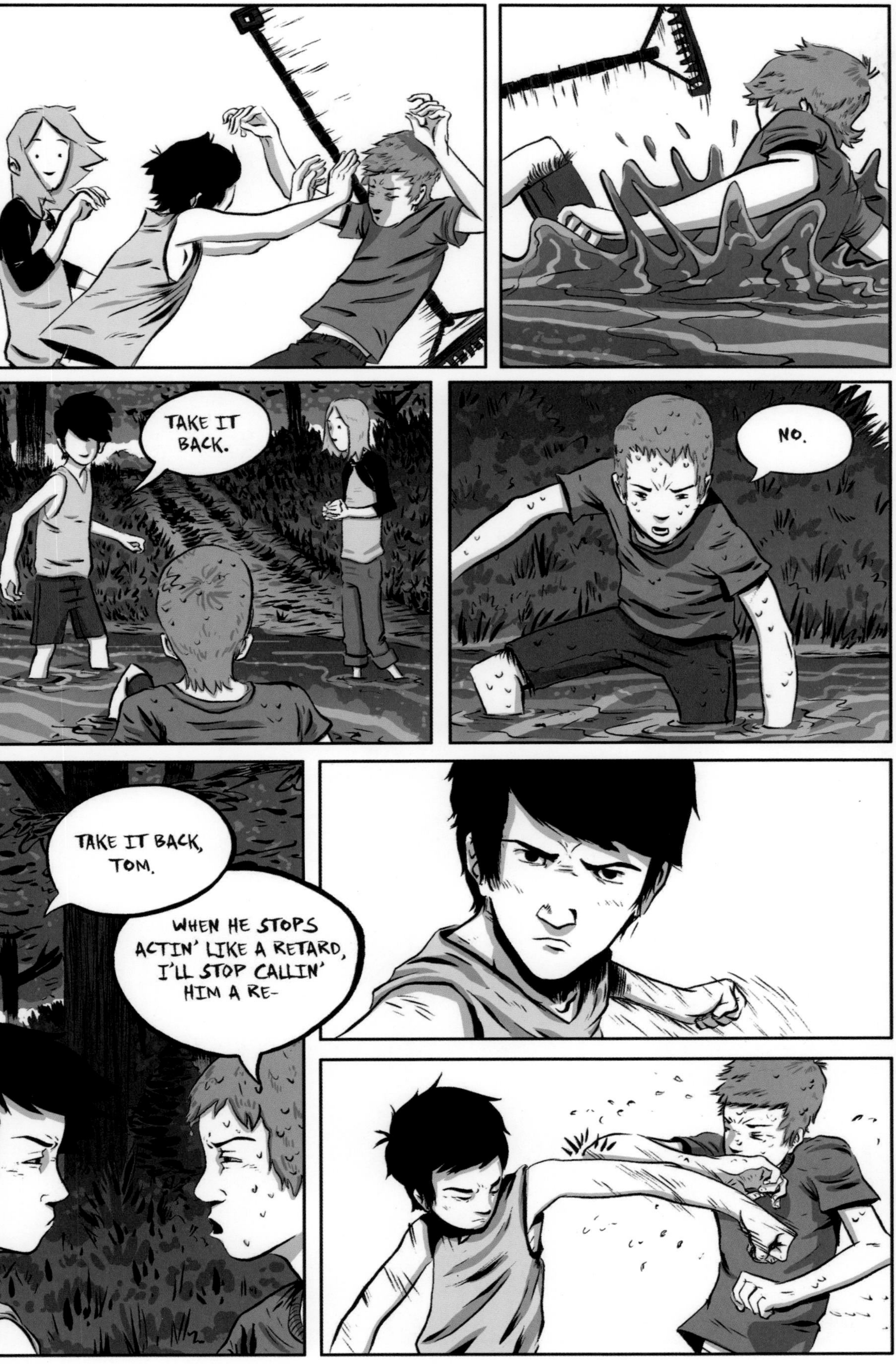
TAKE IT BACK.
NO.
TAKE IT BACK, TOM.
WHEN HE STOPS ACTIN' LIKE A RETARD, I'LL STOP CALLIN' HIM A RE-

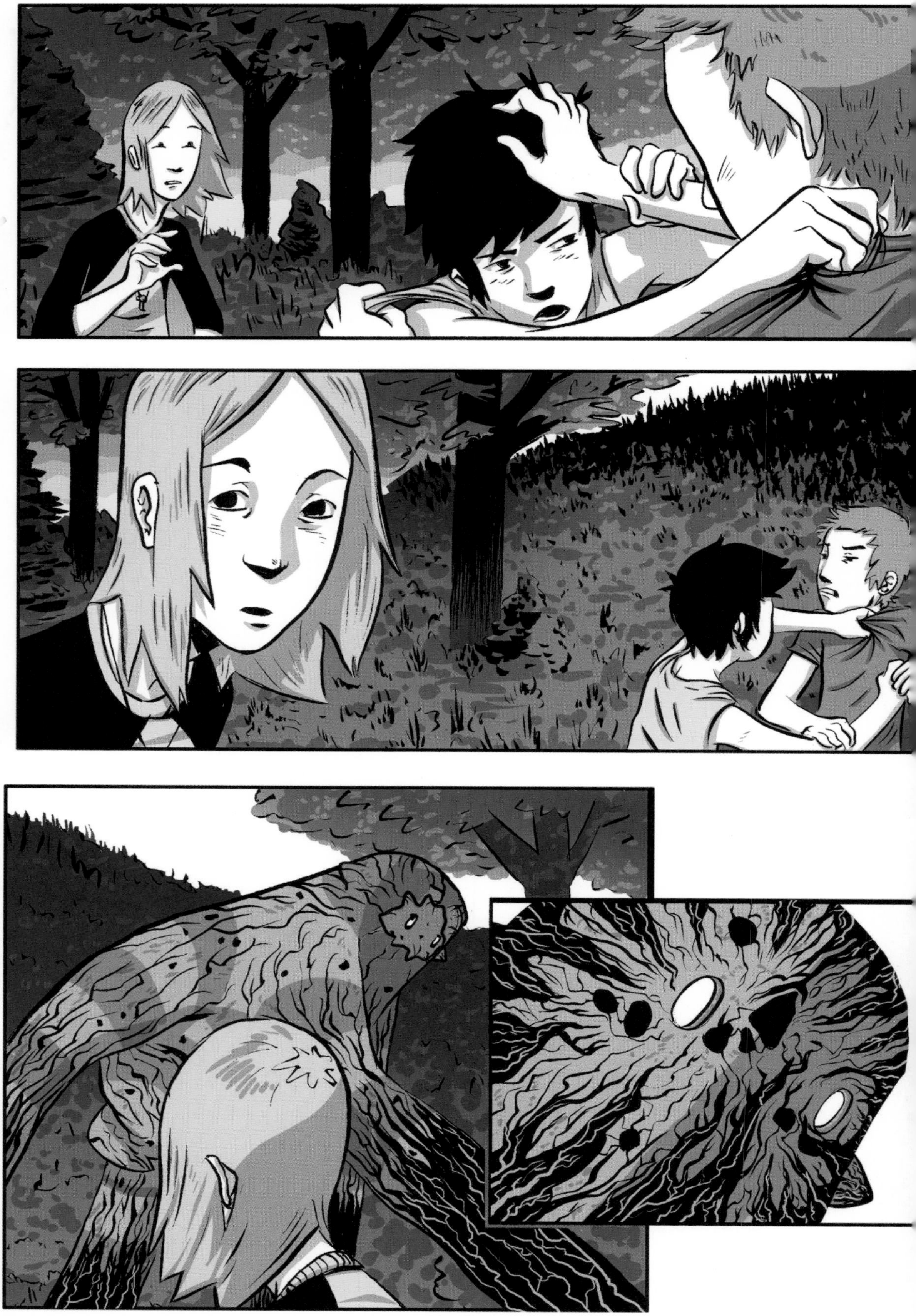

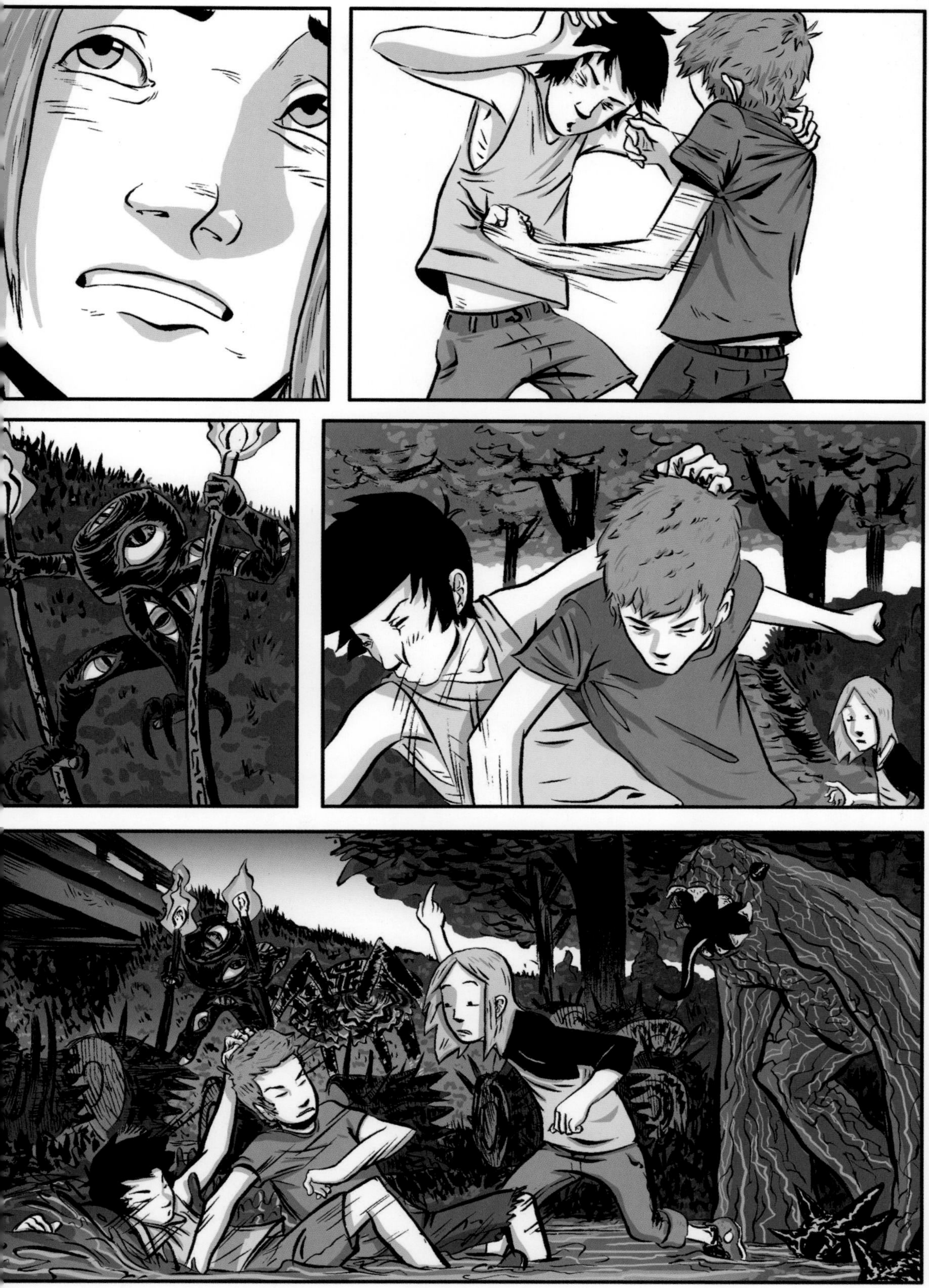

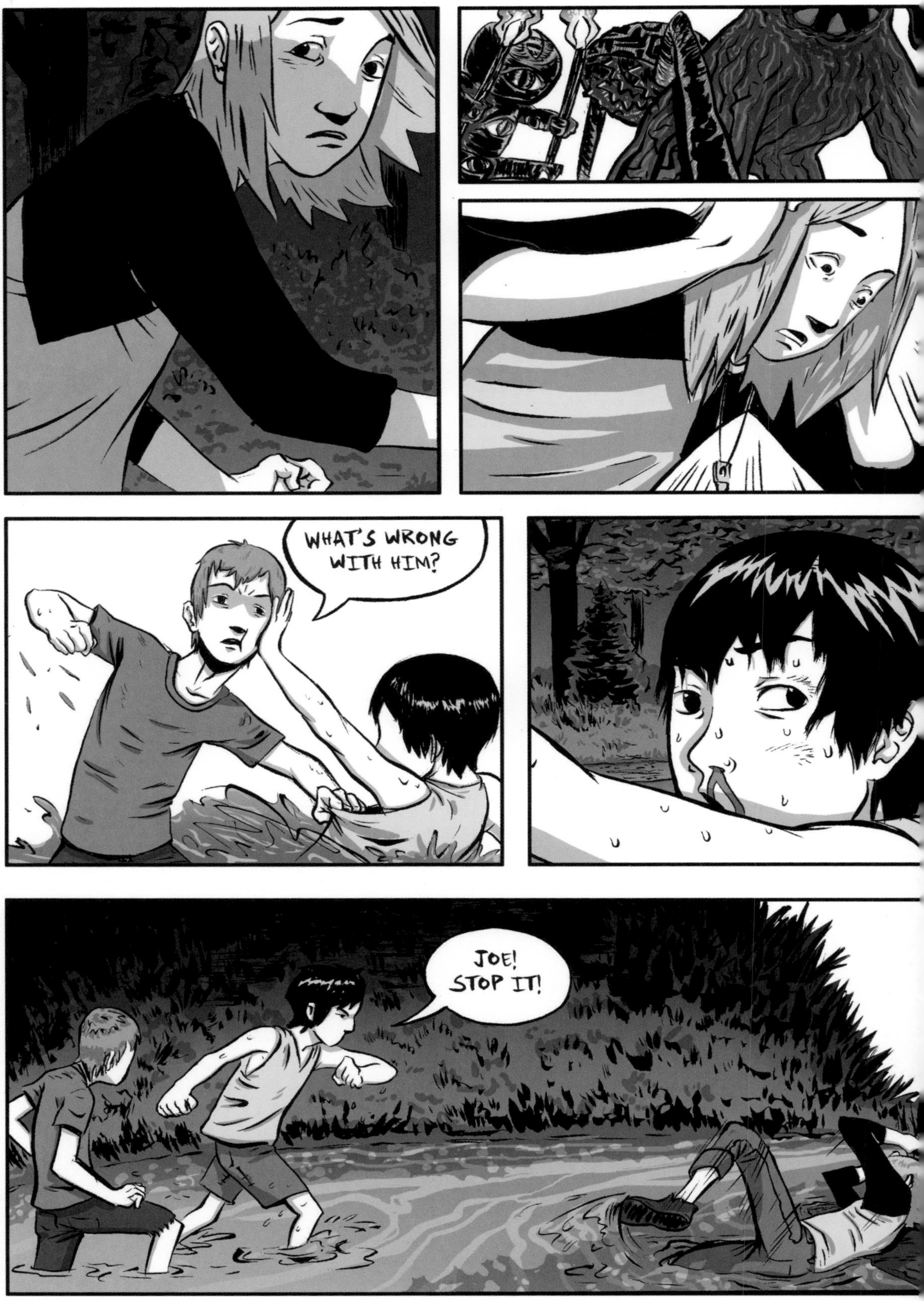
WHAT'S WRONG WITH HIM?
JOE! STOP IT!

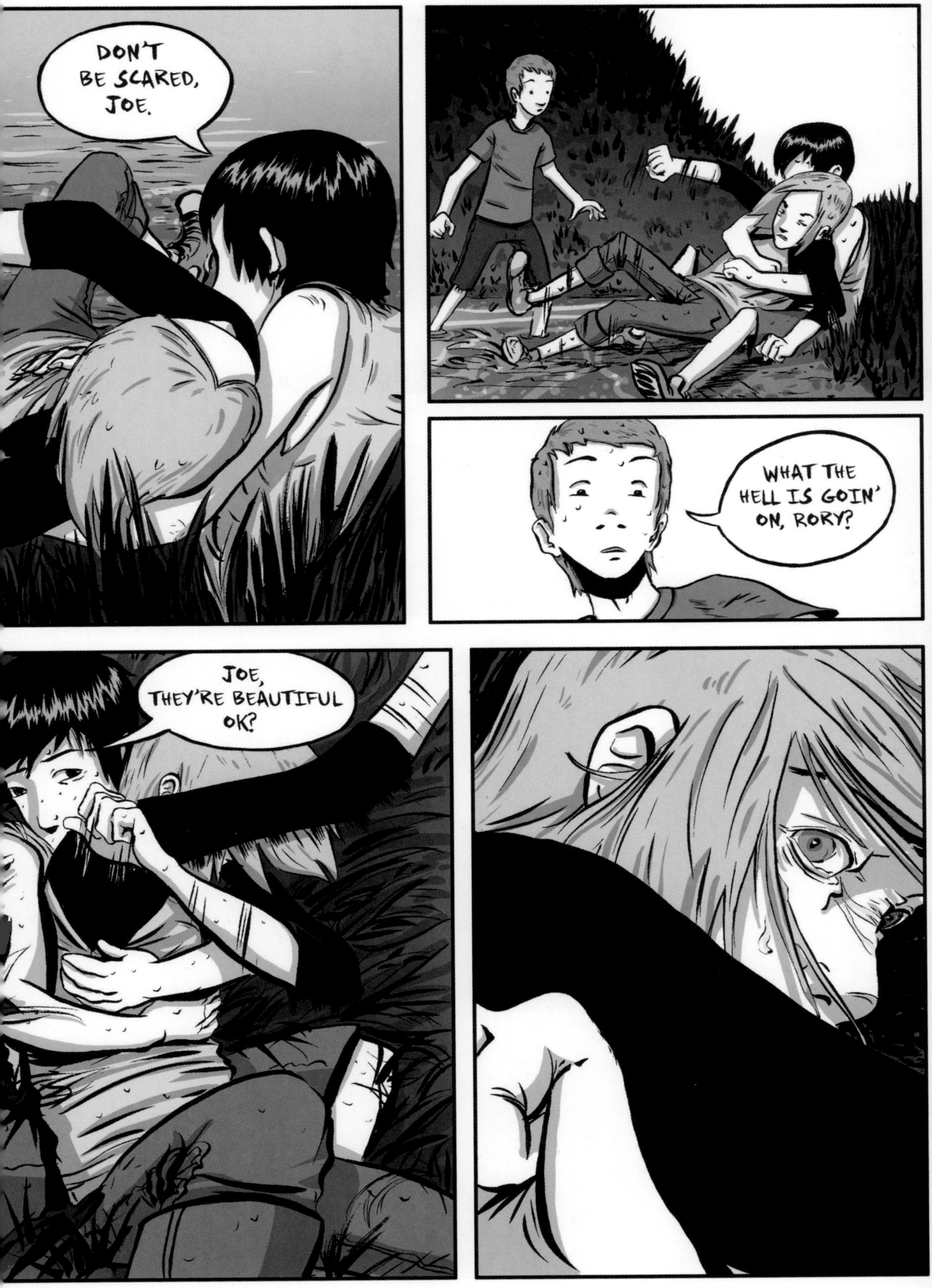
DON'T BE SCARED, JOE.
WHAT THE HELL IS GOIN' ON, RORY?
JOE, THEY'RE BEAUTIFUL OK?

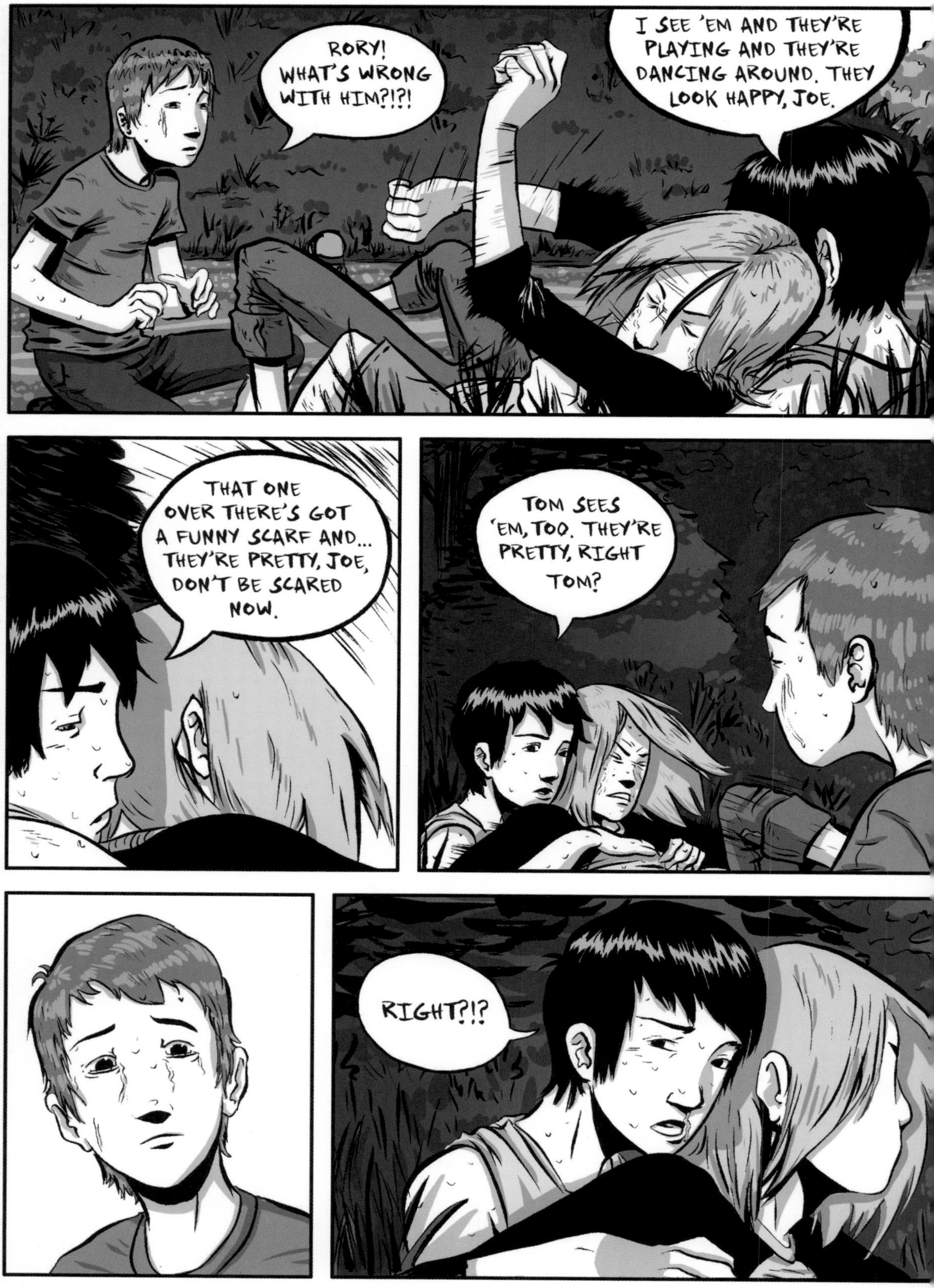
RORY! WHAT'S WRONG WITH HIM?!?!
I SEE 'EM AND THEY'RE PLAYING AND THEY'RE DANCING AROUND. THEY LOOK HAPPY, JOE.
THAT ONE OVER THERE'S GOT A FUNNY SCARF AND... THEY'RE PRETTY, JOE, DON'T BE SCARED NOW.
TOM SEES 'EM, TOO. THEY'RE PRETTY, RIGHT TOM?
RIGHT?!?

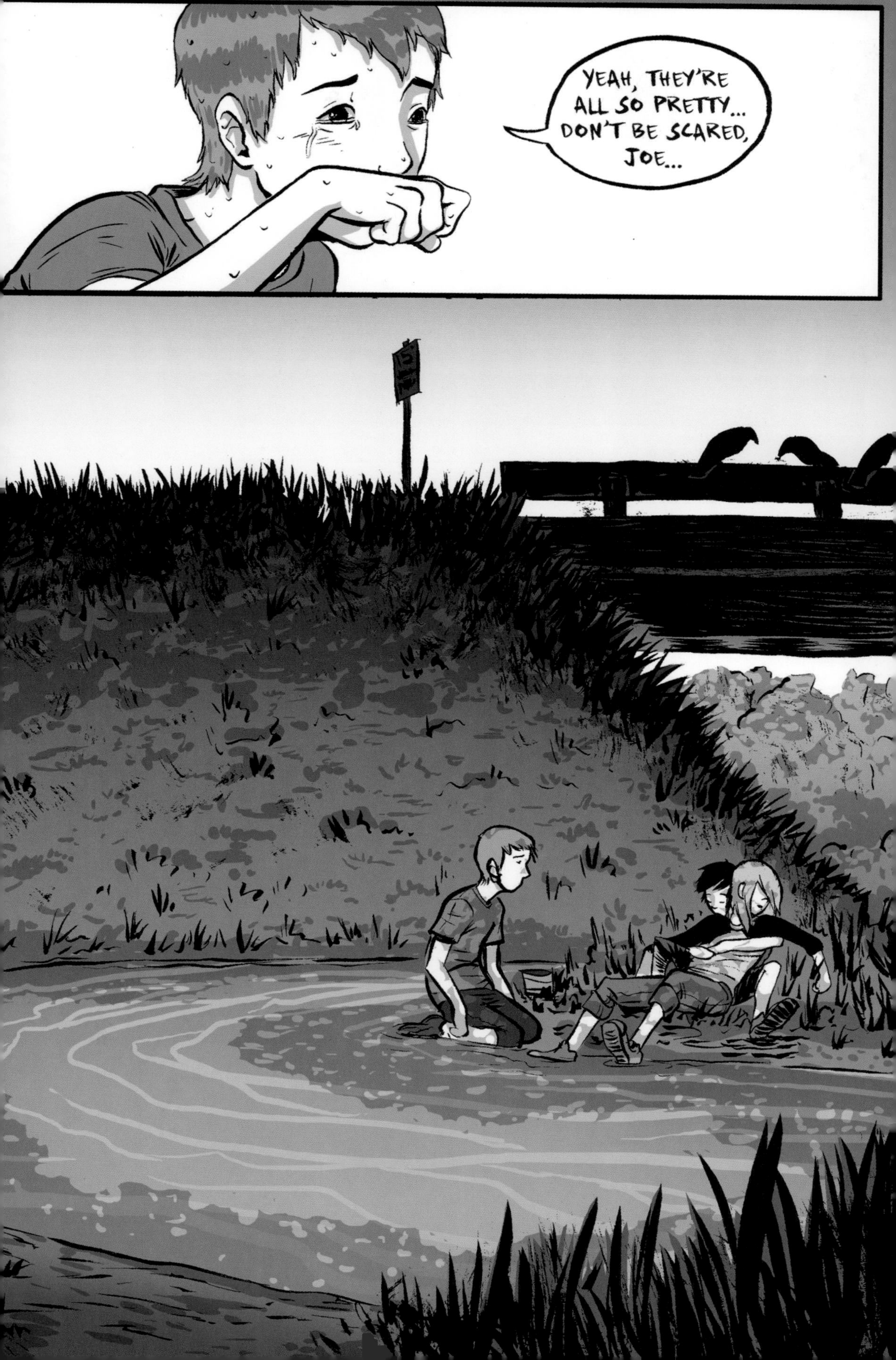
YEAH, THEY'RE ALL SO PRETTY... DON'T BE SCARED, JOE...

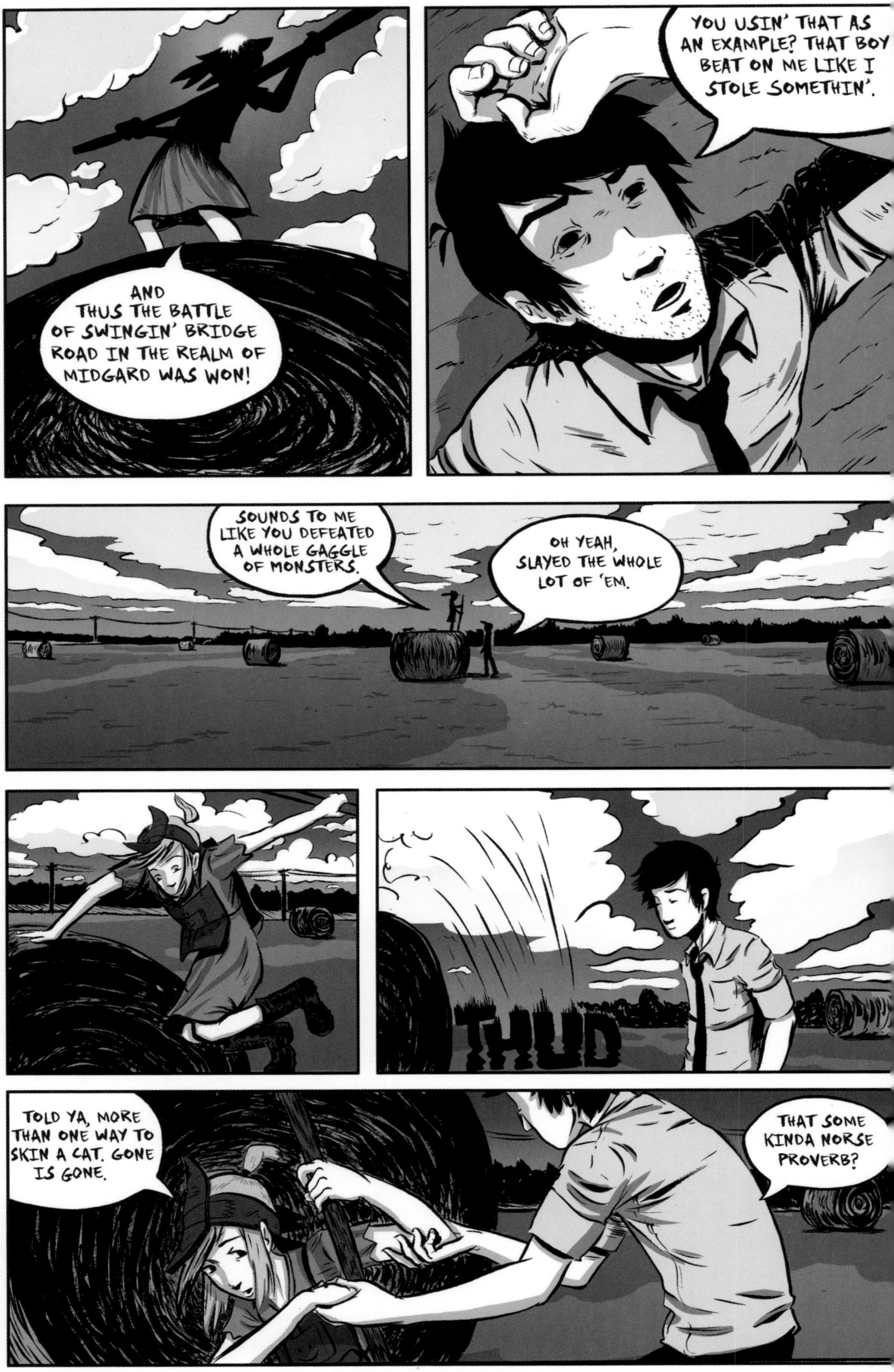
AND THUS THE BATTLE OF SWINGIN' BRIDGE ROAD IN THE REALM OF MIDGARD WAS WON!
YOU USIN' THAT AS AN EXAMPLE? THAT BOY BEAT ON ME LIKE I STOLE SOMETHIN'.
SOUNDS TO ME LIKE YOU DEFEATED A WHOLE GAGGLE OF MONSTERS.
OH YEAH, SLAYED THE WHOLE LOT OF 'EM.
THUD
TOLD YA, MORE THAN ONE WAY TO SKIN A CAT. GONE IS GONE.
THAT SOME KINDA NORSE PROVERB?

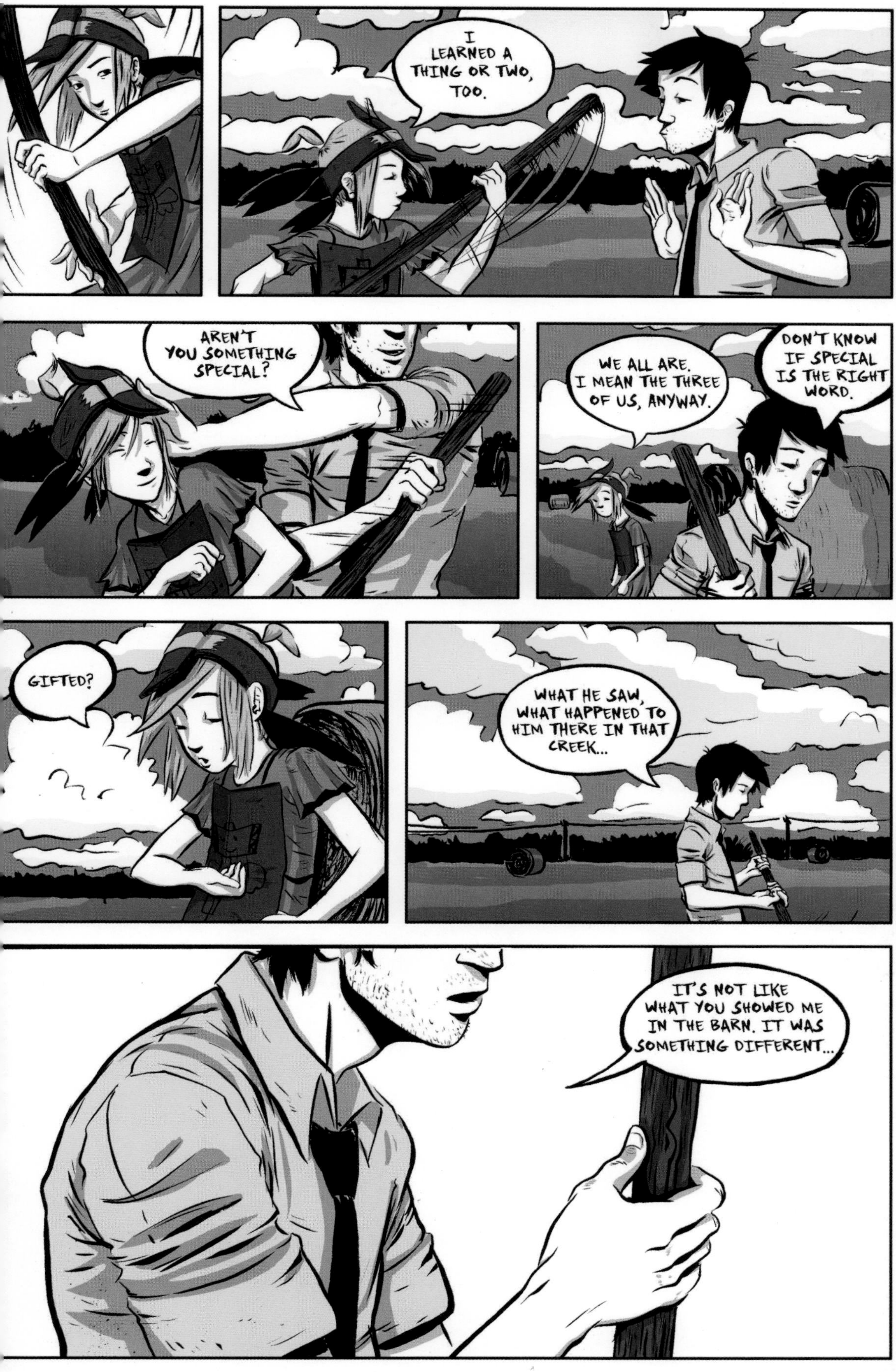
I LEARNED A THING OR TWO, TOO.
AREN'T YOU SOMETHING SPECIAL?
WE ALL ARE. I MEAN THE THREE OF US, ANYWAY.
DON'T KNOW IF SPECIAL IS THE RIGHT WORD.
GIFTED?
WHAT HE SAW, WHAT HAPPENED TO HIM THERE IN THAT CREEK...
IT'S NOT LIKE WHAT YOU SHOWED ME IN THE BARN. IT WAS SOMETHING DIFFERENT...

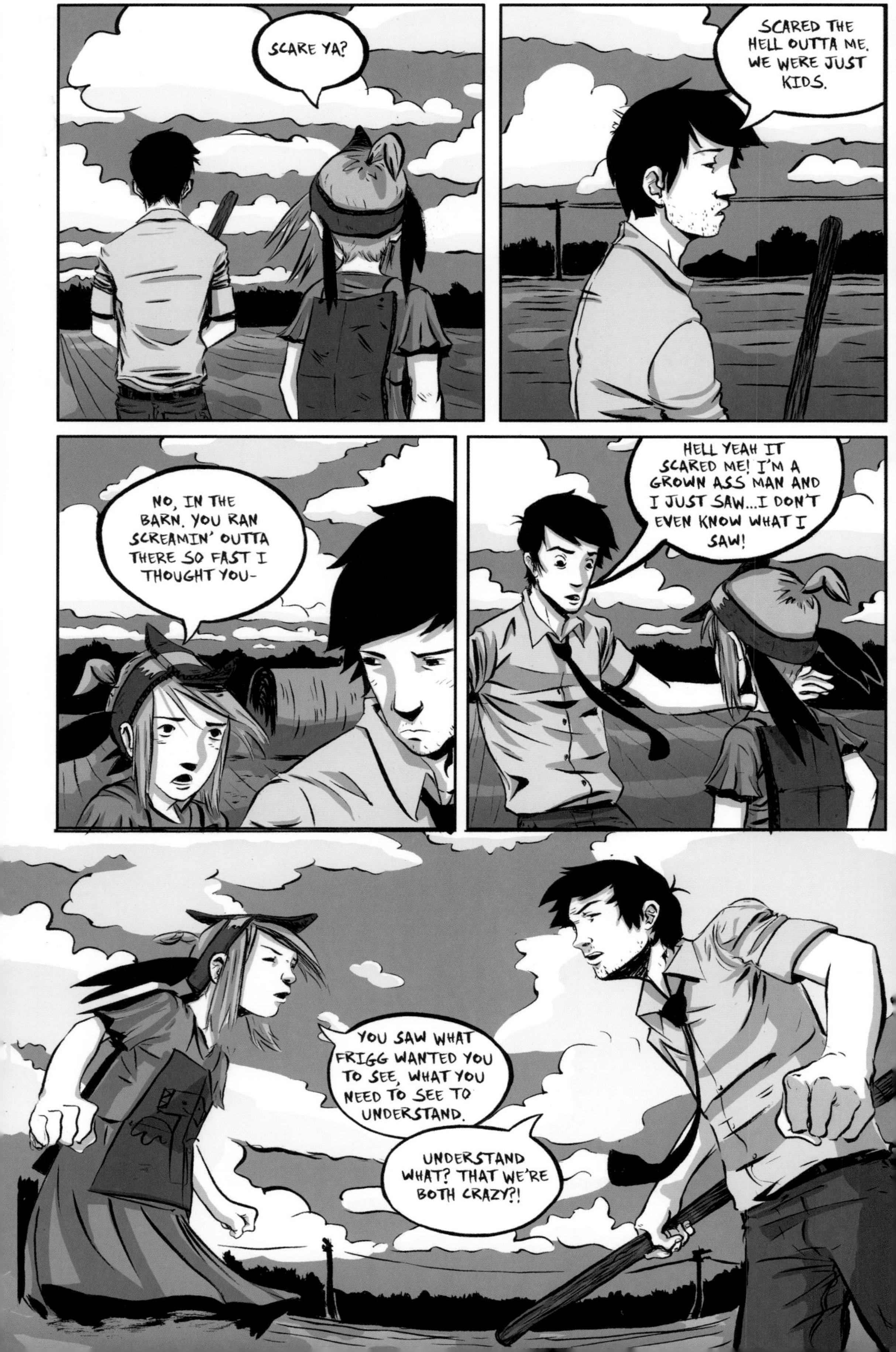
SCARE YA?
SCARED THE HELL OUTTA ME. WE WERE JUST KIDS.
NO, IN THE BARN. YOU RAN SCREAMIN' OUTTA THERE SO FAST I THOUGHT YOU-
HELL YEAH IT SCARED ME! I'M A GROWN ASS MAN AND I JUST SAW...I DON'T EVEN KNOW WHAT I SAW!
YOU SAW WHAT FRIGG WANTED YOU TO SEE, WHAT YOU NEED TO SEE TO UNDERSTAND.
UNDERSTAND WHAT? THAT WE'RE BOTH CRAZY?!

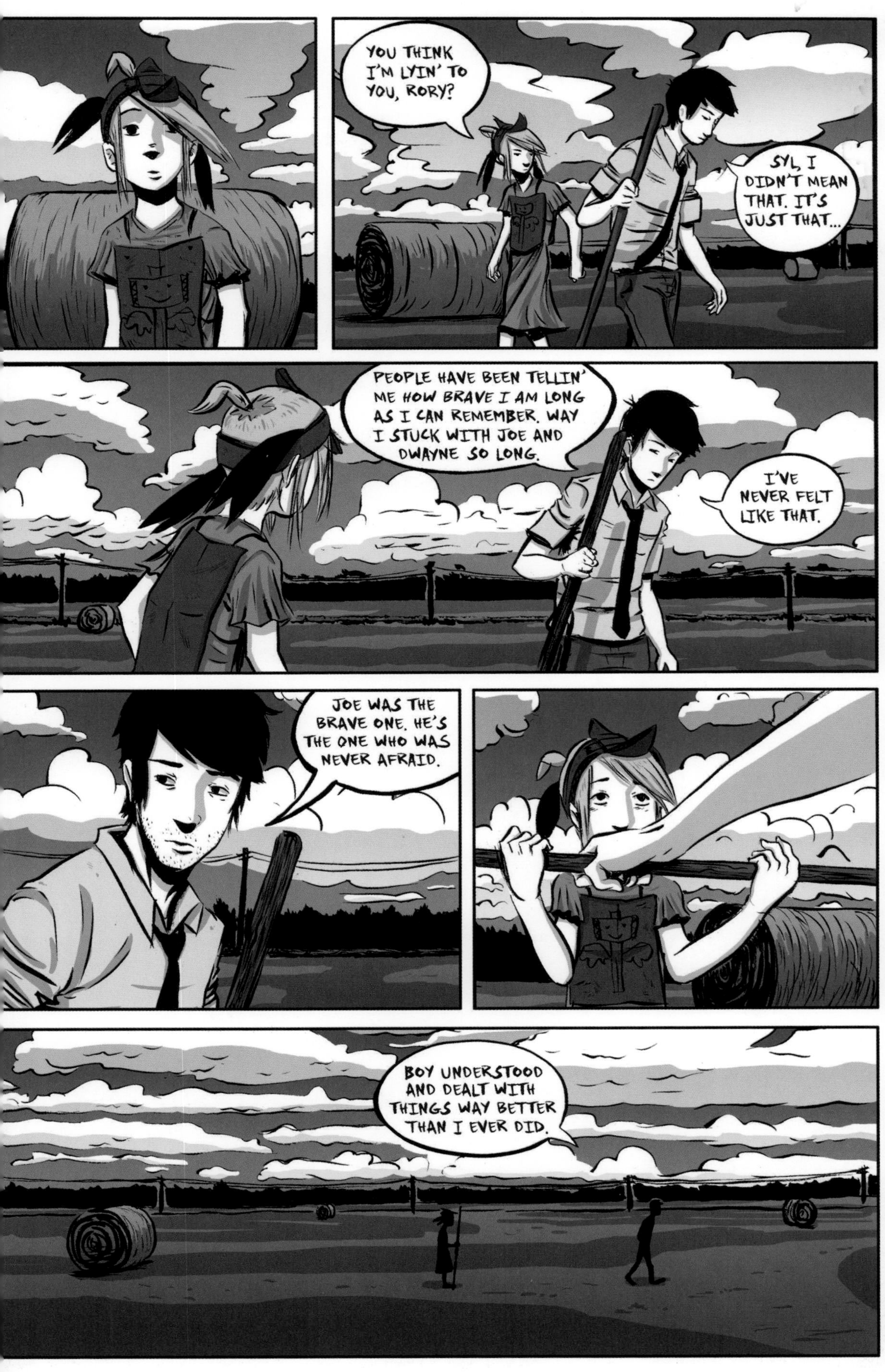

YOU THINK I'M LYIN' TO YOU, RORY?
SYL, I DIDN'T MEAN THAT. IT'S JUST THAT...
PEOPLE HAVE BEEN TELLIN' ME HOW *BRAVE* I AM LONG AS I CAN REMEMBER. WAY I STUCK WITH JOE AND DWAYNE SO LONG.
I'VE NEVER FELT LIKE THAT.
JOE WAS THE BRAVE ONE. HE'S THE ONE WHO WAS NEVER AFRAID.
BOY UNDERSTOOD AND DEALT WITH THINGS WAY BETTER THAN I EVER DID.

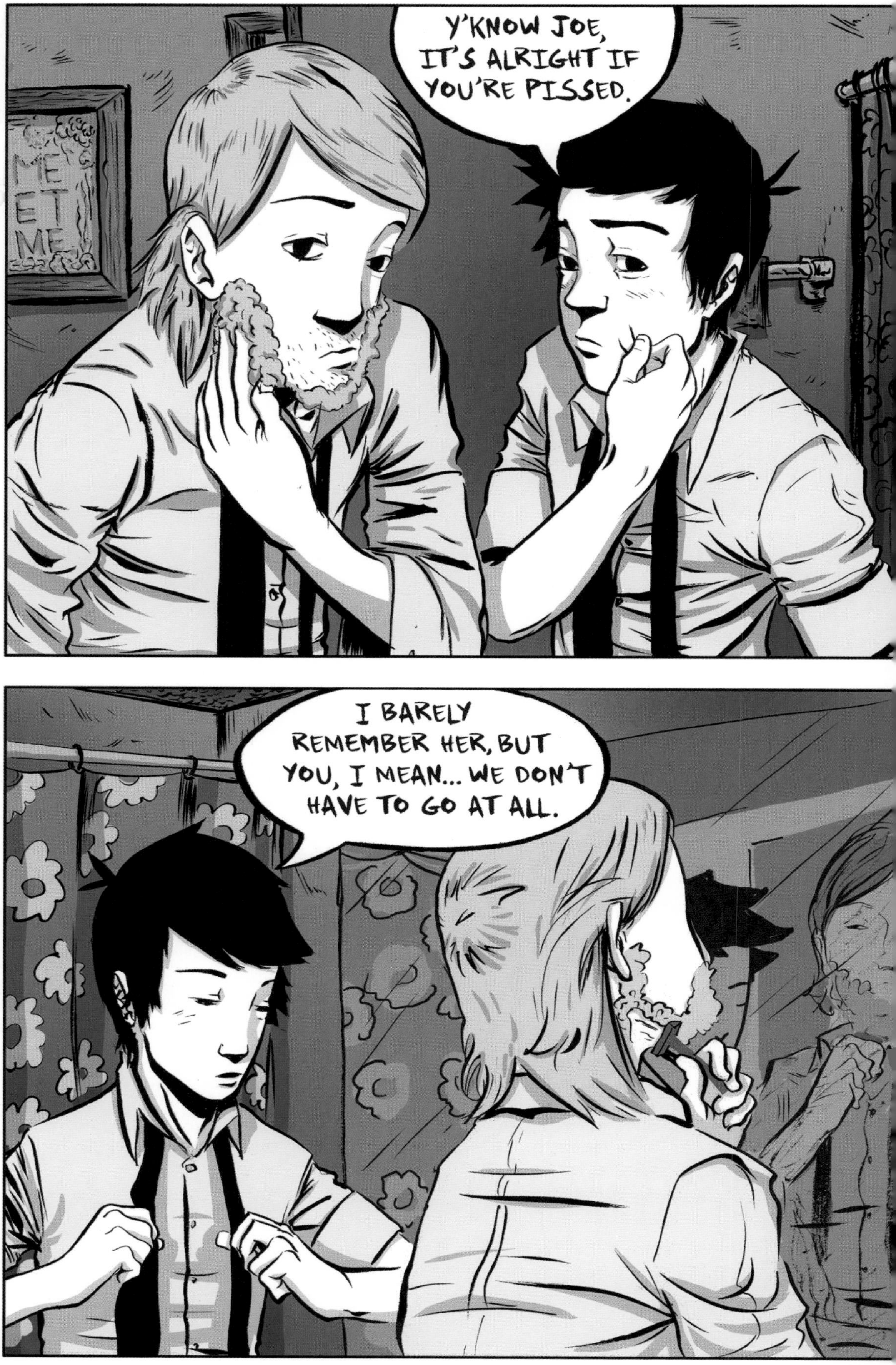
Y'KNOW JOE, IT'S ALRIGHT IF YOU'RE PISSED.
I BARELY REMEMBER HER, BUT YOU, I MEAN... WE DON'T HAVE TO GO AT ALL.

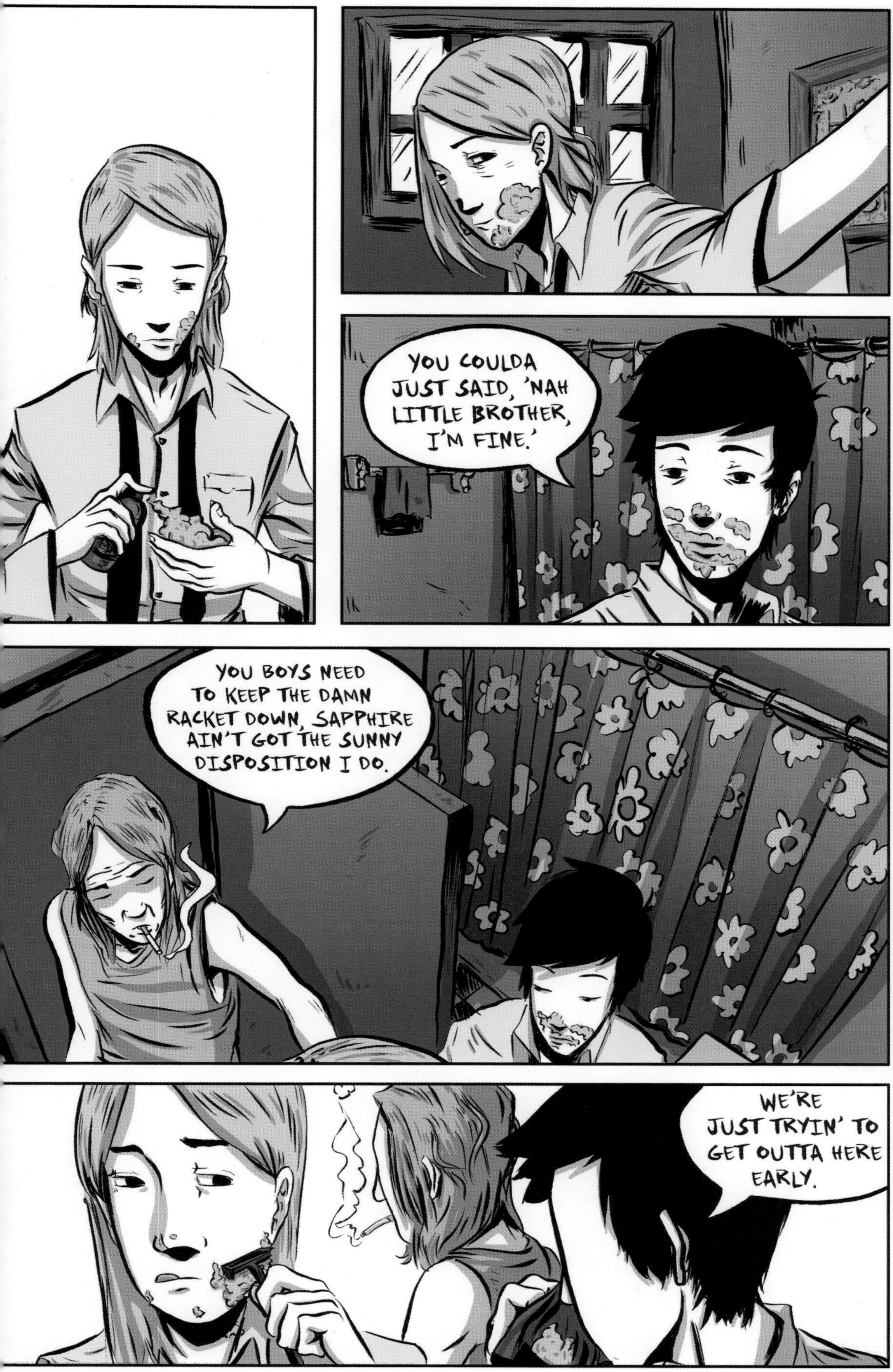
YOU COULDA JUST SAID, 'NAH LITTLE BROTHER, I'M FINE.'
YOU BOYS NEED TO KEEP THE DAMN RACKET DOWN, SAPPHIRE AIN'T GOT THE SUNNY DISPOSITION I DO.
WE'RE JUST TRYIN' TO GET OUTTA HERE EARLY.

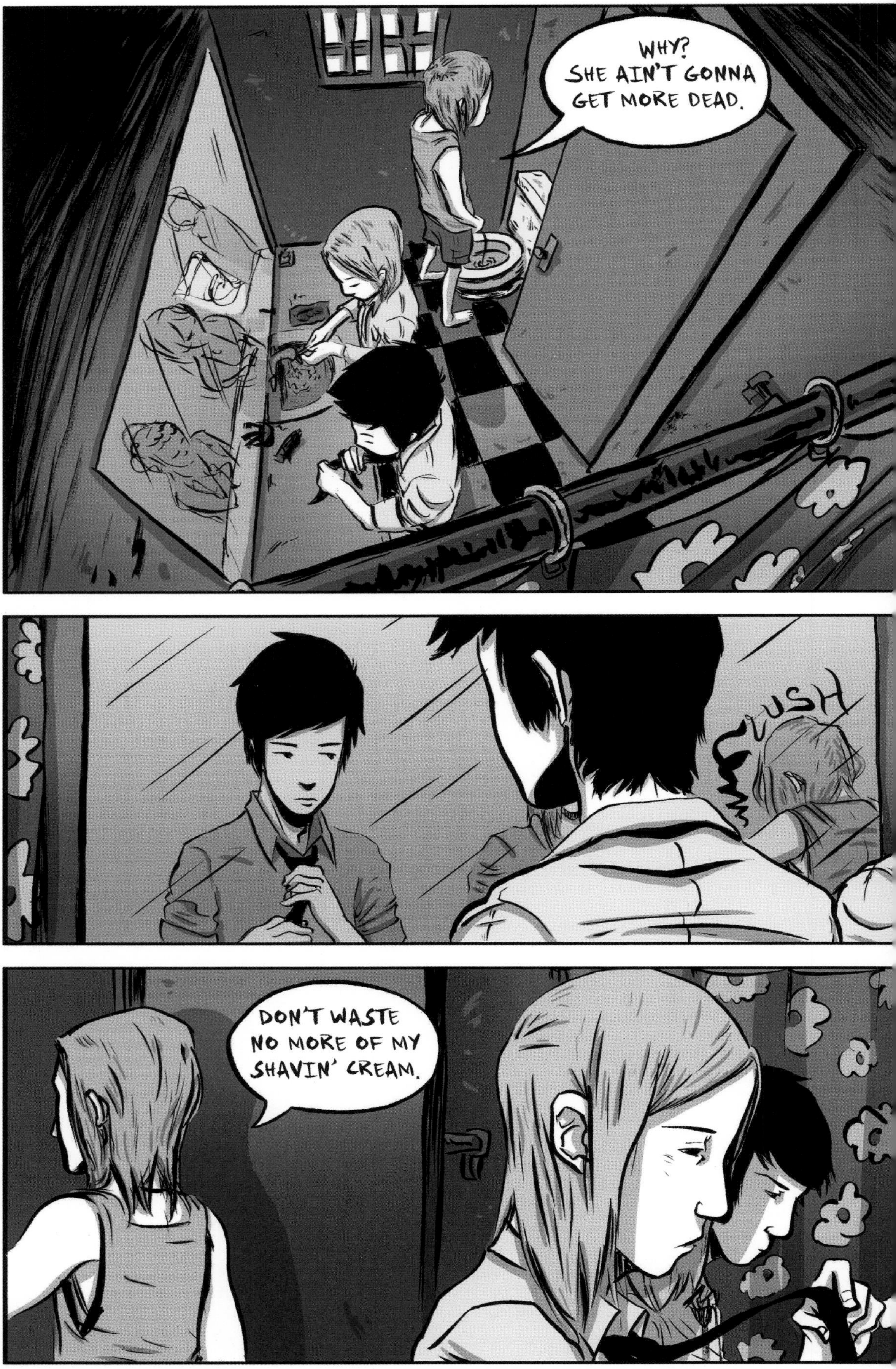
WHY? SHE AIN'T GONNA GET MORE DEAD.
DON'T WASTE NO MORE OF MY SHAVIN' CREAM.

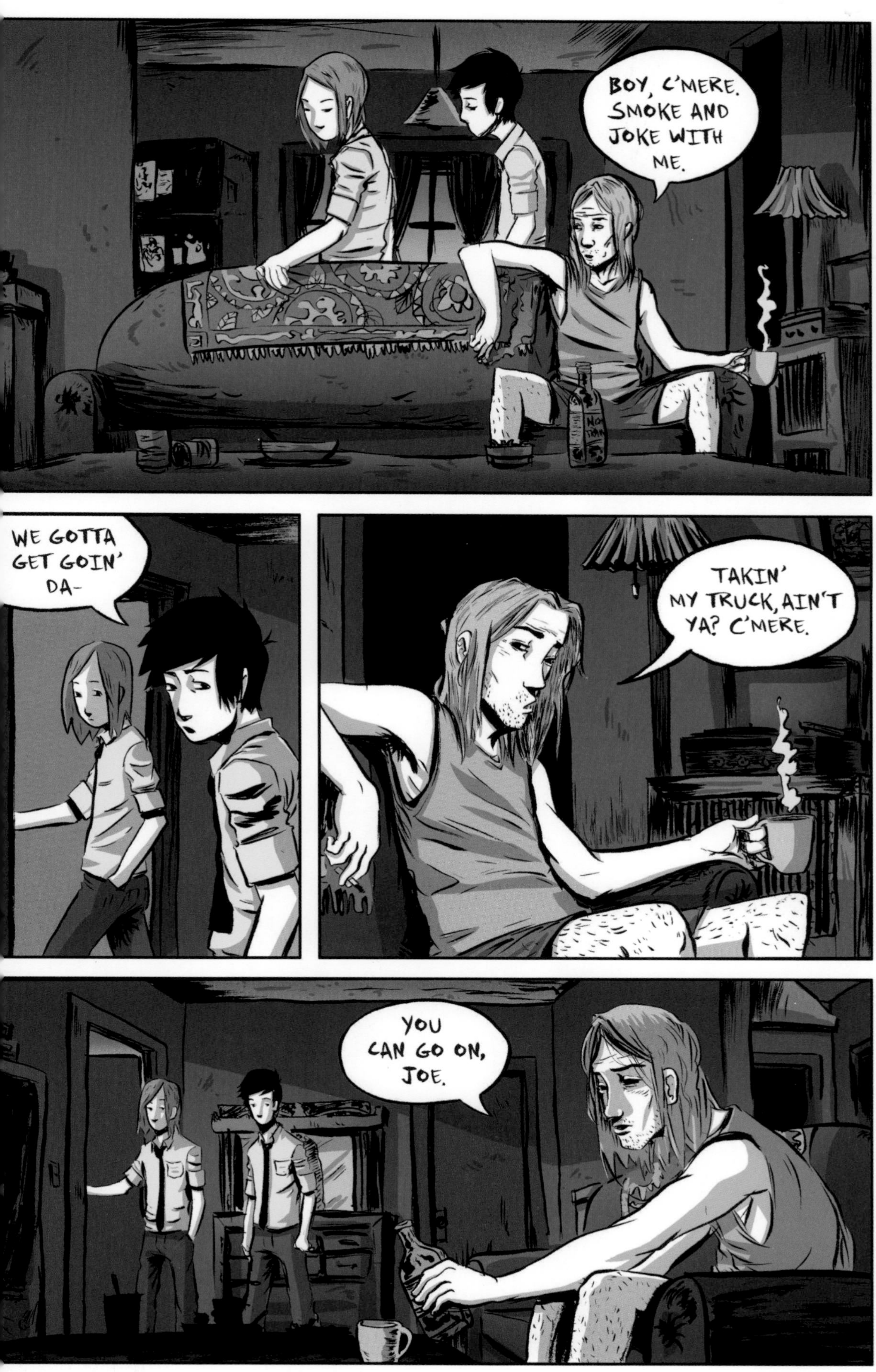
BOY, C'MERE. SMOKE AND JOKE WITH ME.
WE GOTTA GET GOIN' DA-
TAKIN' MY TRUCK, AIN'T YA? C'MERE.
YOU CAN GO ON, JOE.

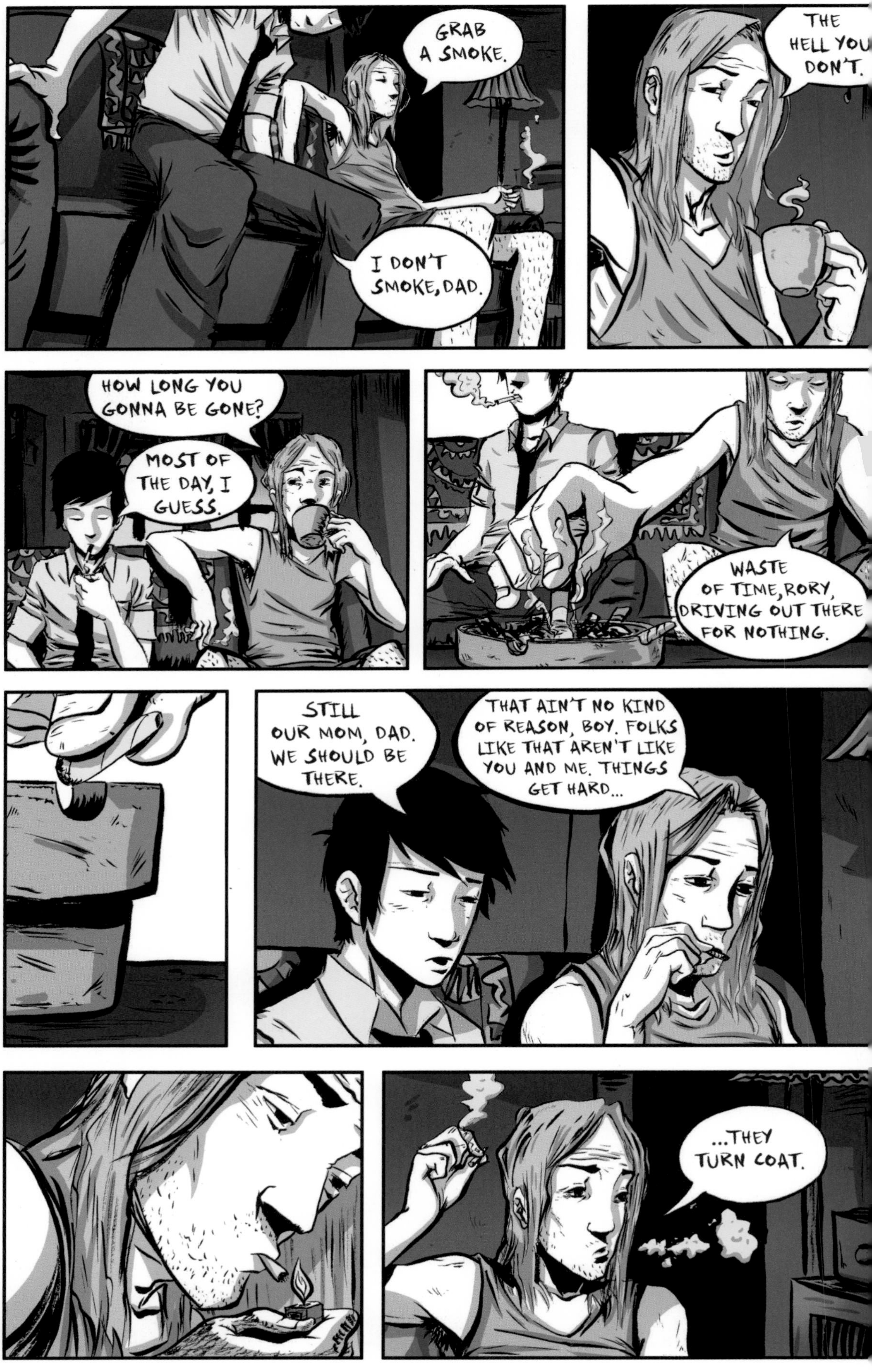
GRAB A SMOKE.
I DON'T SMOKE, DAD.
THE HELL YOU DON'T.
HOW LONG YOU GONNA BE GONE?
MOST OF THE DAY, I GUESS.
WASTE OF TIME, RORY, DRIVING OUT THERE FOR NOTHING.
STILL OUR MOM, DAD. WE SHOULD BE THERE.
THAT AIN'T NO KIND OF REASON, BOY. FOLKS LIKE THAT AREN'T LIKE YOU AND ME. THINGS GET HARD...
...THEY TURN COAT.

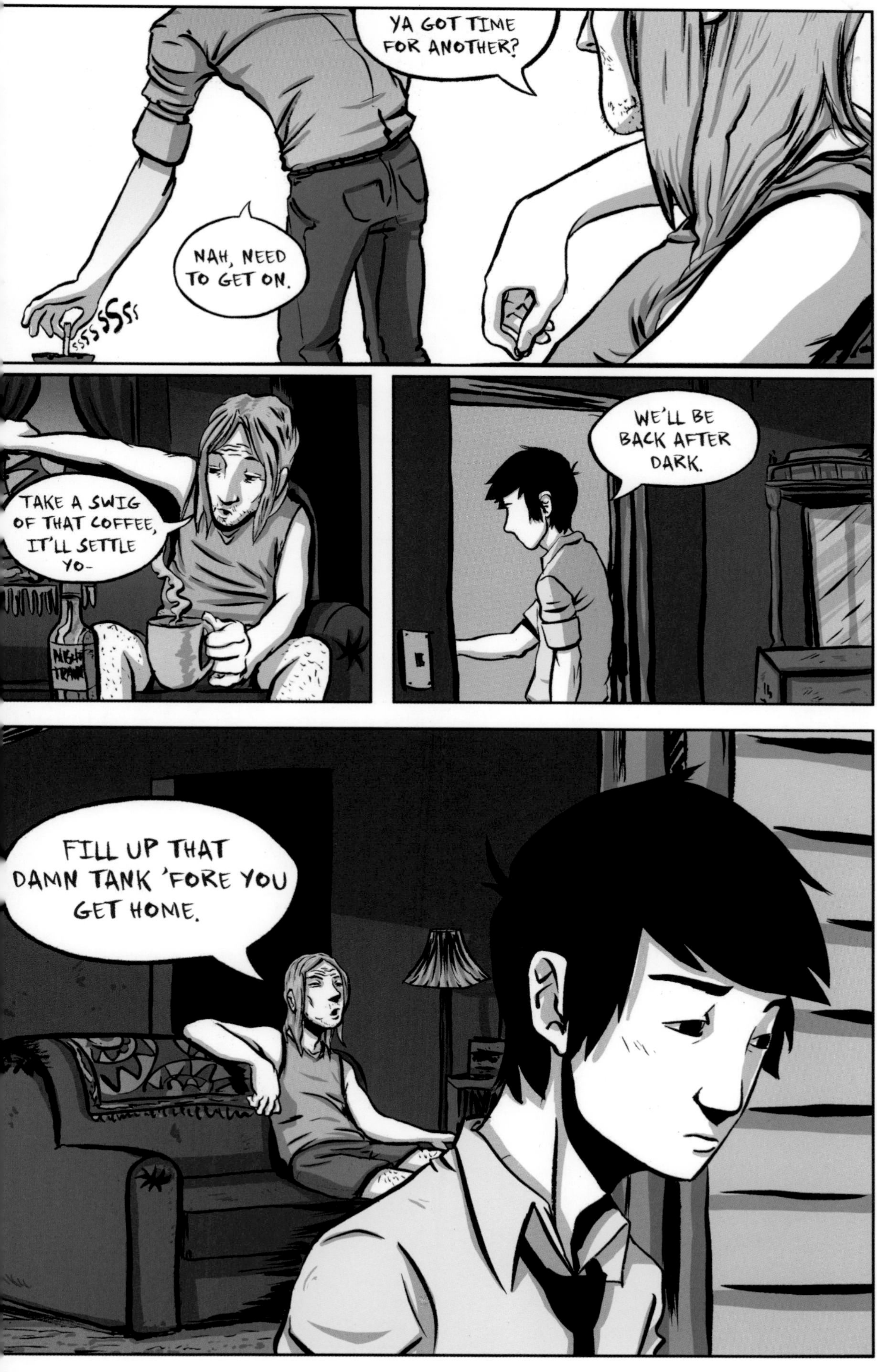
YA GOT TIME FOR ANOTHER?
NAH, NEED TO GET ON.
SSSSSSSSS
TAKE A SWIG OF THAT COFFEE, IT'LL SETTLE YO-
WE'LL BE BACK AFTER DARK.
FILL UP THAT DAMN TANK 'FORE YOU GET HOME.

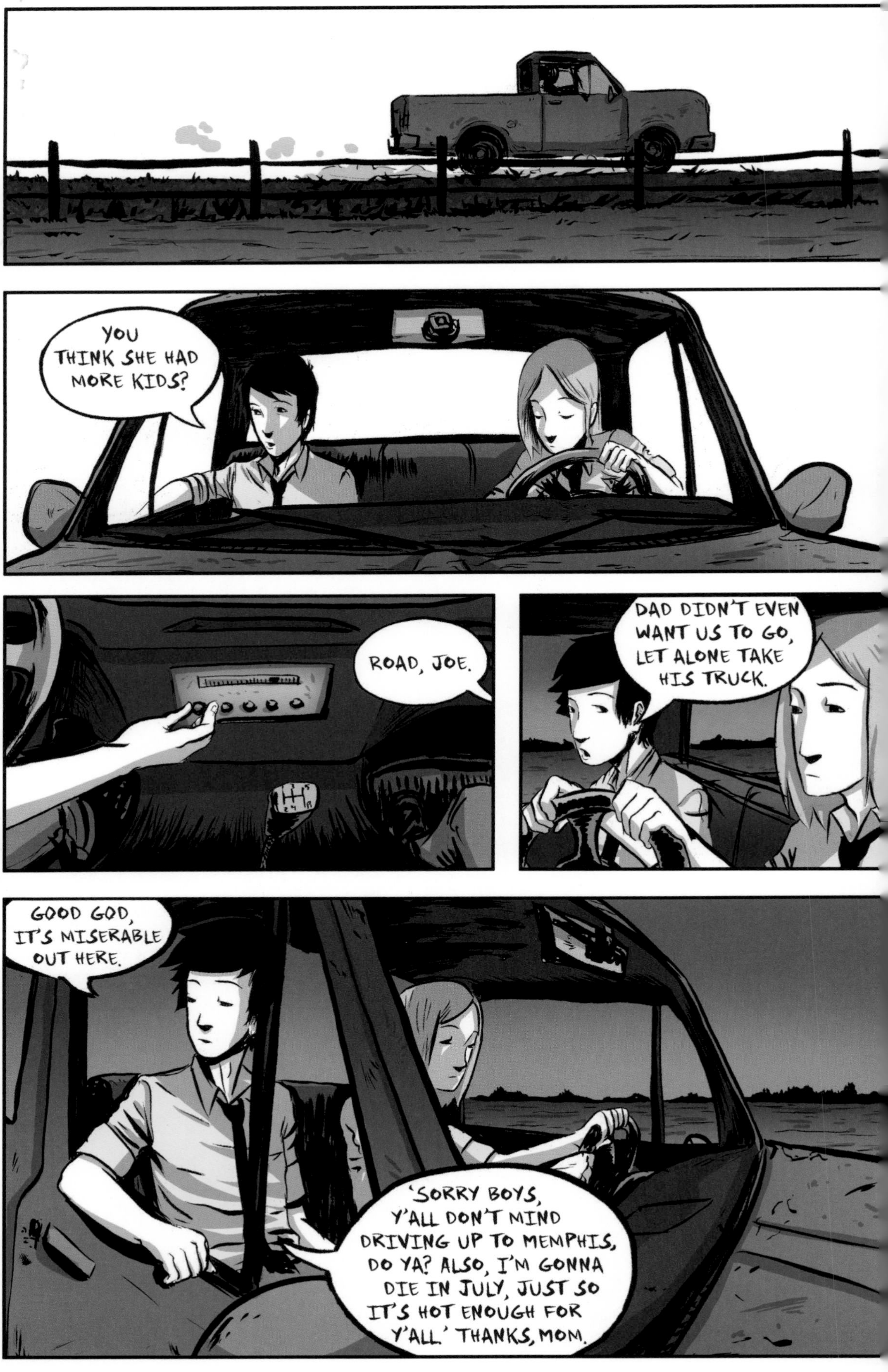
YOU THINK SHE HAD MORE KIDS?
ROAD, JOE.
DAD DIDN'T EVEN WANT US TO GO, LET ALONE TAKE HIS TRUCK.
GOOD GOD, IT'S MISERABLE OUT HERE.
'SORRY BOYS, Y'ALL DON'T MIND DRIVING UP TO MEMPHIS, DO YA? ALSO, I'M GONNA DIE IN JULY, JUST SO IT'S HOT ENOUGH FOR Y'ALL.' THANKS, MOM.

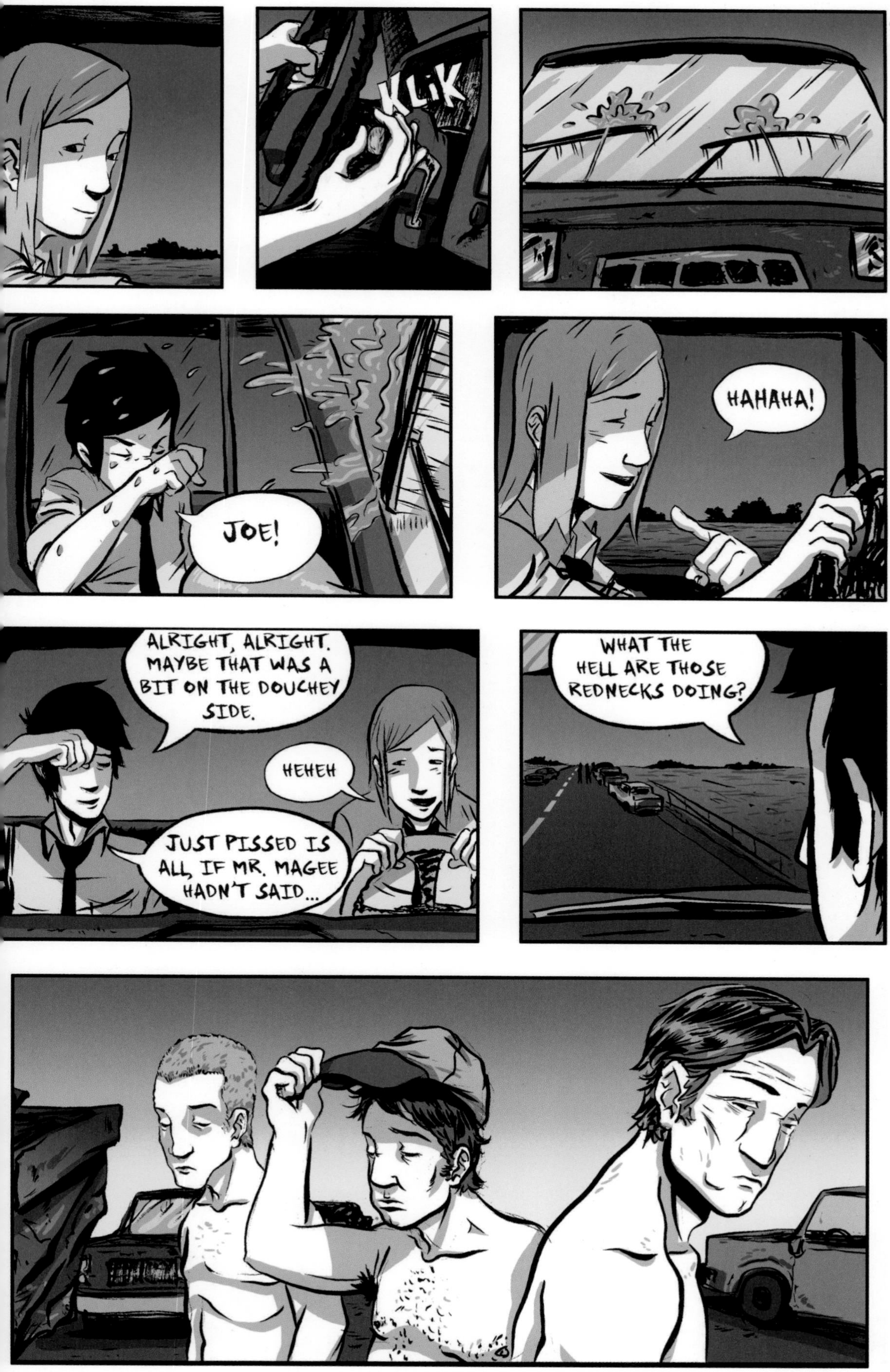
KLiK
JOE!
HAHAHA!
ALRIGHT, ALRIGHT. MAYBE THAT WAS A BIT ON THE DOUCHEY SIDE.
HEHEH
JUST PISSED IS ALL, IF MR. MAGEE HADN'T SAID...
WHAT THE HELL ARE THOSE REDNECKS DOING?

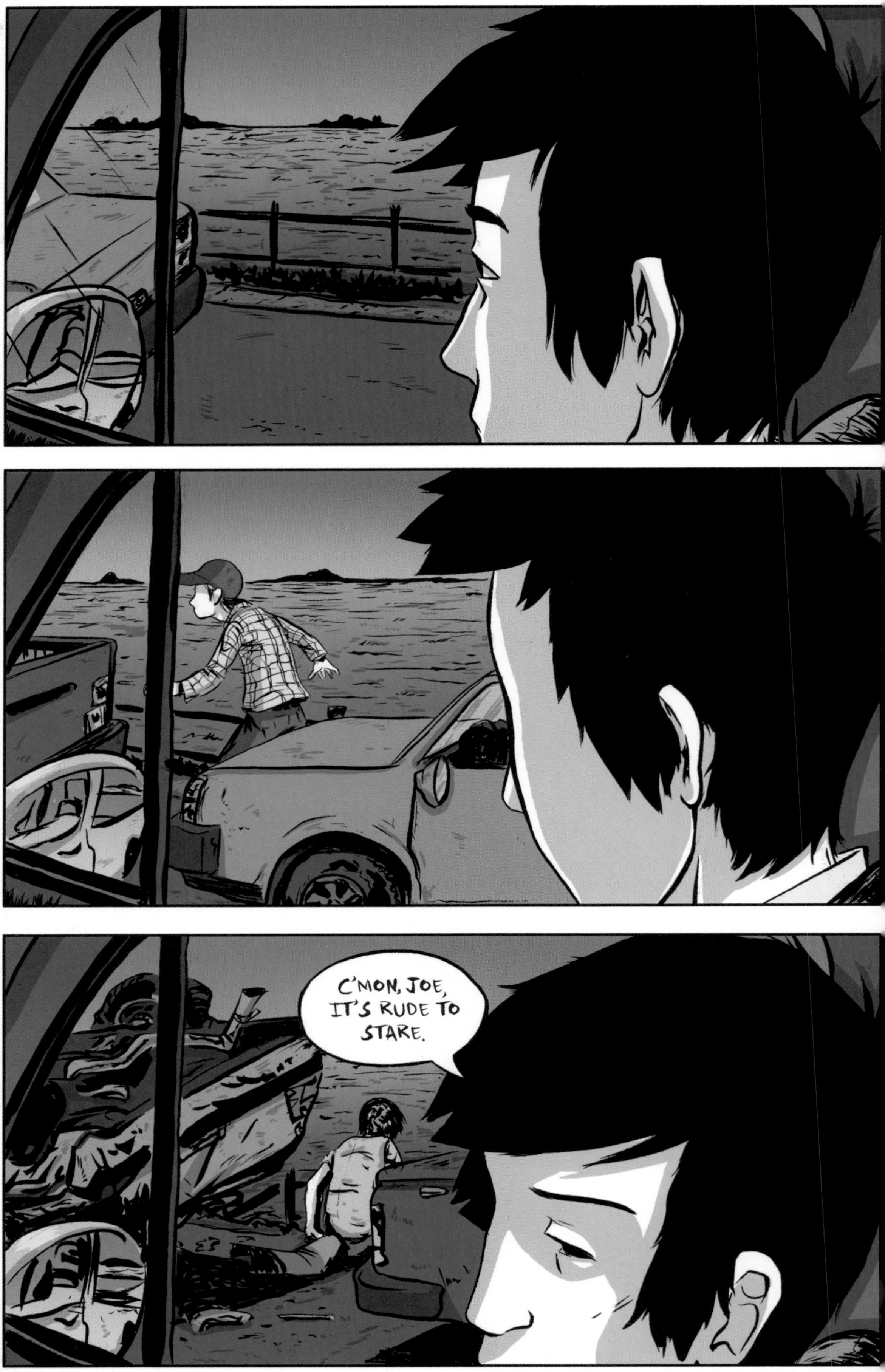
C'MON, JOE, IT'S RUDE TO STARE.

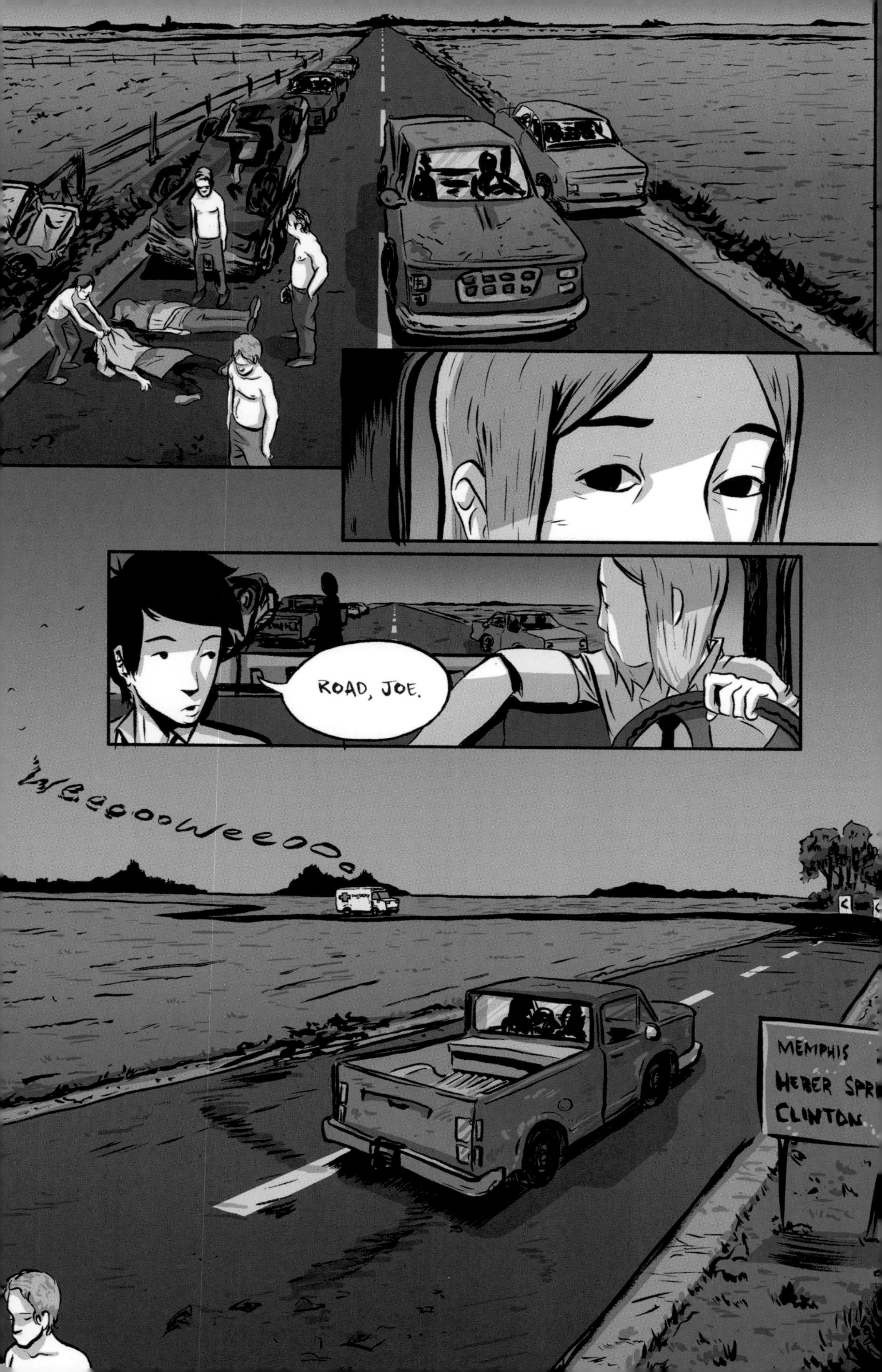
ROAD, JOE.
WEEOOOWEEOOO
MEMPHIS
HEBER SPR
CLINTON

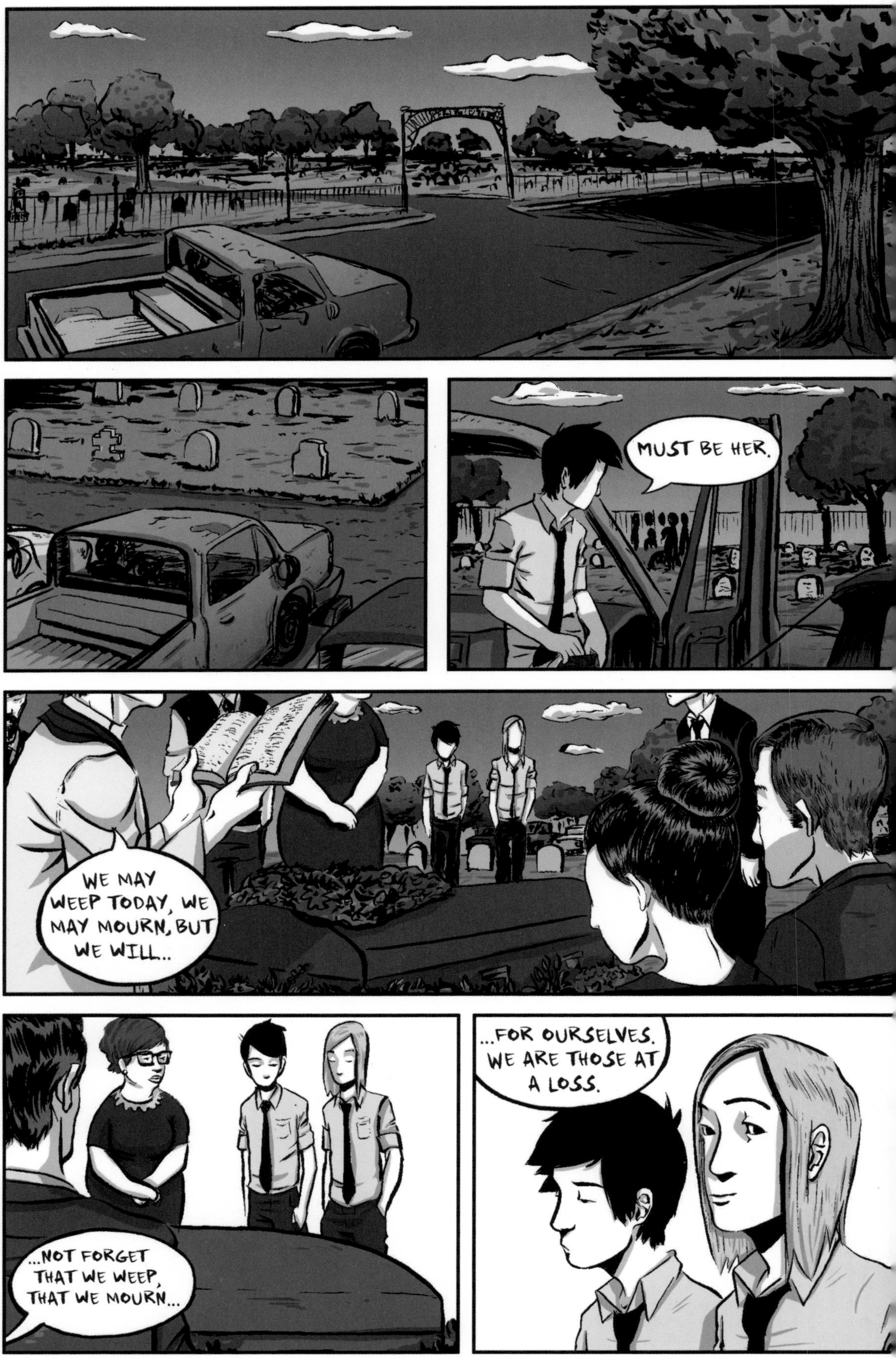
MUST BE HER.
WE MAY WEEP TODAY, WE MAY MOURN, BUT WE WILL..
...NOT FORGET THAT WE WEEP, THAT WE MOURN...
...FOR OURSELVES. WE ARE THOSE AT A LOSS.

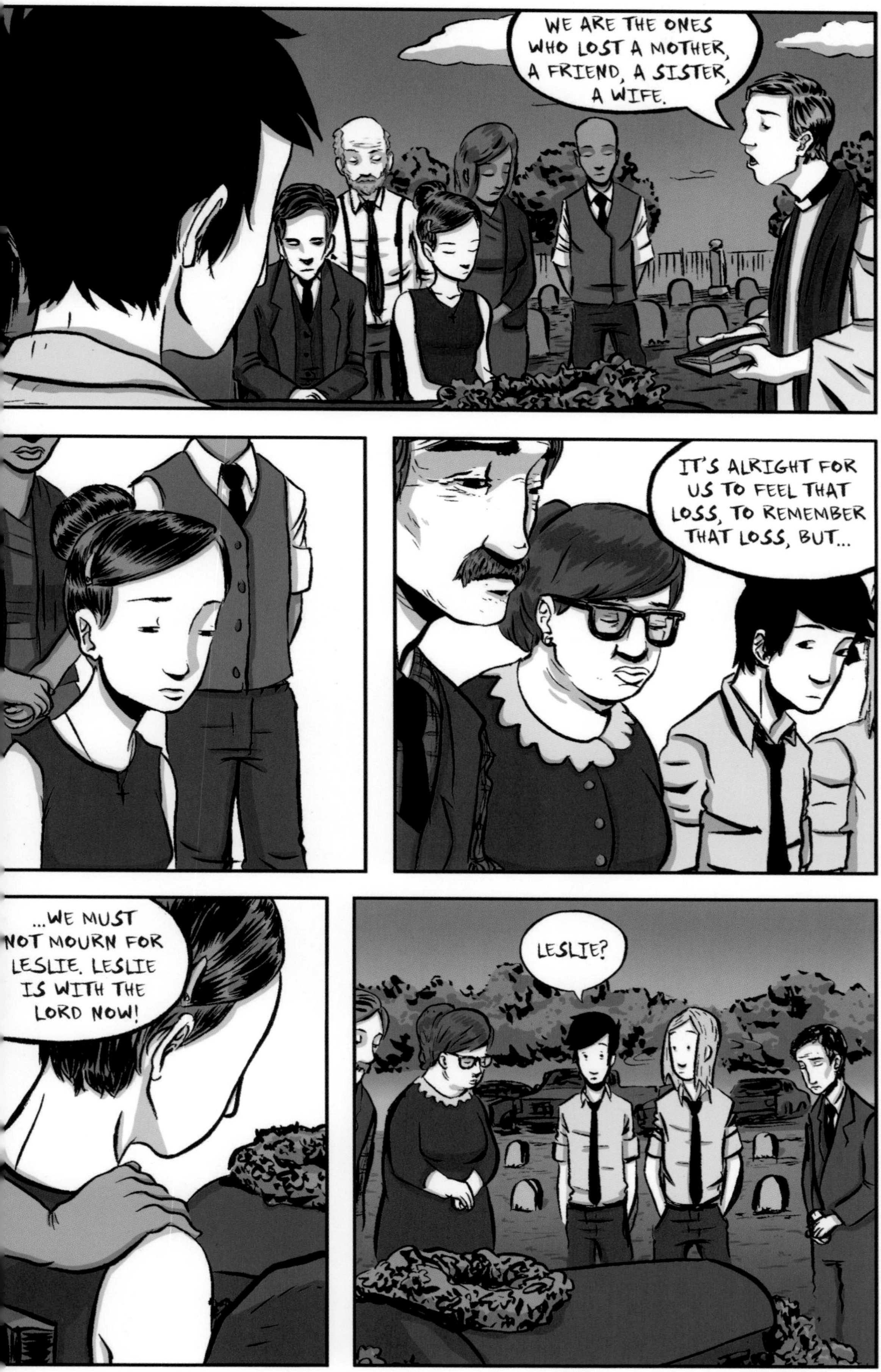
WE ARE THE ONES WHO LOST A MOTHER, A FRIEND, A SISTER, A WIFE.
IT'S ALRIGHT FOR US TO FEEL THAT LOSS, TO REMEMBER THAT LOSS, BUT...
...WE MUST NOT MOURN FOR LESLIE. LESLIE IS WITH THE LORD NOW!
LESLIE?

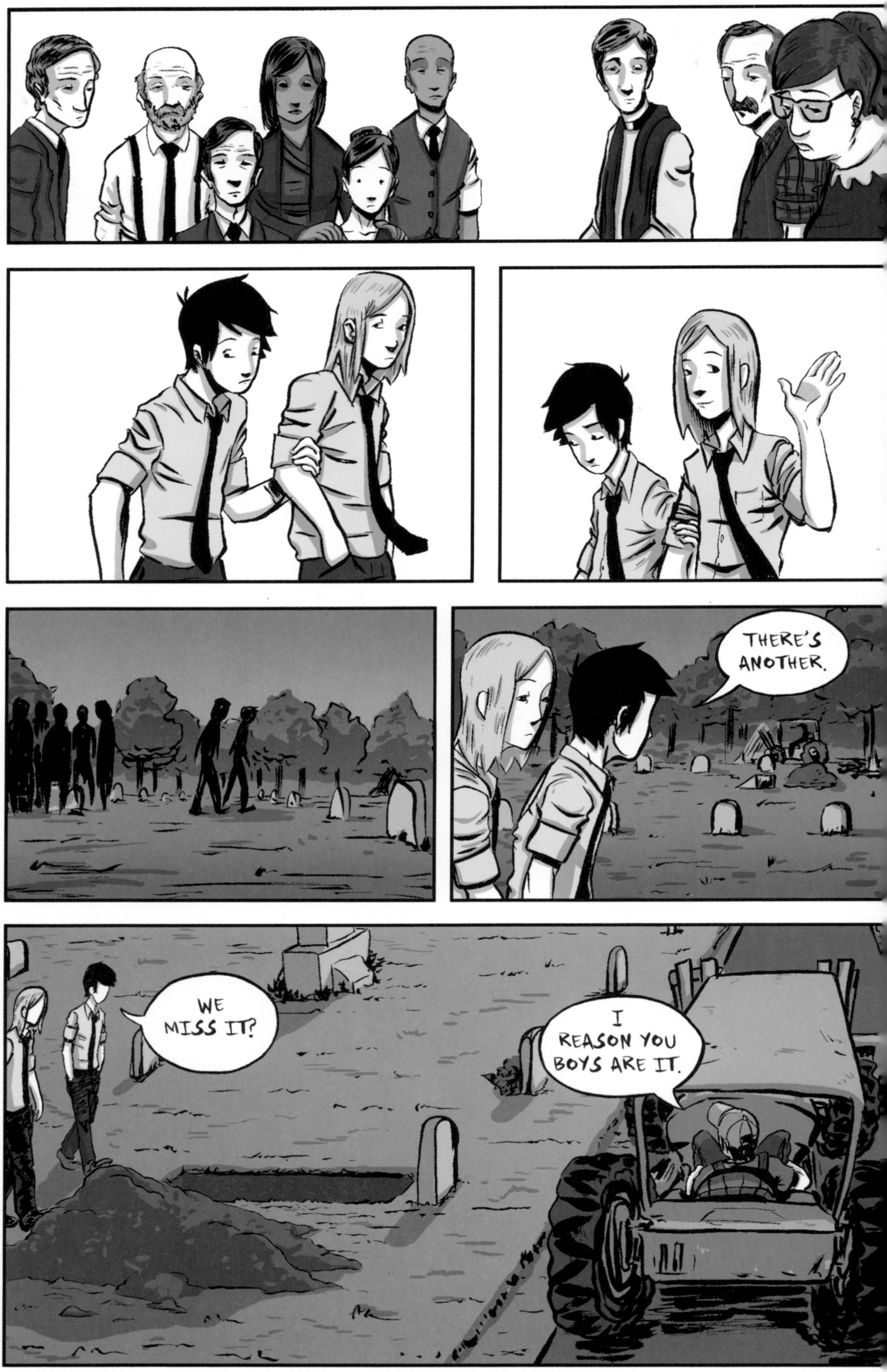
THERE'S ANOTHER.
WE MISS IT?
I REASON YOU BOYS ARE IT.

I'LL GIVE Y'ALL A MOMENT.

SEEMS MORE RIGHT.

I'M SORRY I THOUGHT YOU LEFT US FOR SOMETHING BETTER.

BELOVED DAUGHTER AND

WHAT THE HELL ARE YOU DOING, JOE?

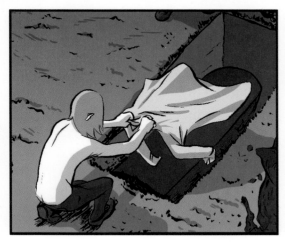

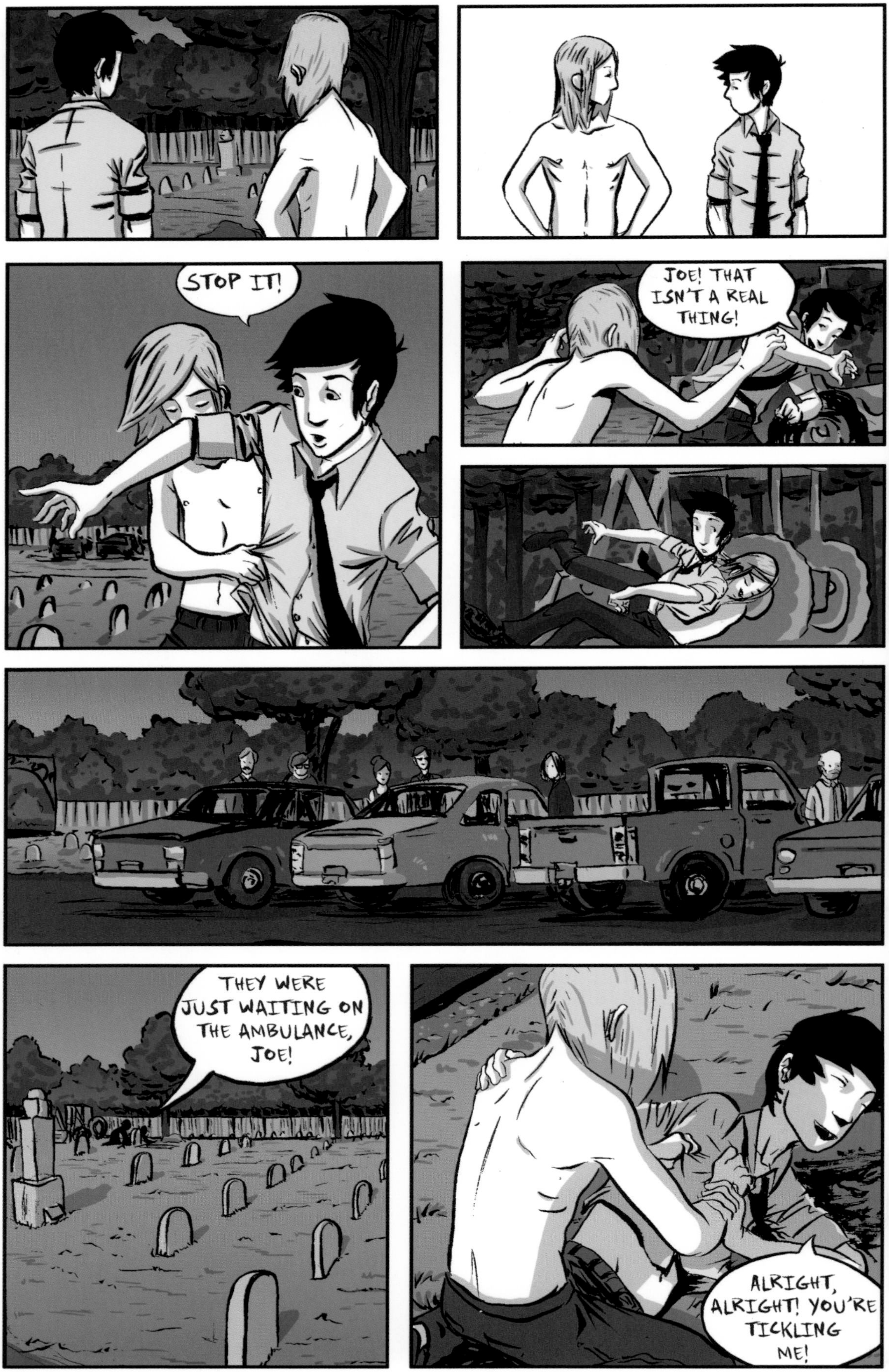
STOP IT!
JOE! THAT ISN'T A REAL THING!
THEY WERE JUST WAITING ON THE AMBULANCE, JOE!
ALRIGHT, ALRIGHT! YOU'RE TICKLING ME!

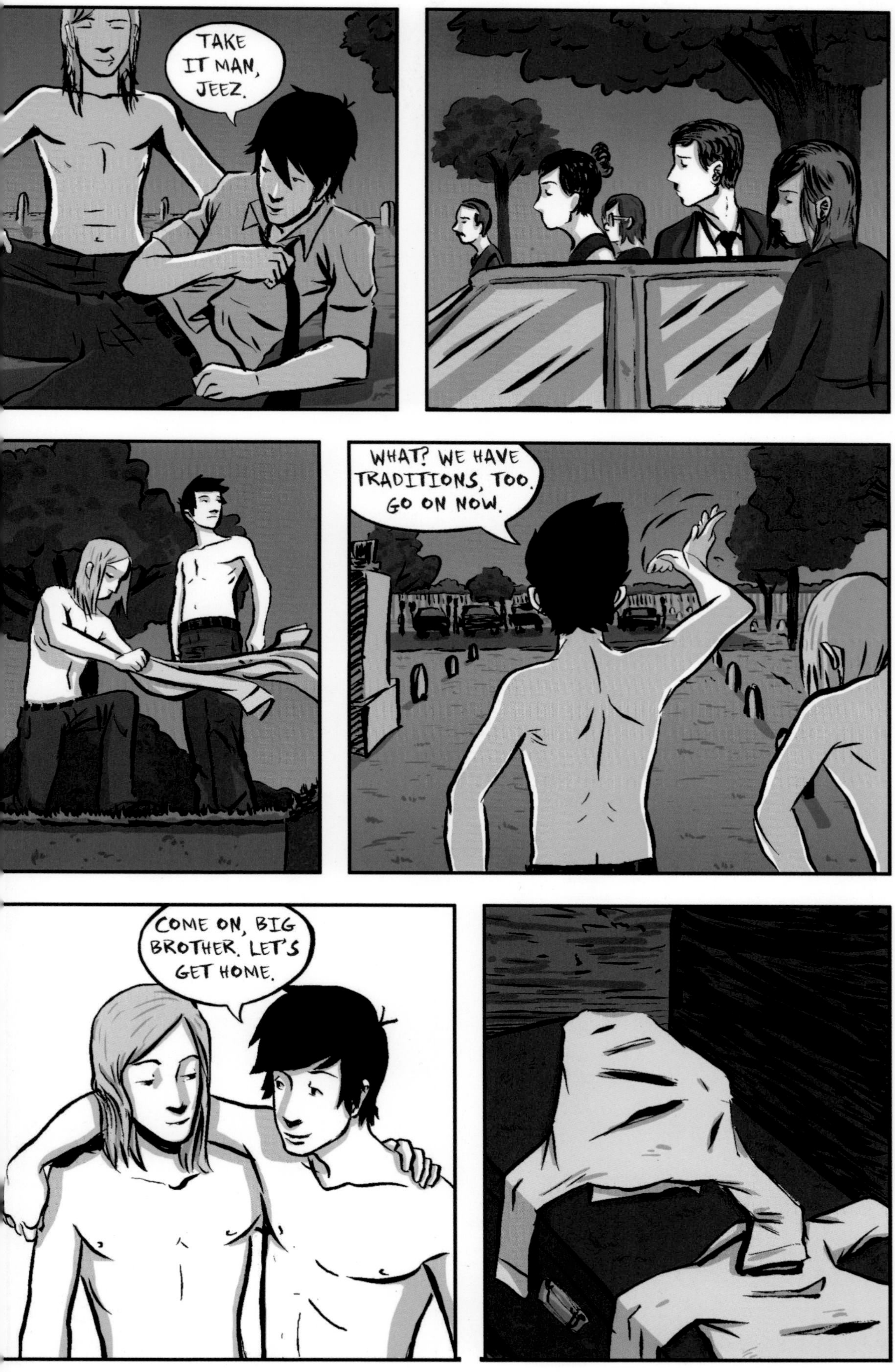
TAKE IT MAN, JEEZ.
WHAT? WE HAVE TRADITIONS, TOO. GO ON NOW.
COME ON, BIG BROTHER. LET'S GET HOME.

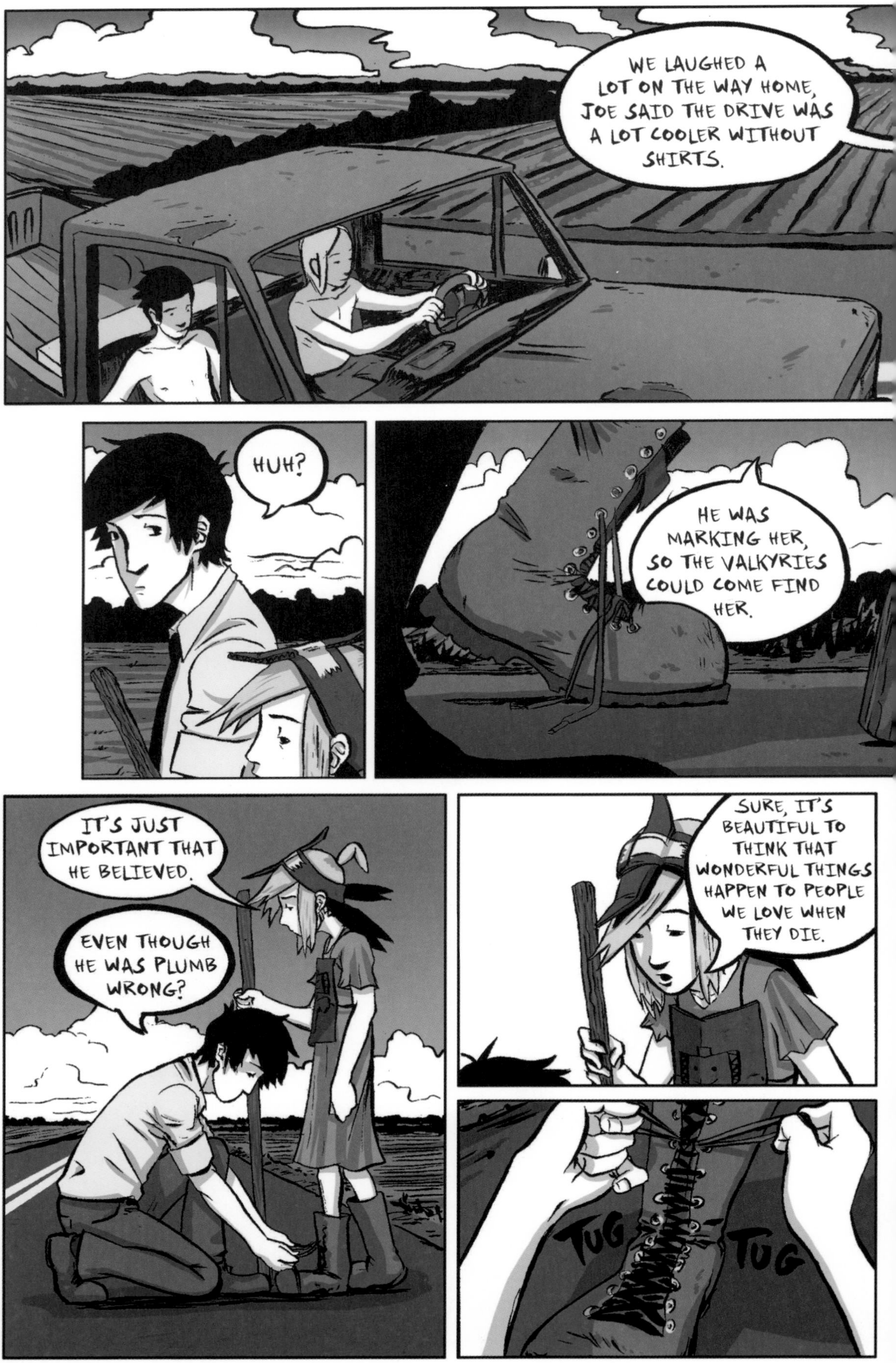
WE LAUGHED A LOT ON THE WAY HOME, JOE SAID THE DRIVE WAS A LOT COOLER WITHOUT SHIRTS.
HUH?
HE WAS MARKING HER, SO THE VALKYRIES COULD COME FIND HER.
IT'S JUST IMPORTANT THAT HE BELIEVED.
EVEN THOUGH HE WAS PLUMB WRONG?
SURE, IT'S BEAUTIFUL TO THINK THAT WONDERFUL THINGS HAPPEN TO PEOPLE WE LOVE WHEN THEY DIE.
TUG
TUG

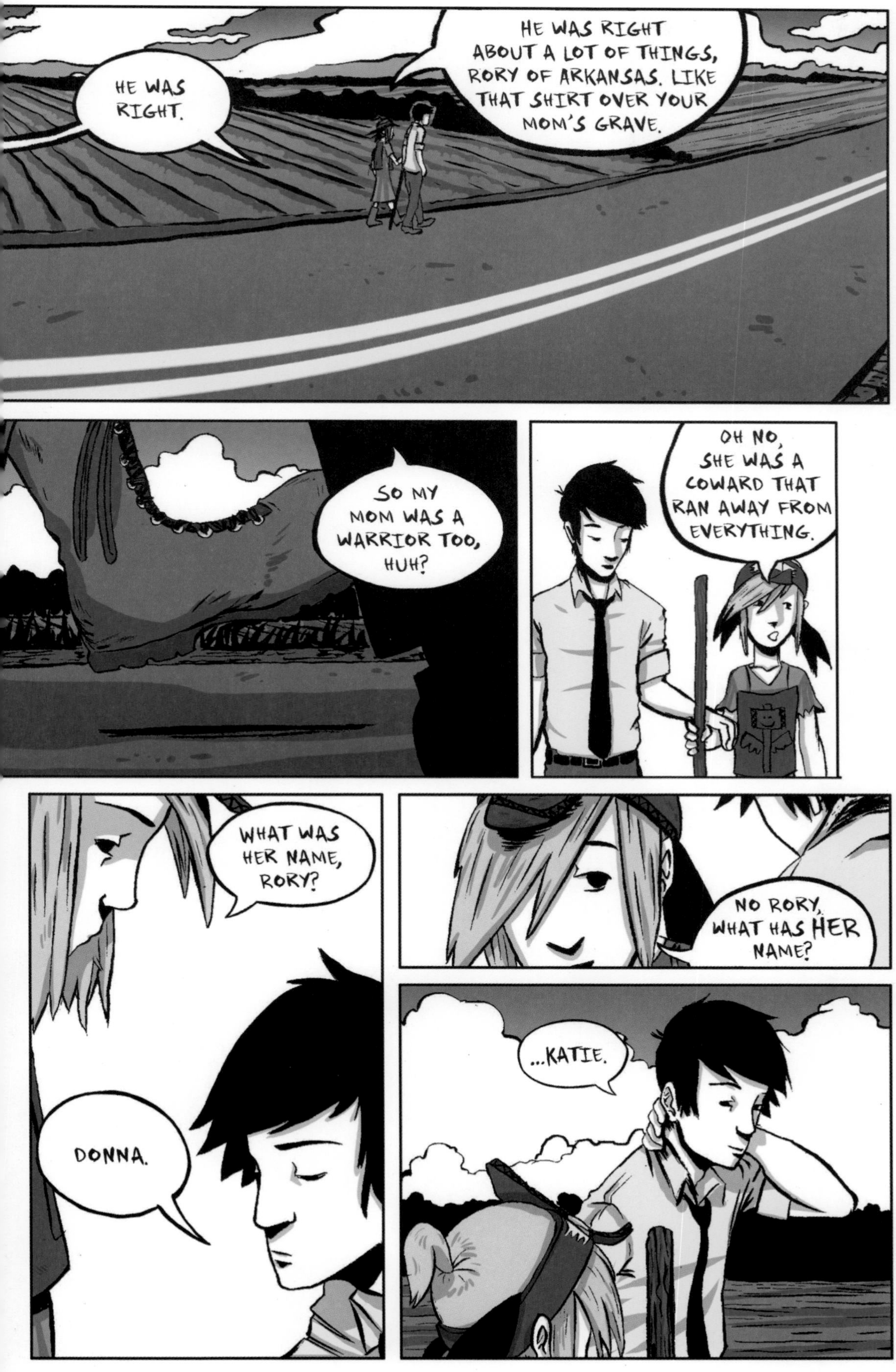
HE WAS RIGHT.
HE WAS RIGHT ABOUT A LOT OF THINGS, RORY OF ARKANSAS. LIKE THAT SHIRT OVER YOUR MOM'S GRAVE.
SO MY MOM WAS A WARRIOR TOO, HUH?
OH NO, SHE WAS A COWARD THAT RAN AWAY FROM EVERYTHING.
WHAT WAS HER NAME, RORY?
DONNA.
NO RORY, WHAT HAS HER NAME?
...KATIE.

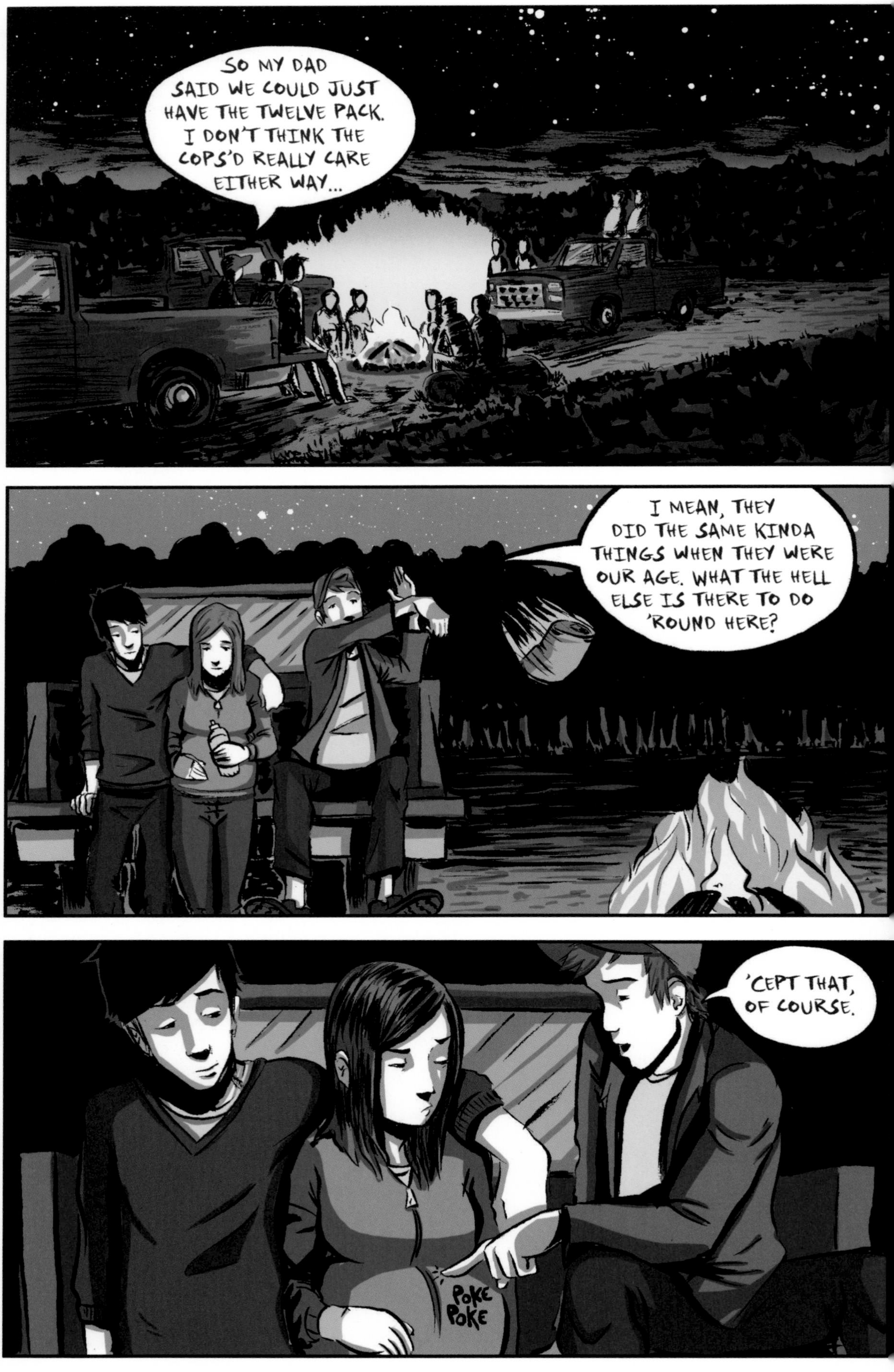
SO MY DAD SAID WE COULD JUST HAVE THE TWELVE PACK. I DON'T THINK THE COPS'D REALLY CARE EITHER WAY...
I MEAN, THEY DID THE SAME KINDA THINGS WHEN THEY WERE OUR AGE. WHAT THE HELL ELSE IS THERE TO DO 'ROUND HERE?
'CEPT THAT, OF COURSE.
POKE POKE

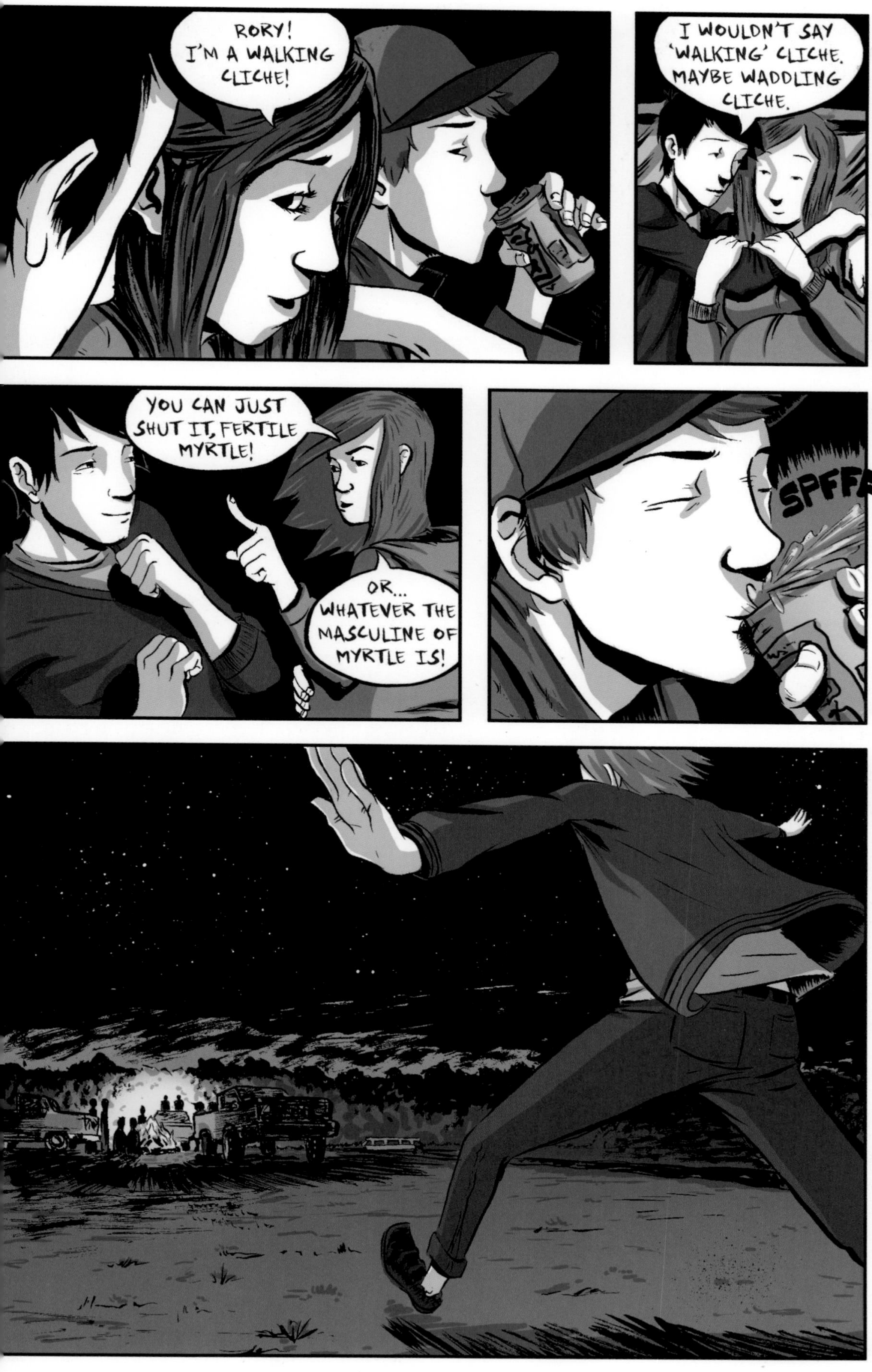
RORY! I'M A WALKING CLICHE!
I WOULDN'T SAY 'WALKING' CLICHE. MAYBE WADDLING CLICHE.
YOU CAN JUST SHUT IT, FERTILE MYRTLE!
OR... WHATEVER THE MASCULINE OF MYRTLE IS!
SPFFF

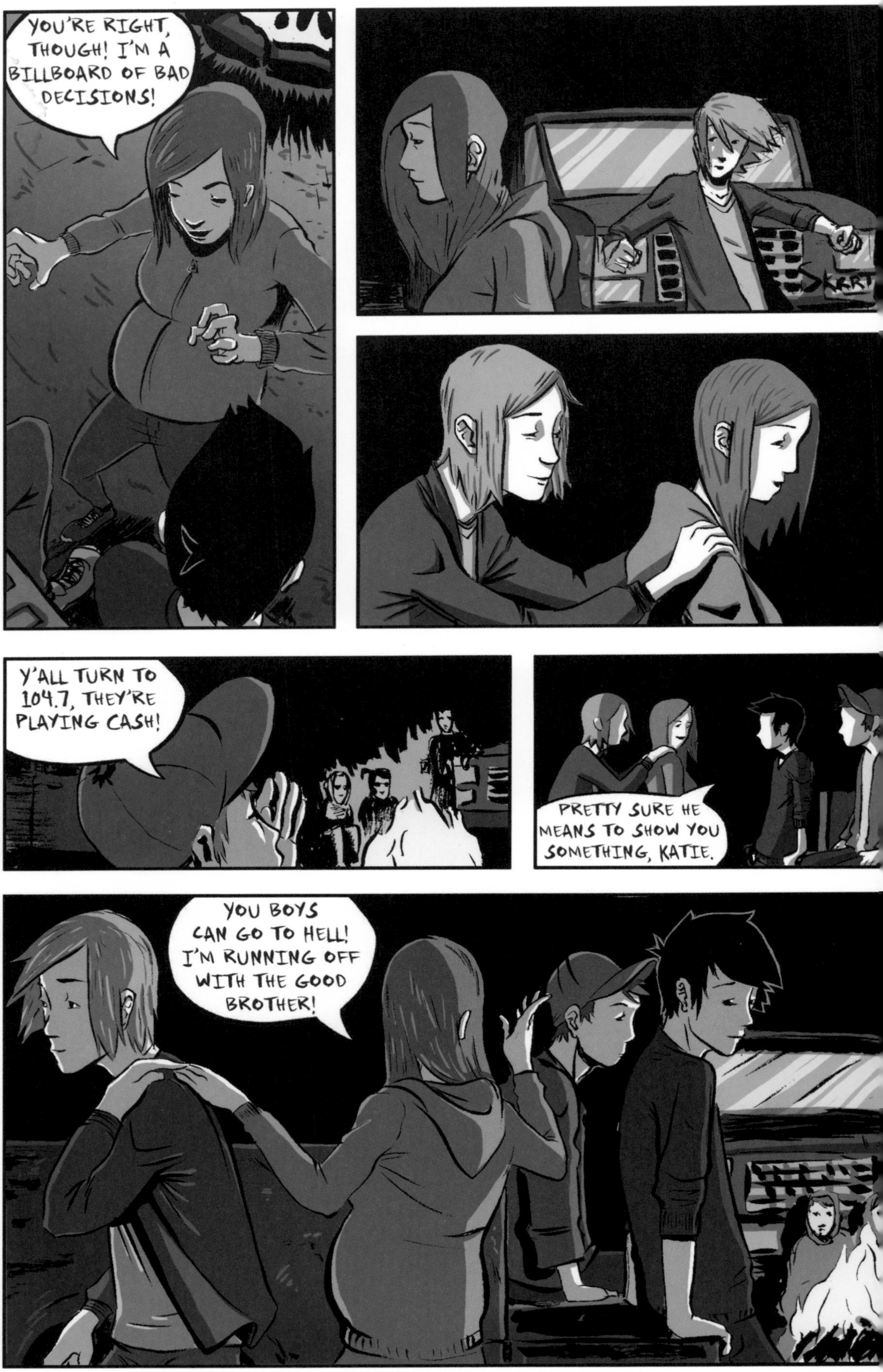
YOU'RE RIGHT, THOUGH! I'M A BILLBOARD OF BAD DECISIONS!
SKRRT
Y'ALL TURN TO 104.7, THEY'RE PLAYING CASH!
PRETTY SURE HE MEANS TO SHOW YOU SOMETHING, KATIE.
YOU BOYS CAN GO TO HELL! I'M RUNNING OFF WITH THE GOOD BROTHER!

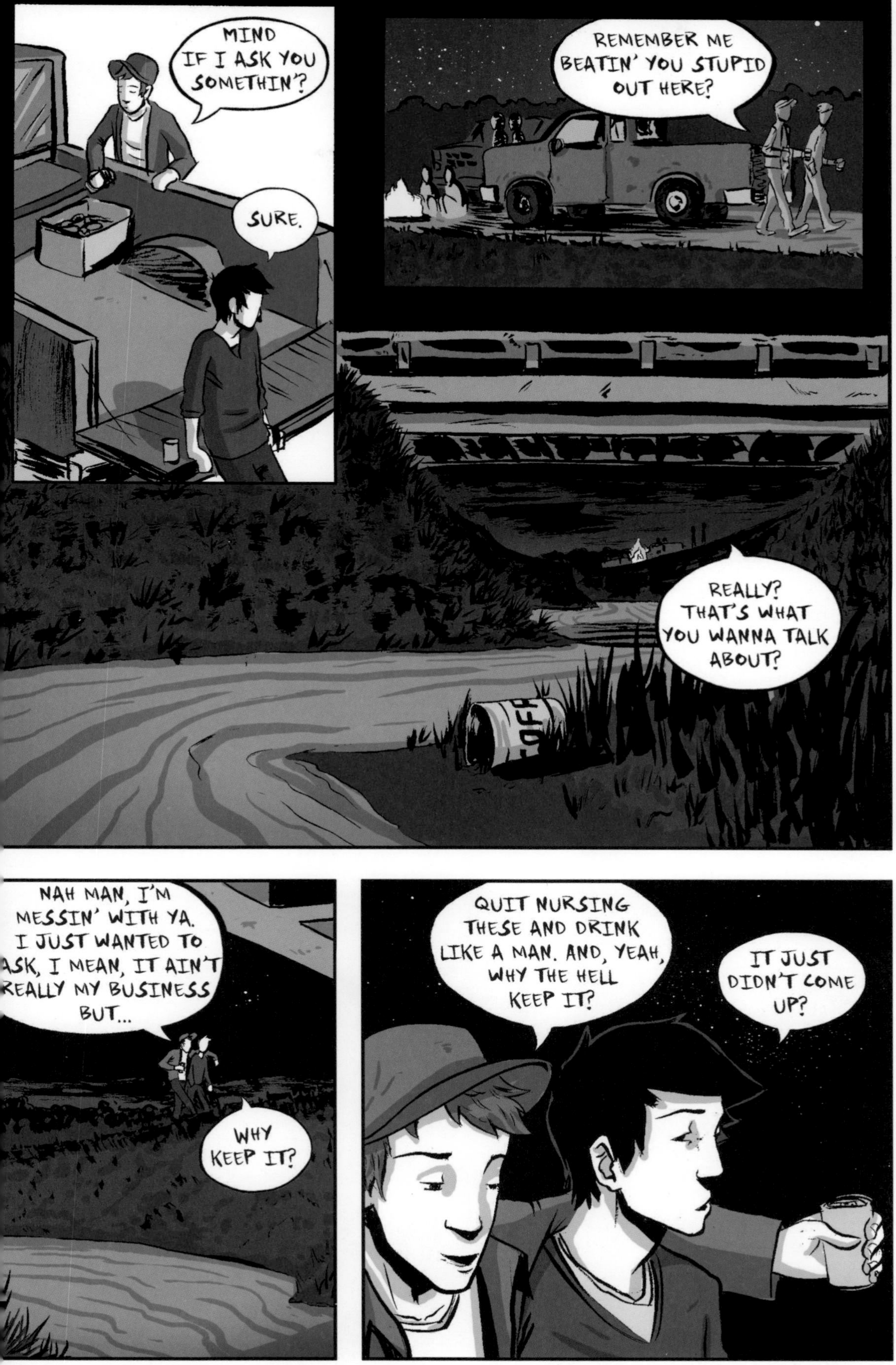

MIND IF I ASK YOU SOMETHIN'?
SURE.
REMEMBER ME BEATIN' YOU STUPID OUT HERE?
REALLY? THAT'S WHAT YOU WANNA TALK ABOUT?
NAH MAN, I'M MESSIN' WITH YA. I JUST WANTED TO ASK, I MEAN, IT AIN'T REALLY MY BUSINESS BUT...
WHY KEEP IT?
QUIT NURSING THESE AND DRINK LIKE A MAN. AND, YEAH, WHY THE HELL KEEP IT?
IT JUST DIDN'T COME UP?

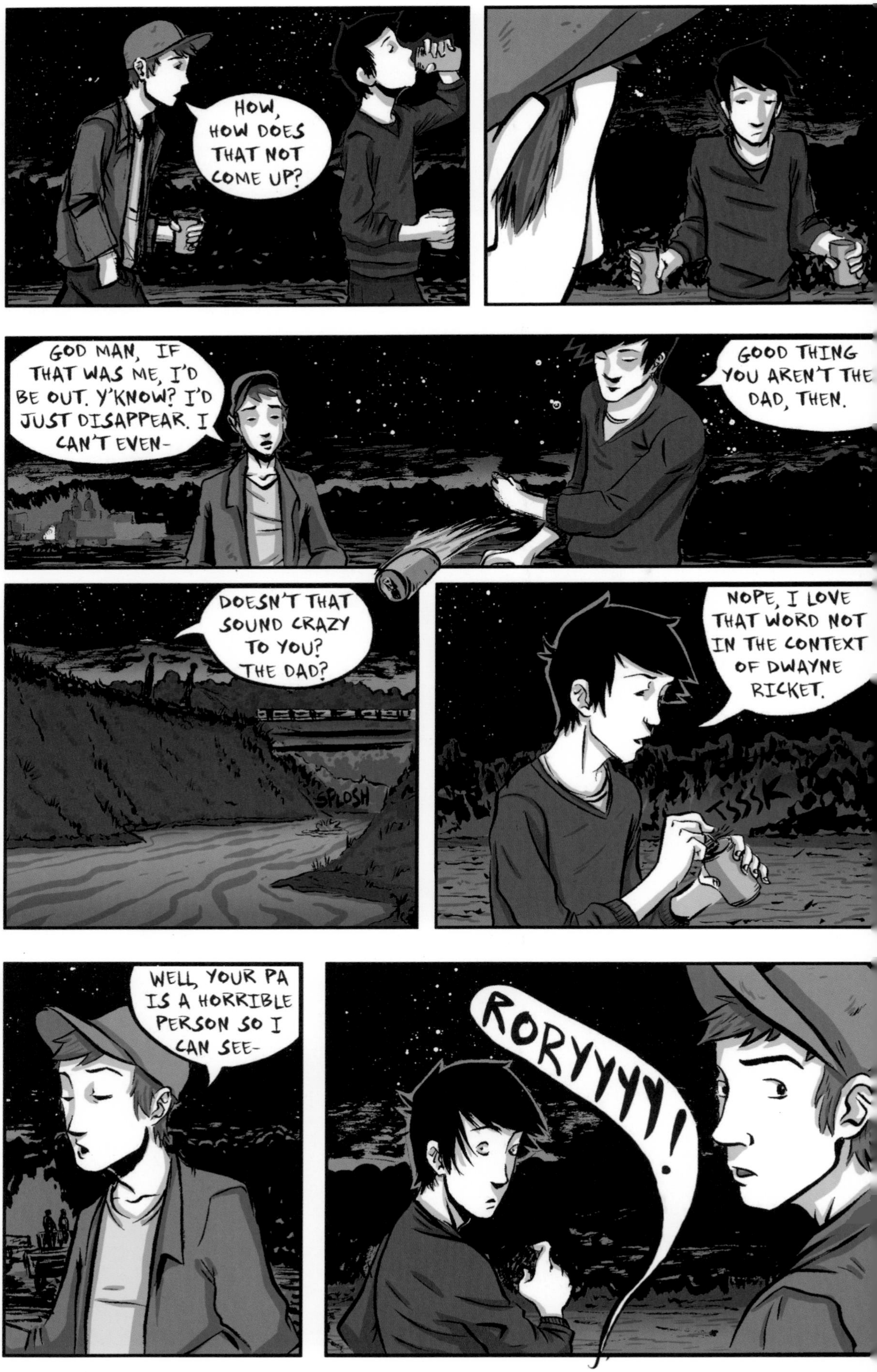
HOW, HOW DOES THAT NOT COME UP?
GOD MAN, IF THAT WAS ME, I'D BE OUT. Y'KNOW? I'D JUST DISAPPEAR. I CAN'T EVEN-
GOOD THING YOU AREN'T THE DAD, THEN.
DOESN'T THAT SOUND CRAZY TO YOU? THE DAD?
SPLOSH
NOPE, I LOVE THAT WORD NOT IN THE CONTEXT OF DWAYNE RICKET.
TSSSK
WELL, YOUR PA IS A HORRIBLE PERSON SO I CAN SEE-
RORYYYY!

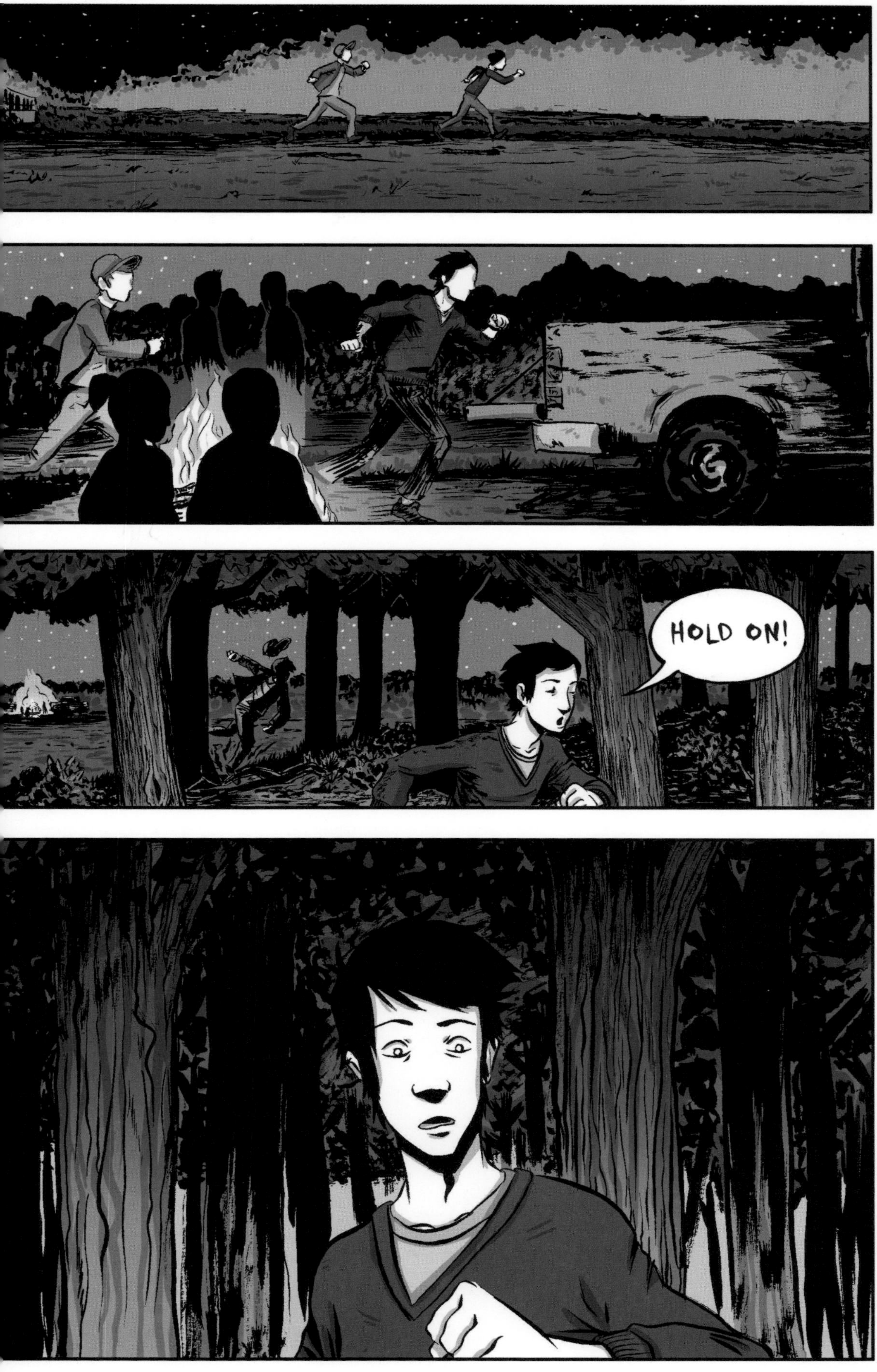
HOLD ON!

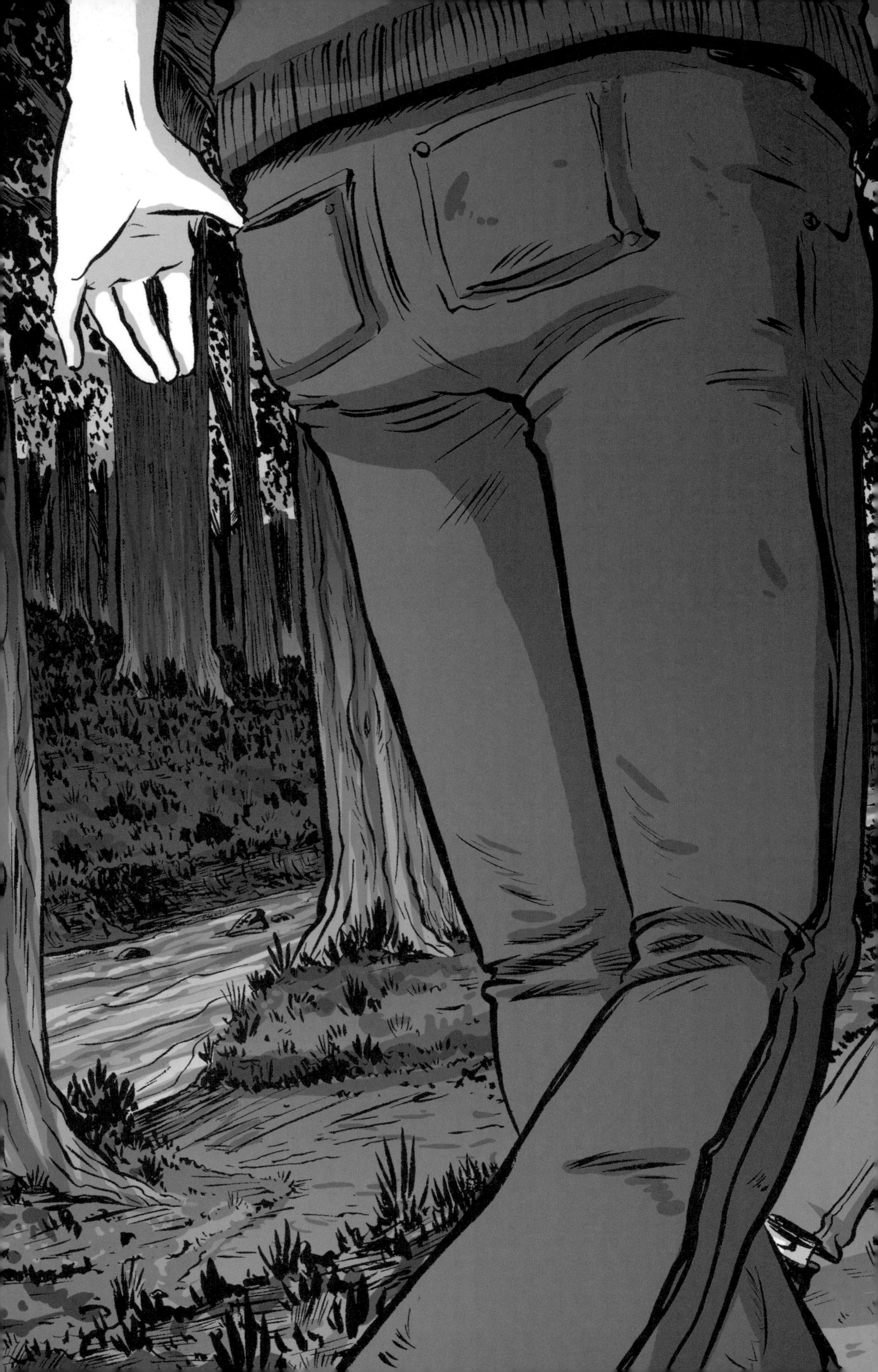

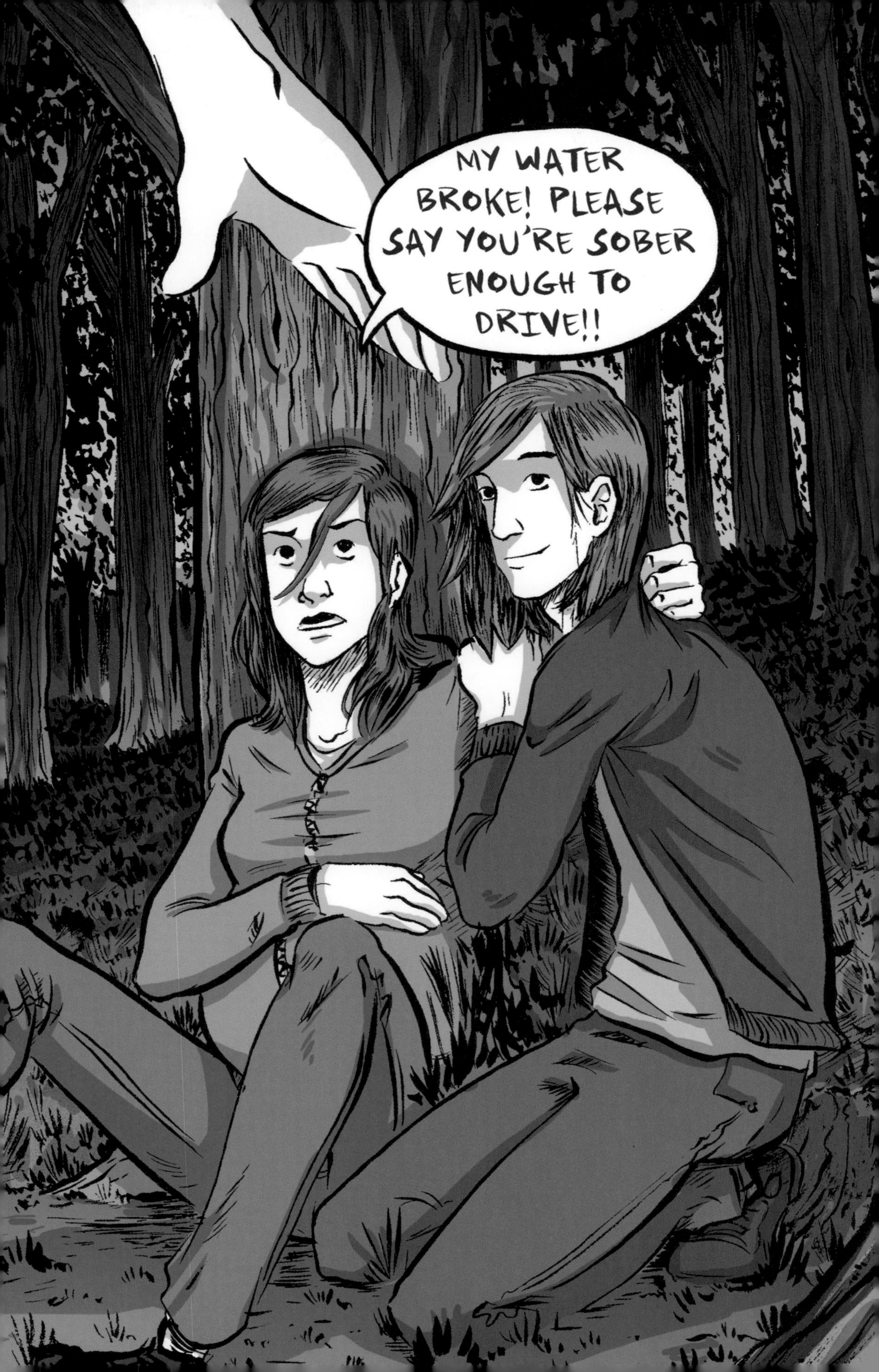
MY WATER BROKE! PLEASE SAY YOU'RE SOBER ENOUGH TO DRIVE!!

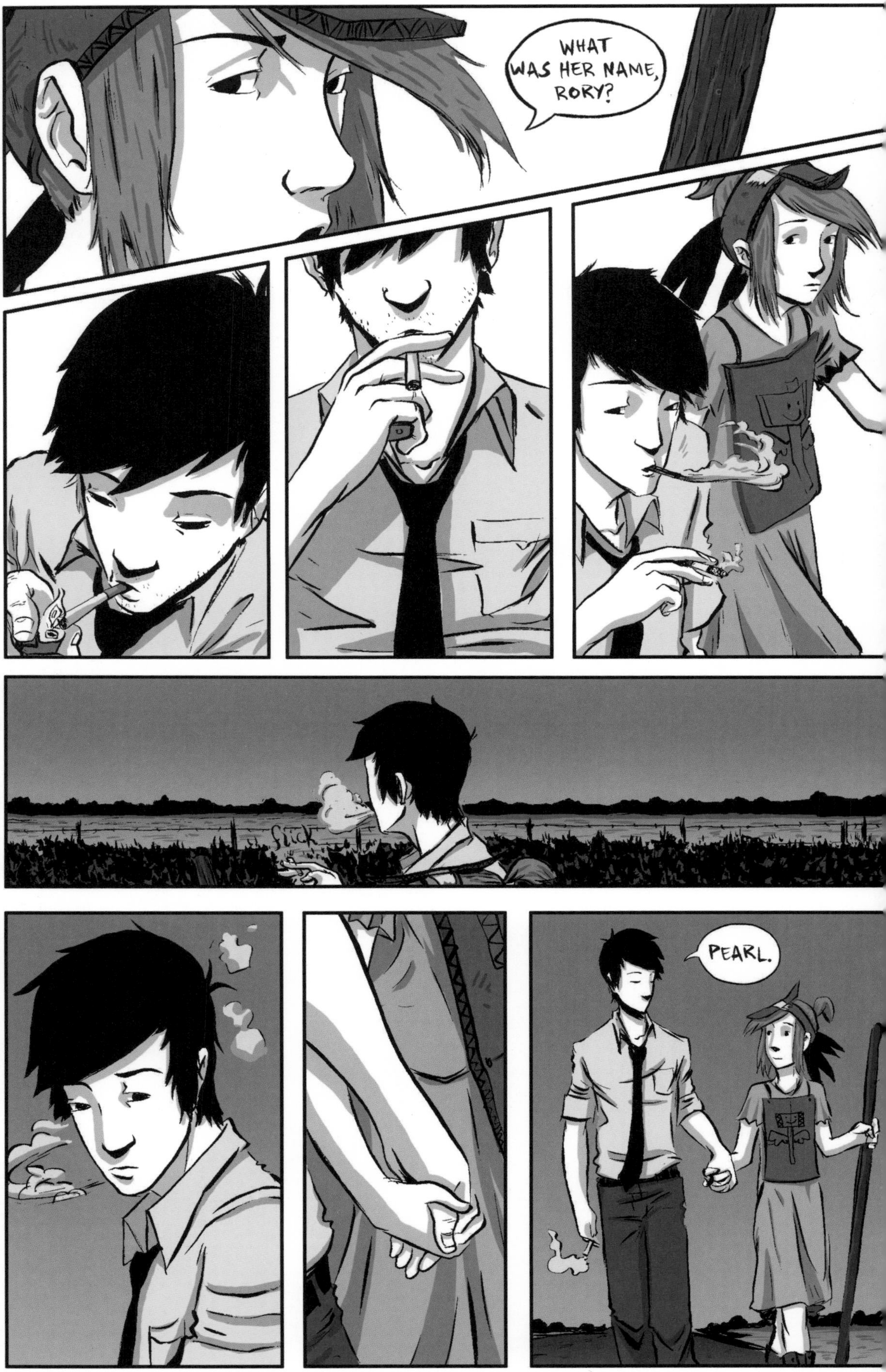
WHAT WAS HER NAME, RORY?
FLICK
PEARL.

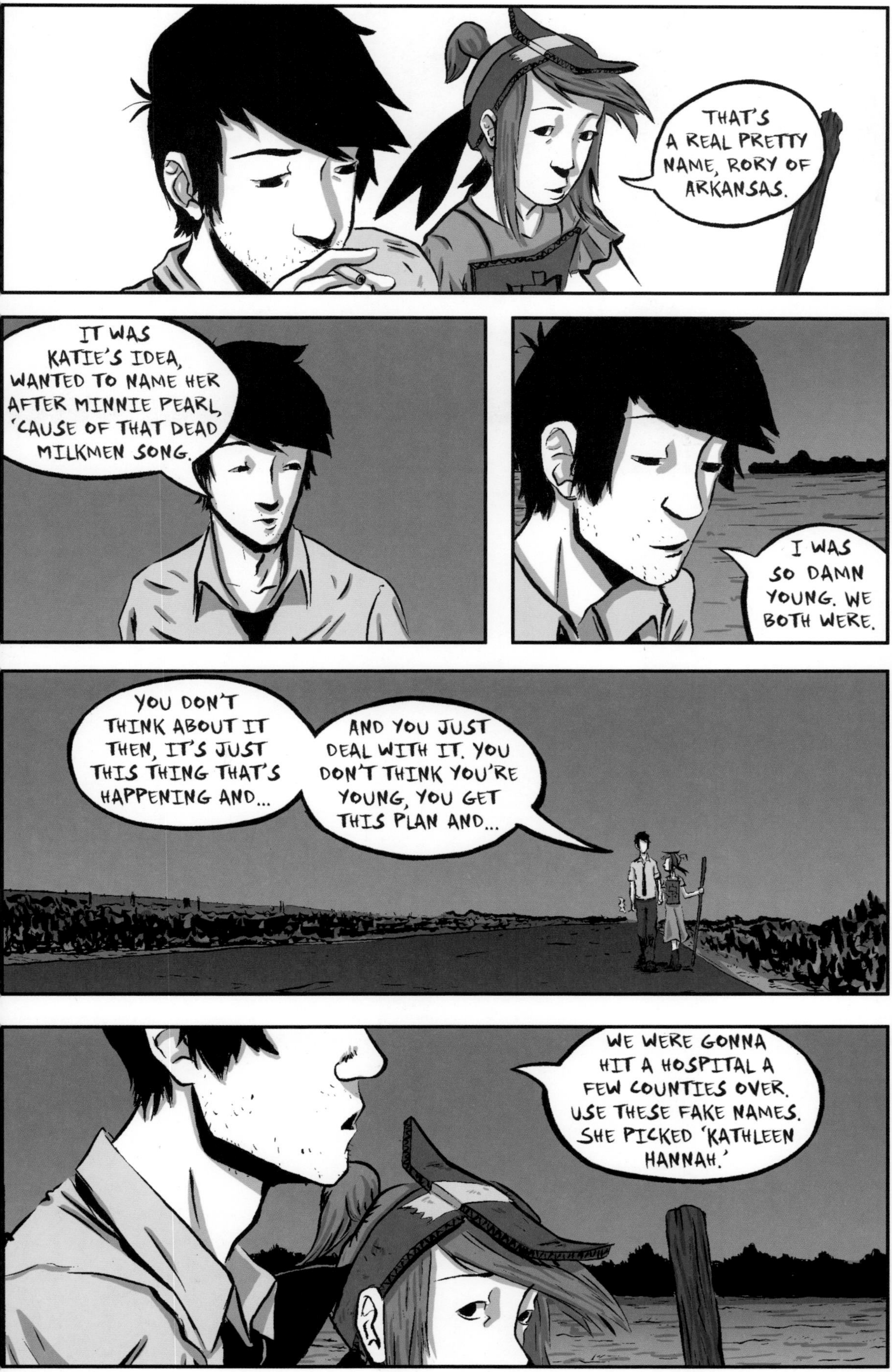
THAT'S A REAL PRETTY NAME, RORY OF ARKANSAS.
IT WAS KATIE'S IDEA, WANTED TO NAME HER AFTER MINNIE PEARL, 'CAUSE OF THAT DEAD MILKMEN SONG.
I WAS SO DAMN YOUNG. WE BOTH WERE.
YOU DON'T THINK ABOUT IT THEN, IT'S JUST THIS THING THAT'S HAPPENING AND...
AND YOU JUST DEAL WITH IT. YOU DON'T THINK YOU'RE YOUNG, YOU GET THIS PLAN AND...
WE WERE GONNA HIT A HOSPITAL A FEW COUNTIES OVER. USE THESE FAKE NAMES. SHE PICKED 'KATHLEEN HANNAH.'

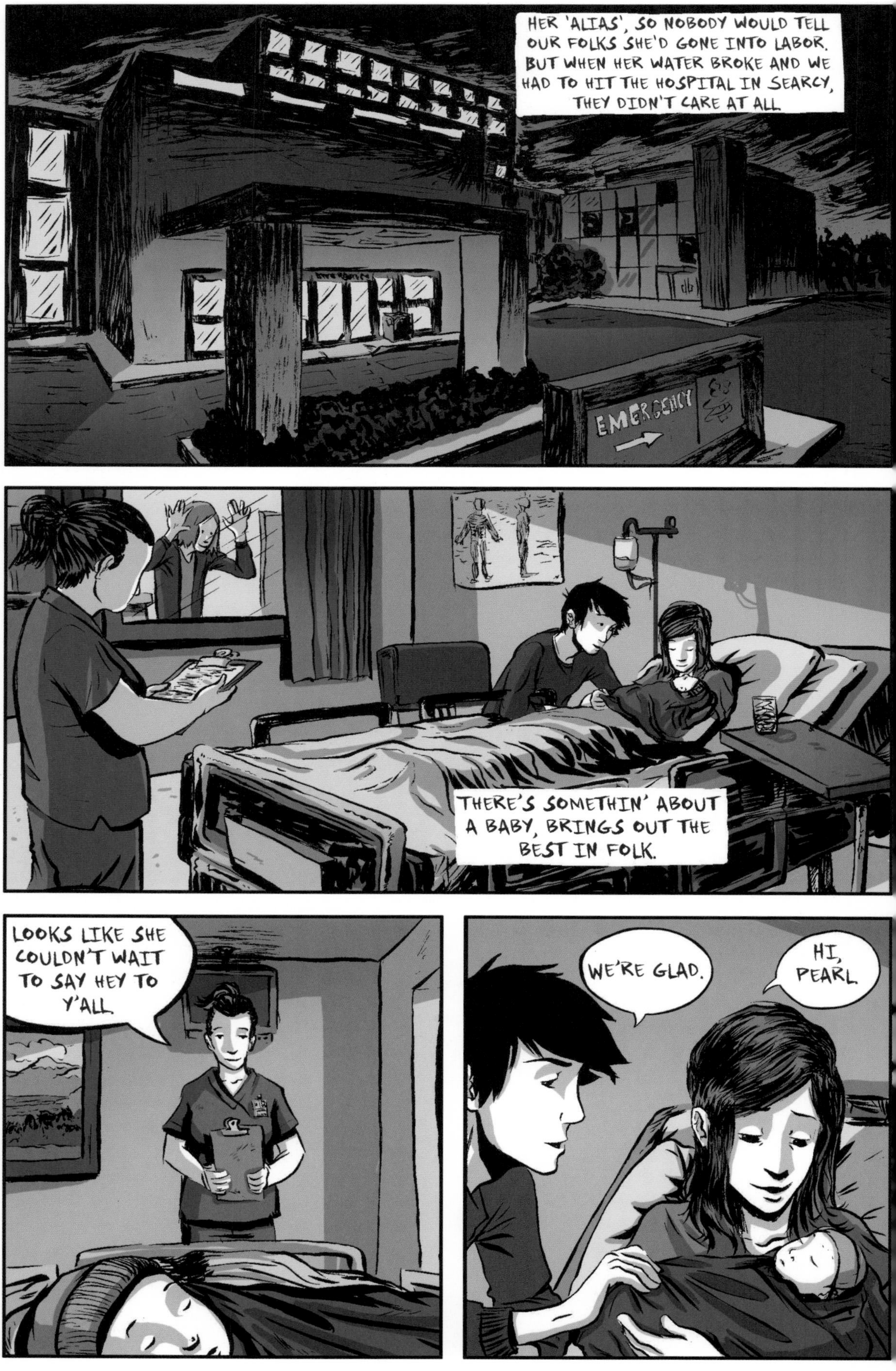
HER 'ALIAS', SO NOBODY WOULD TELL OUR FOLKS SHE'D GONE INTO LABOR. BUT WHEN HER WATER BROKE AND WE HAD TO HIT THE HOSPITAL IN SEARCY, THEY DIDN'T CARE AT ALL
EMERGENCY
THERE'S SOMETHIN' ABOUT A BABY, BRINGS OUT THE BEST IN FOLK.
LOOKS LIKE SHE COULDN'T WAIT TO SAY HEY TO Y'ALL.
WE'RE GLAD.
HI, PEARL.

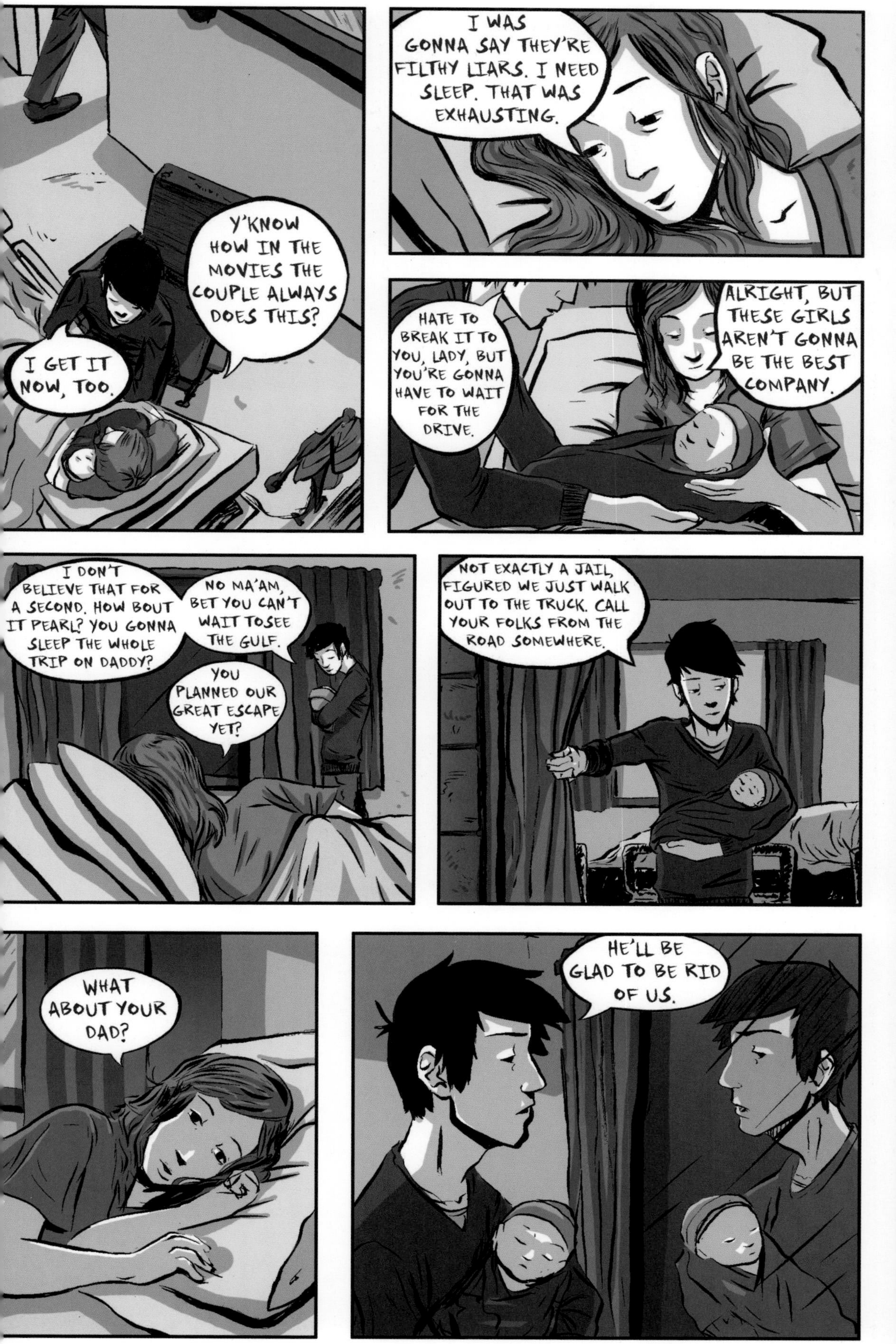
Y'KNOW HOW IN THE MOVIES THE COUPLE ALWAYS DOES THIS?
I GET IT NOW, TOO.
I WAS GONNA SAY THEY'RE FILTHY LIARS. I NEED SLEEP. THAT WAS EXHAUSTING.
HATE TO BREAK IT TO YOU, LADY, BUT YOU'RE GONNA HAVE TO WAIT FOR THE DRIVE.
ALRIGHT, BUT THESE GIRLS AREN'T GONNA BE THE BEST COMPANY.
I DON'T BELIEVE THAT FOR A SECOND. HOW BOUT IT PEARL? YOU GONNA SLEEP THE WHOLE TRIP ON DADDY?
NO MA'AM, BET YOU CAN'T WAIT TOSEE THE GULF.
YOU PLANNED OUR GREAT ESCAPE YET?
NOT EXACTLY A JAIL, FIGURED WE JUST WALK OUT TO THE TRUCK. CALL YOUR FOLKS FROM THE ROAD SOMEWHERE.
WHAT ABOUT YOUR DAD?
HE'LL BE GLAD TO BE RID OF US.

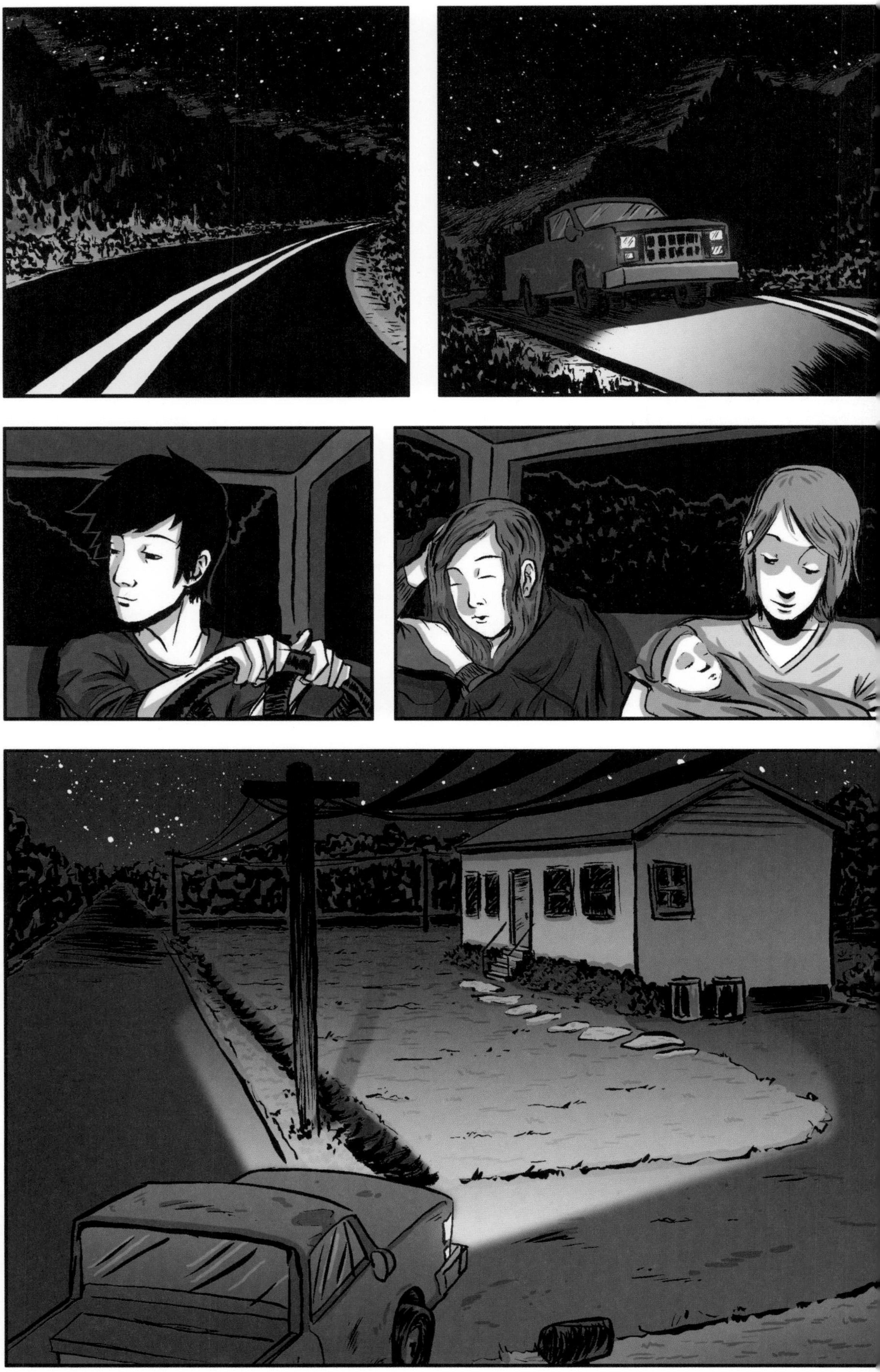

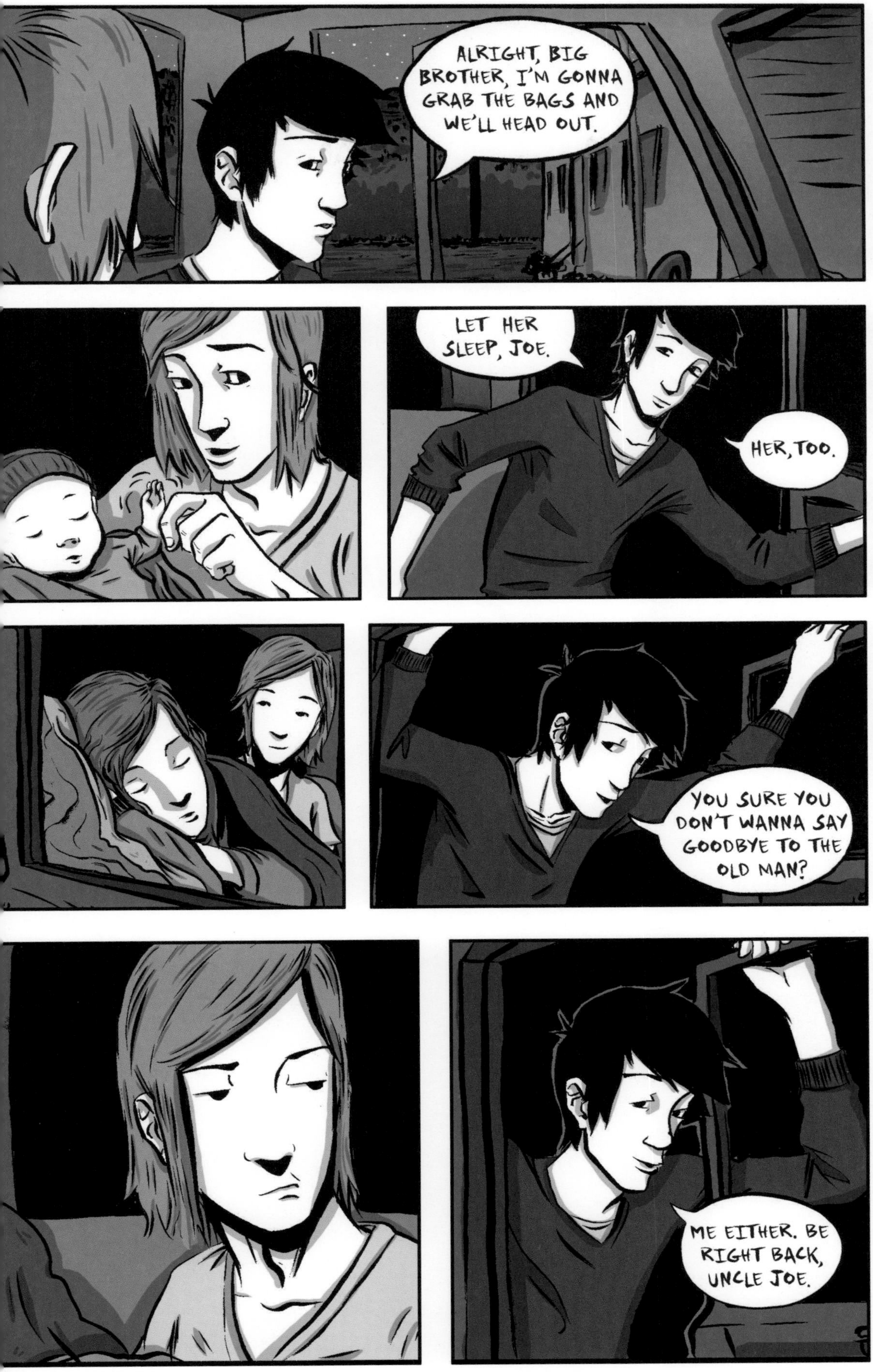
ALRIGHT, BIG BROTHER, I'M GONNA GRAB THE BAGS AND WE'LL HEAD OUT.
LET HER SLEEP, JOE.
HER, TOO.
YOU SURE YOU DON'T WANNA SAY GOODBYE TO THE OLD MAN?
ME EITHER. BE RIGHT BACK, UNCLE JOE.

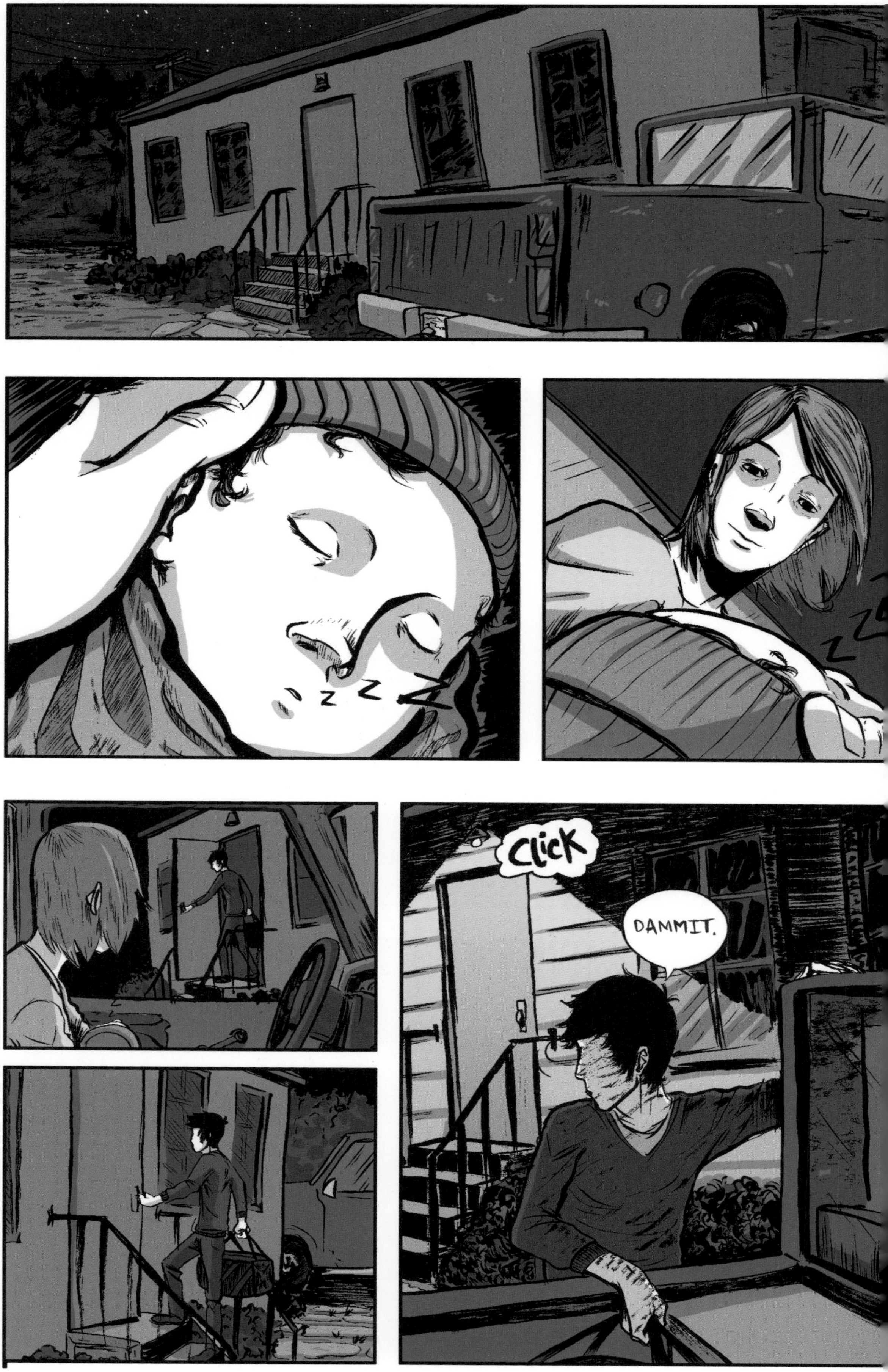
CLICK
DAMMIT.

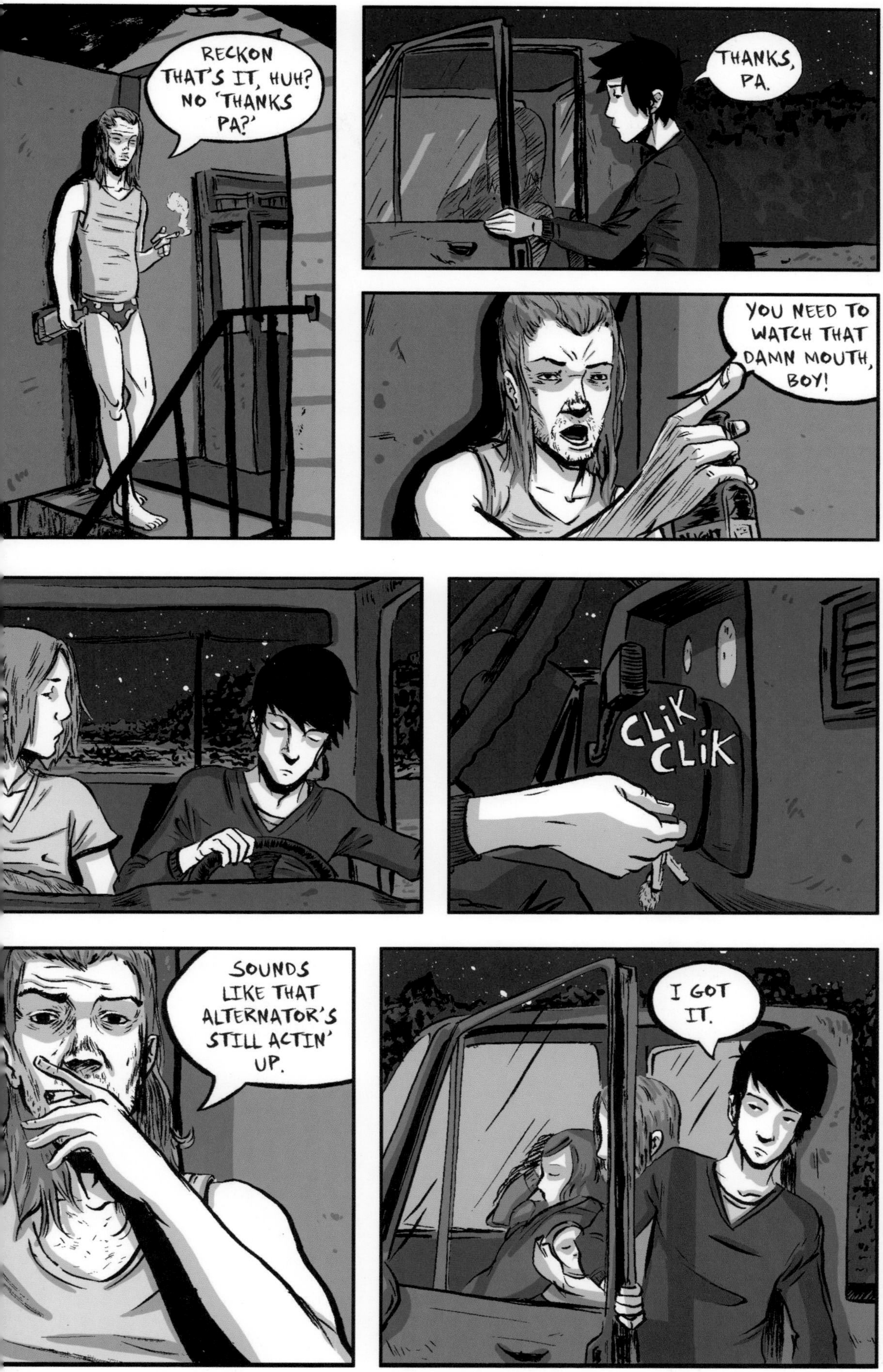
RECKON THAT'S IT, HUH? NO 'THANKS PA?'
THANKS, PA.
YOU NEED TO WATCH THAT DAMN MOUTH, BOY!
CLIK CLIK
SOUNDS LIKE THAT ALTERNATOR'S STILL ACTIN' UP.
I GOT IT.

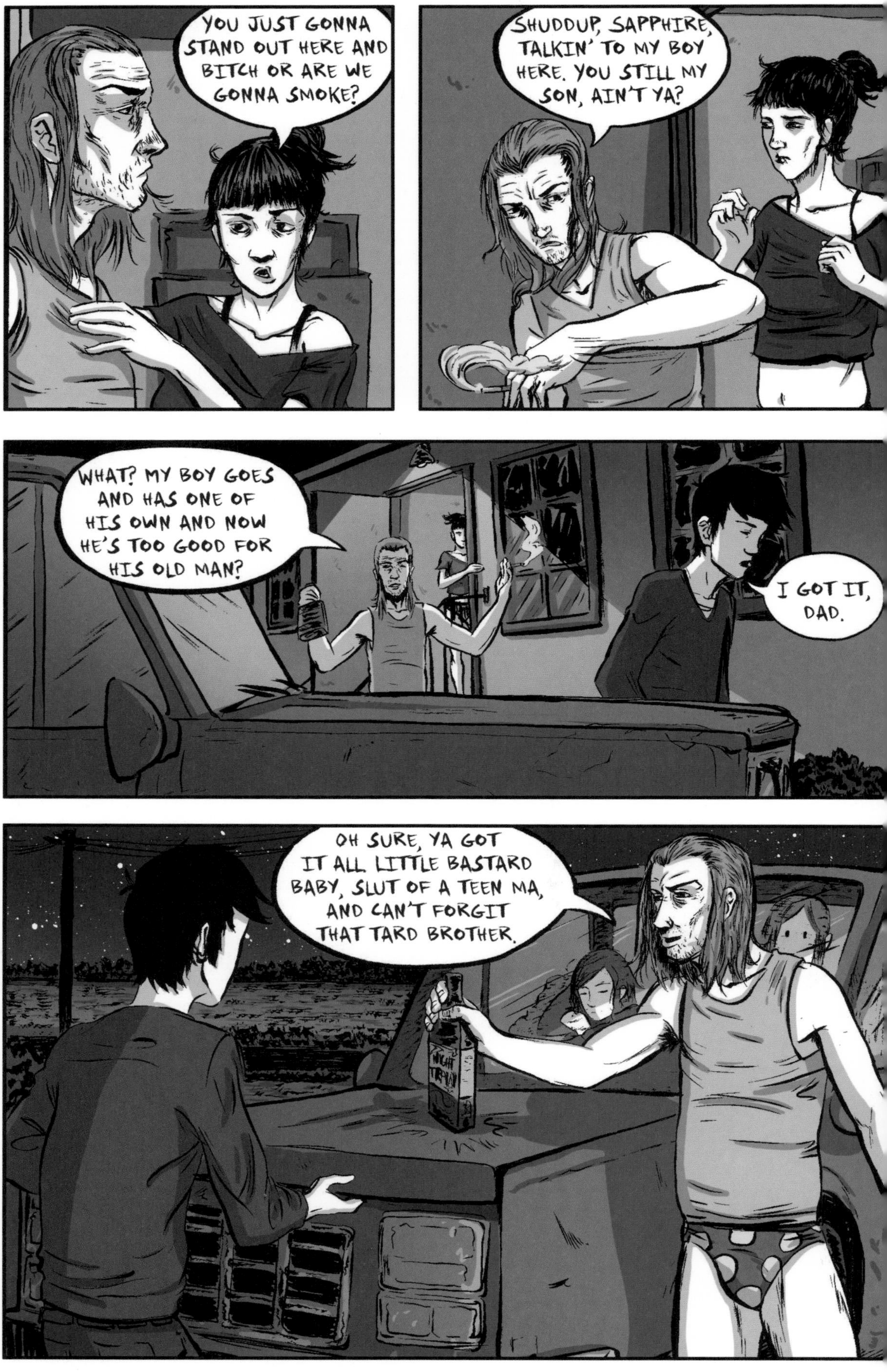
YOU JUST GONNA STAND OUT HERE AND BITCH OR ARE WE GONNA SMOKE?
SHUDDUP, SAPPHIRE, TALKIN' TO MY BOY HERE. YOU STILL MY SON, AIN'T YA?
WHAT? MY BOY GOES AND HAS ONE OF HIS OWN AND NOW HE'S TOO GOOD FOR HIS OLD MAN?
I GOT IT, DAD.
OH SURE, YA GOT IT ALL. LITTLE BASTARD BABY, SLUT OF A TEEN MA, AND CAN'T FORGIT THAT TARD BROTHER.
NIGHT TRAIN

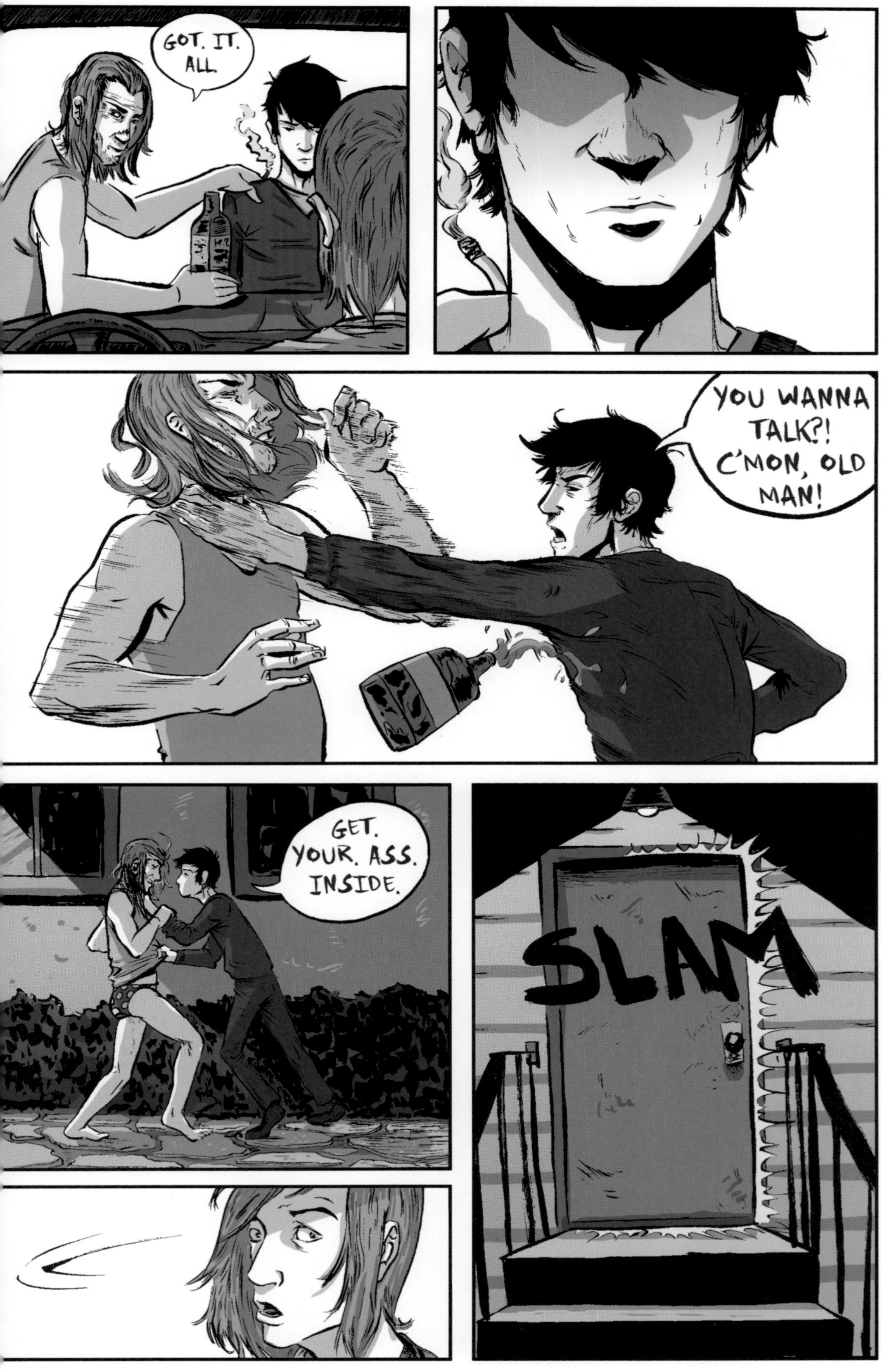
GOT. IT. ALL.
YOU WANNA TALK?! C'MON, OLD MAN!
GET. YOUR. ASS. INSIDE.
SLAM

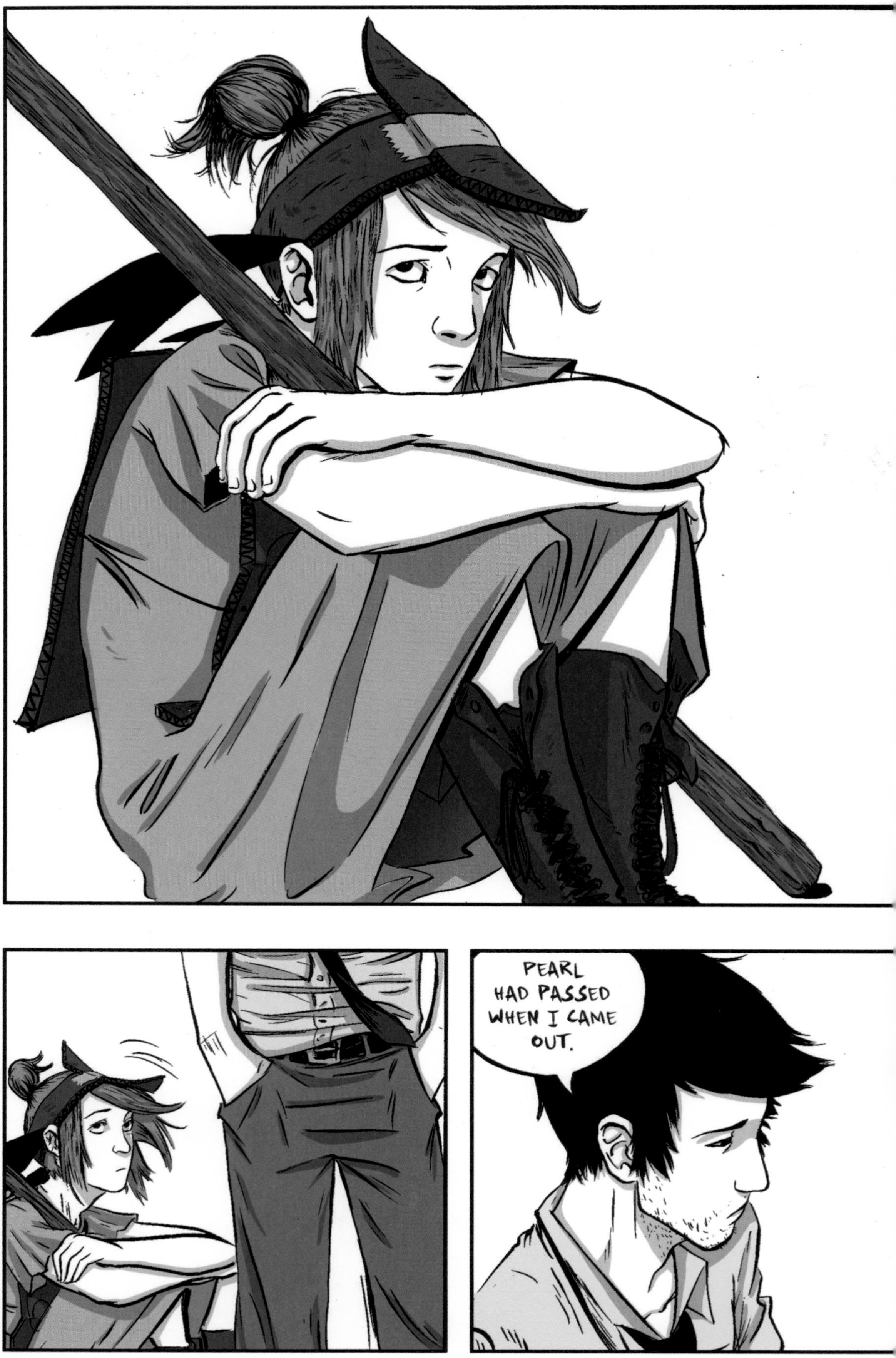
PEARL HAD PASSED WHEN I CAME OUT.

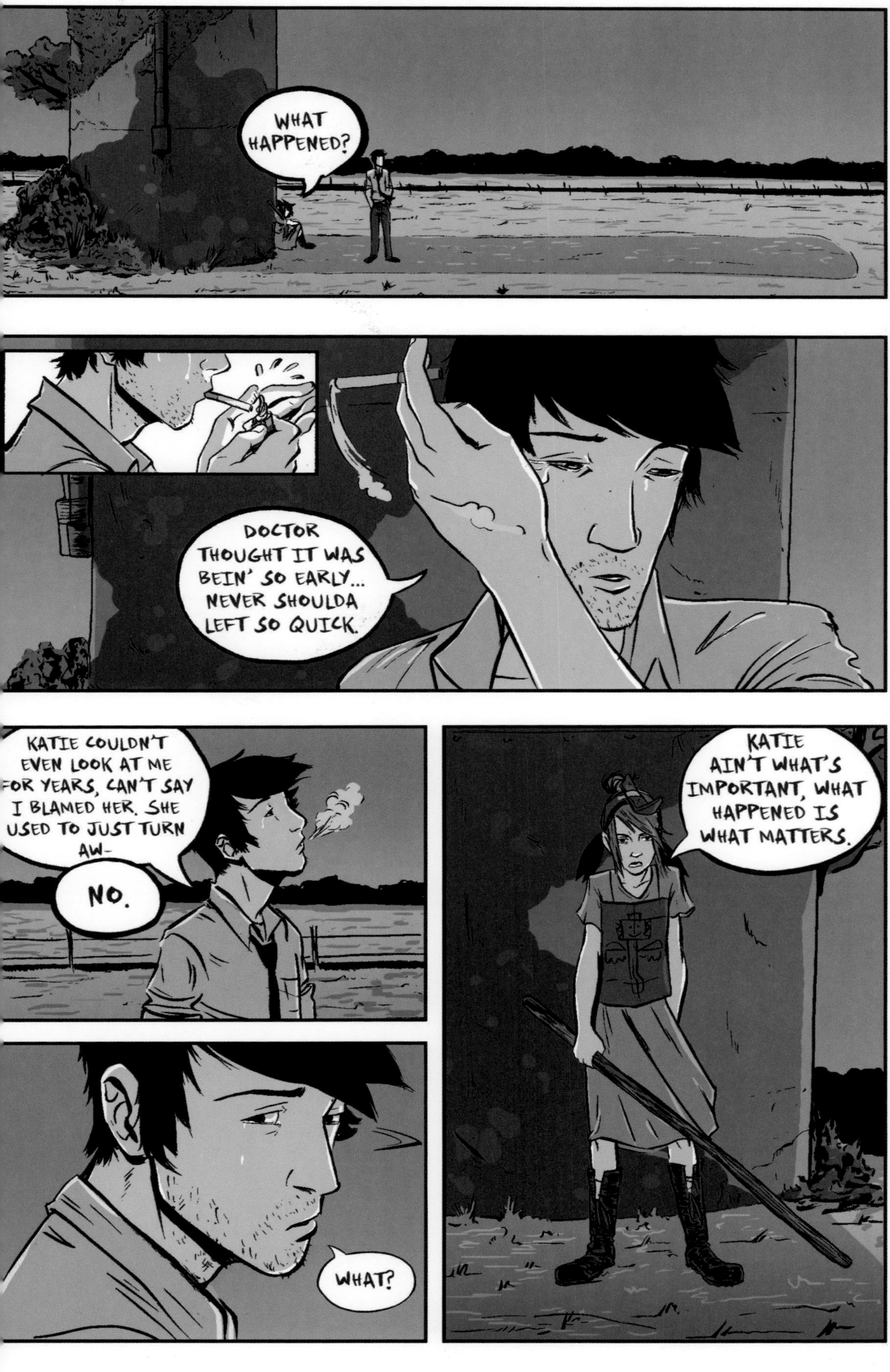
WHAT HAPPENED?
DOCTOR THOUGHT IT WAS BEIN' SO EARLY... NEVER SHOULDA LEFT SO QUICK.
KATIE COULDN'T EVEN LOOK AT ME FOR YEARS, CAN'T SAY I BLAMED HER. SHE USED TO JUST TURN AW-
NO.
WHAT?
KATIE AIN'T WHAT'S IMPORTANT, WHAT HAPPENED IS WHAT MATTERS.

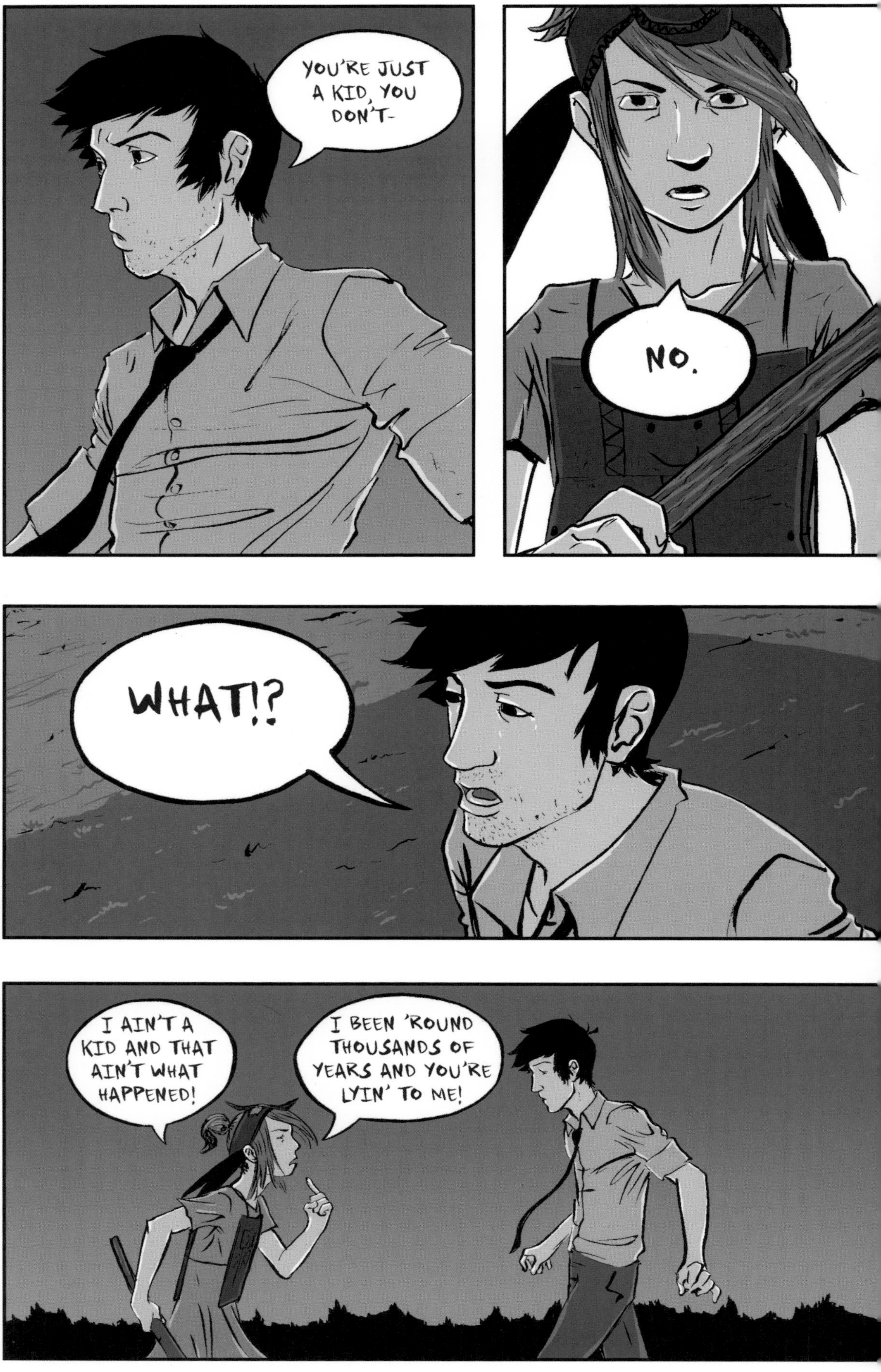
YOU'RE JUST A KID, YOU DON'T-
NO.
WHAT!?
I AIN'T A KID AND THAT AIN'T WHAT HAPPENED!
I BEEN 'ROUND THOUSANDS OF YEARS AND YOU'RE LYIN' TO ME!

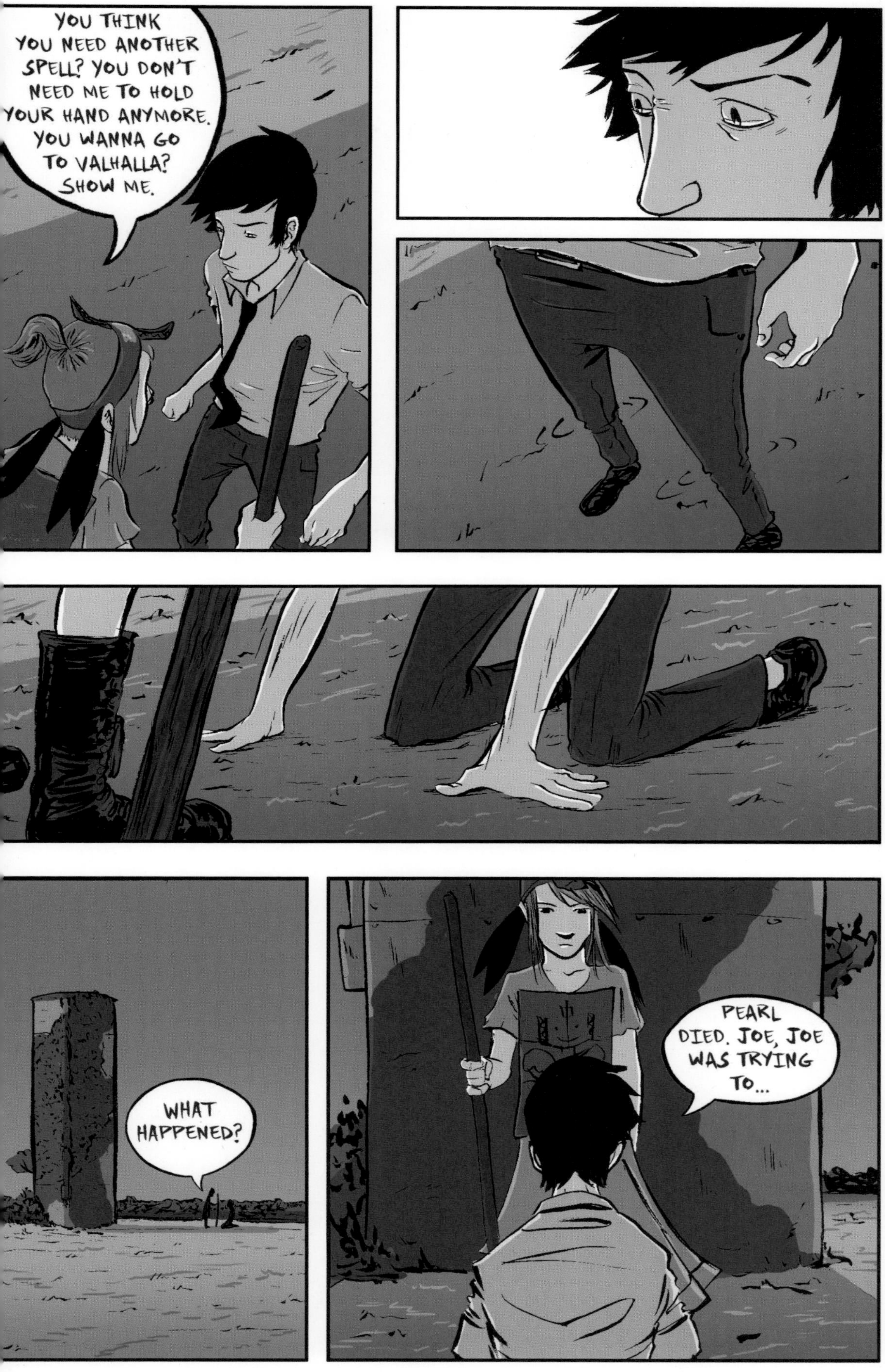
YOU THINK YOU NEED ANOTHER SPELL? YOU DON'T NEED ME TO HOLD YOUR HAND ANYMORE. YOU WANNA GO TO VALHALLA? SHOW ME.
WHAT HAPPENED?
PEARL DIED. JOE, JOE WAS TRYING TO...

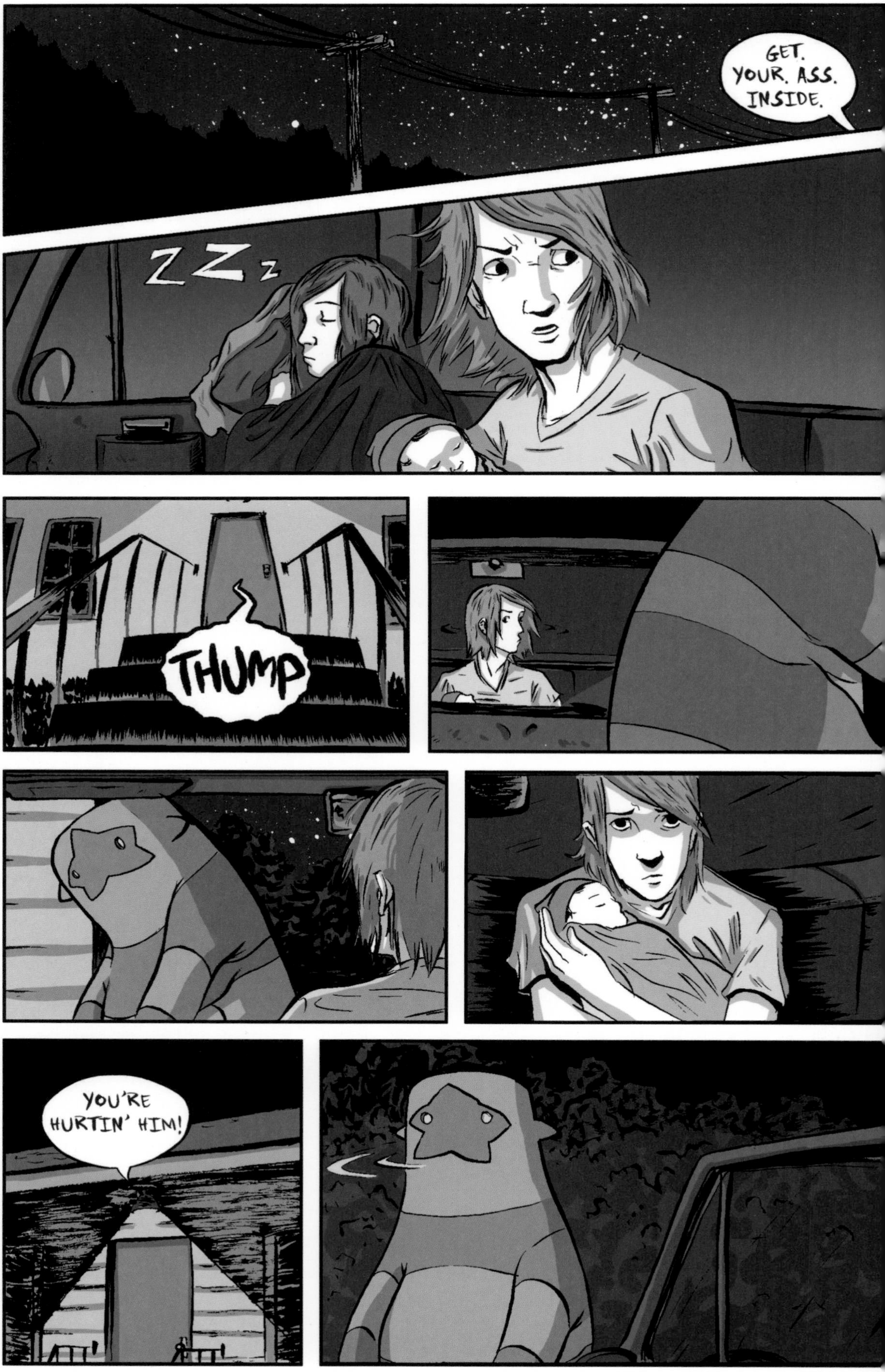
GET. YOUR. ASS. INSIDE.
ZZZ
THUMP
YOU'RE HURTIN' HIM!

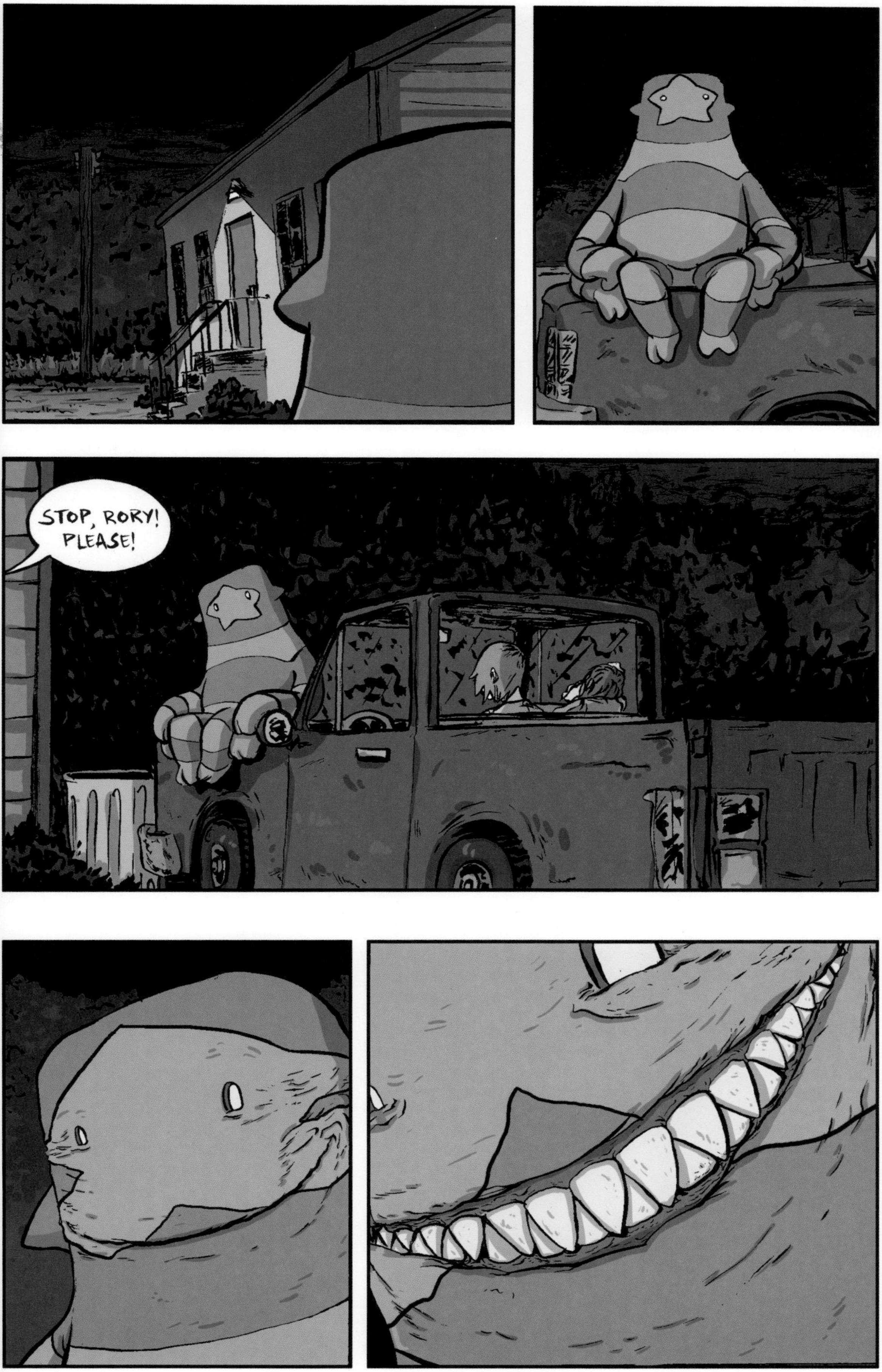
STOP, RORY! PLEASE!

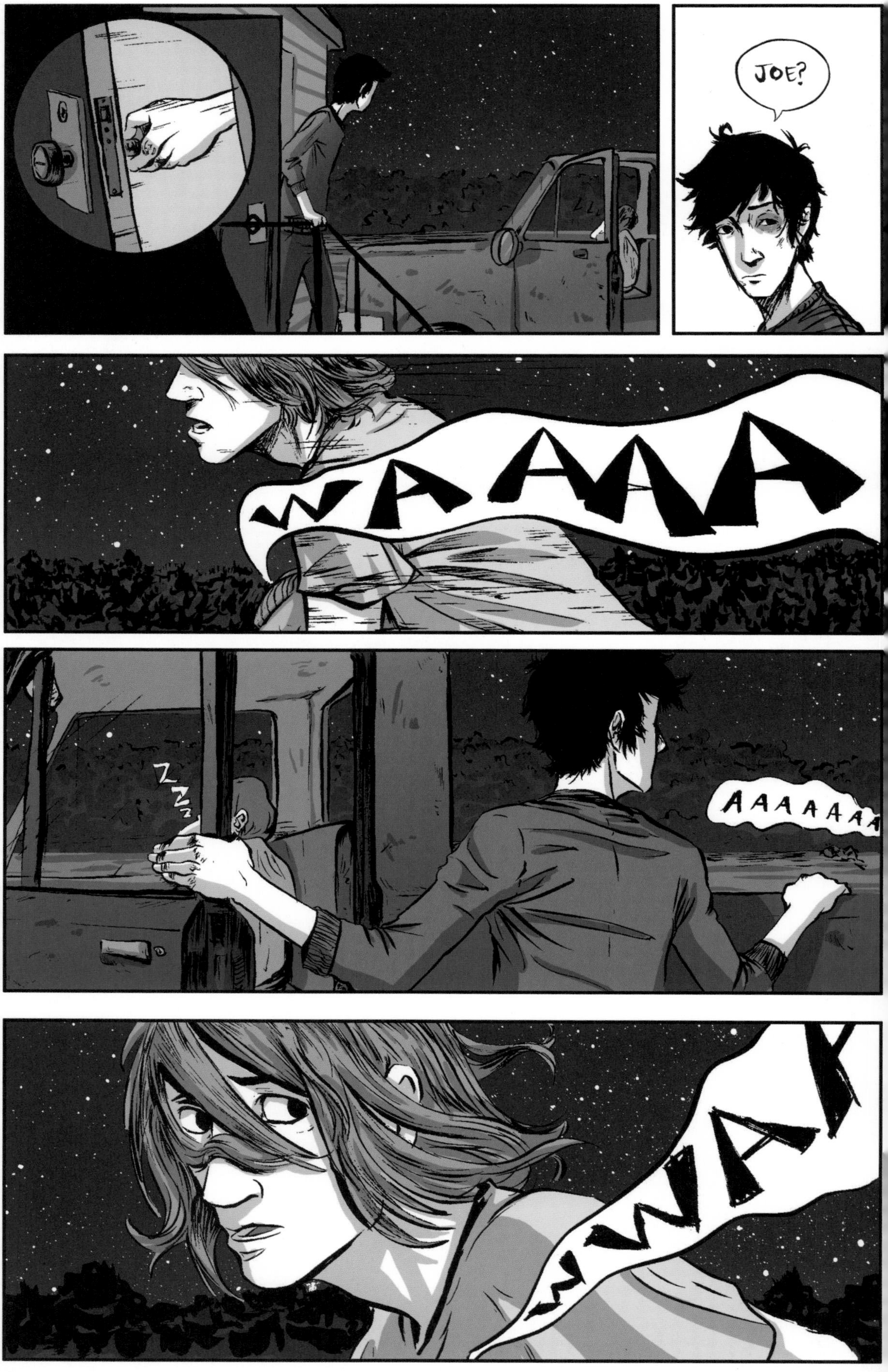
JOE?
WAAAA
ZZZ
AAAAAAA
WAA

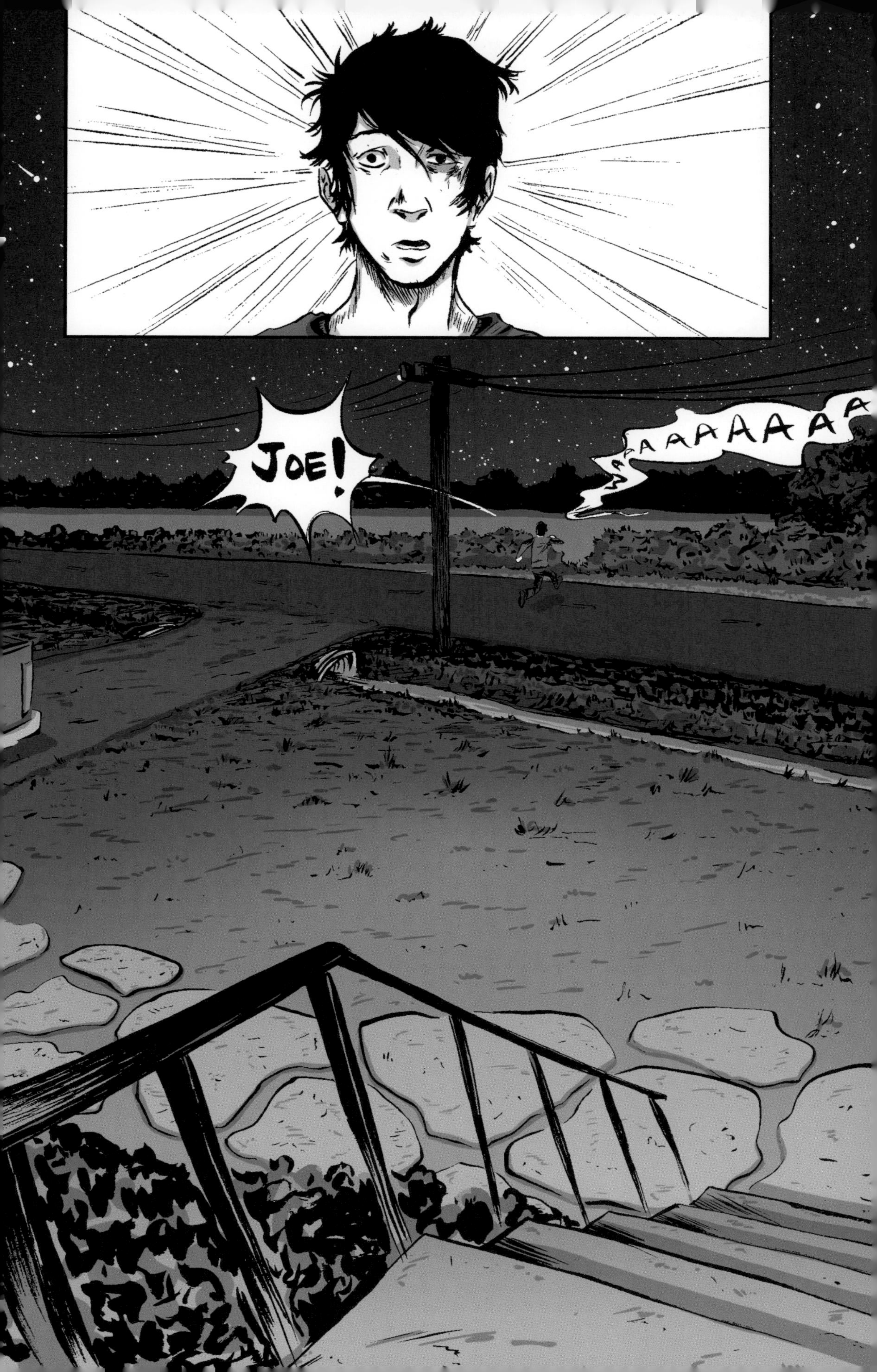
JOE!
AAAAAAAAAA

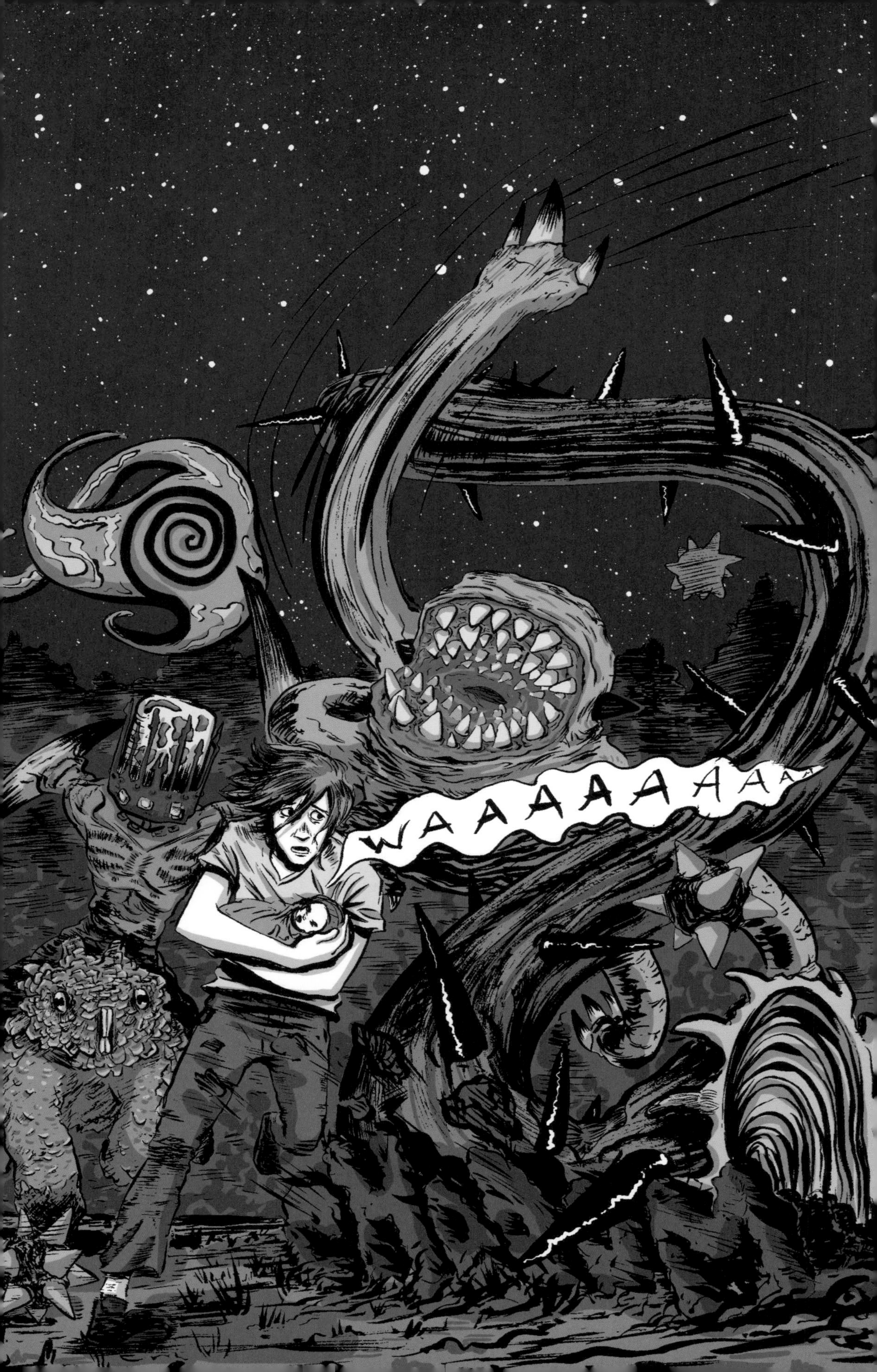
WAAAAAAAAA

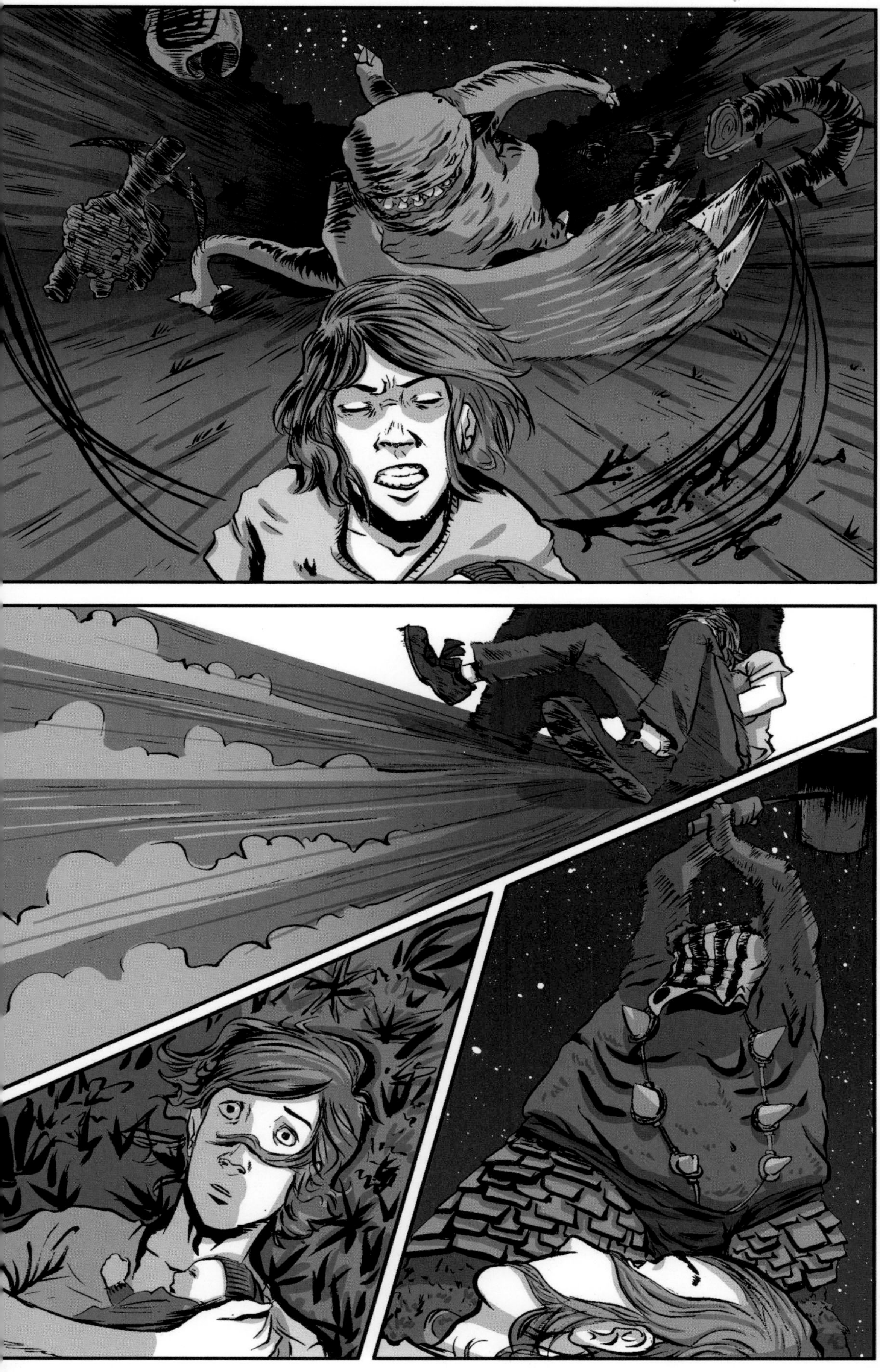

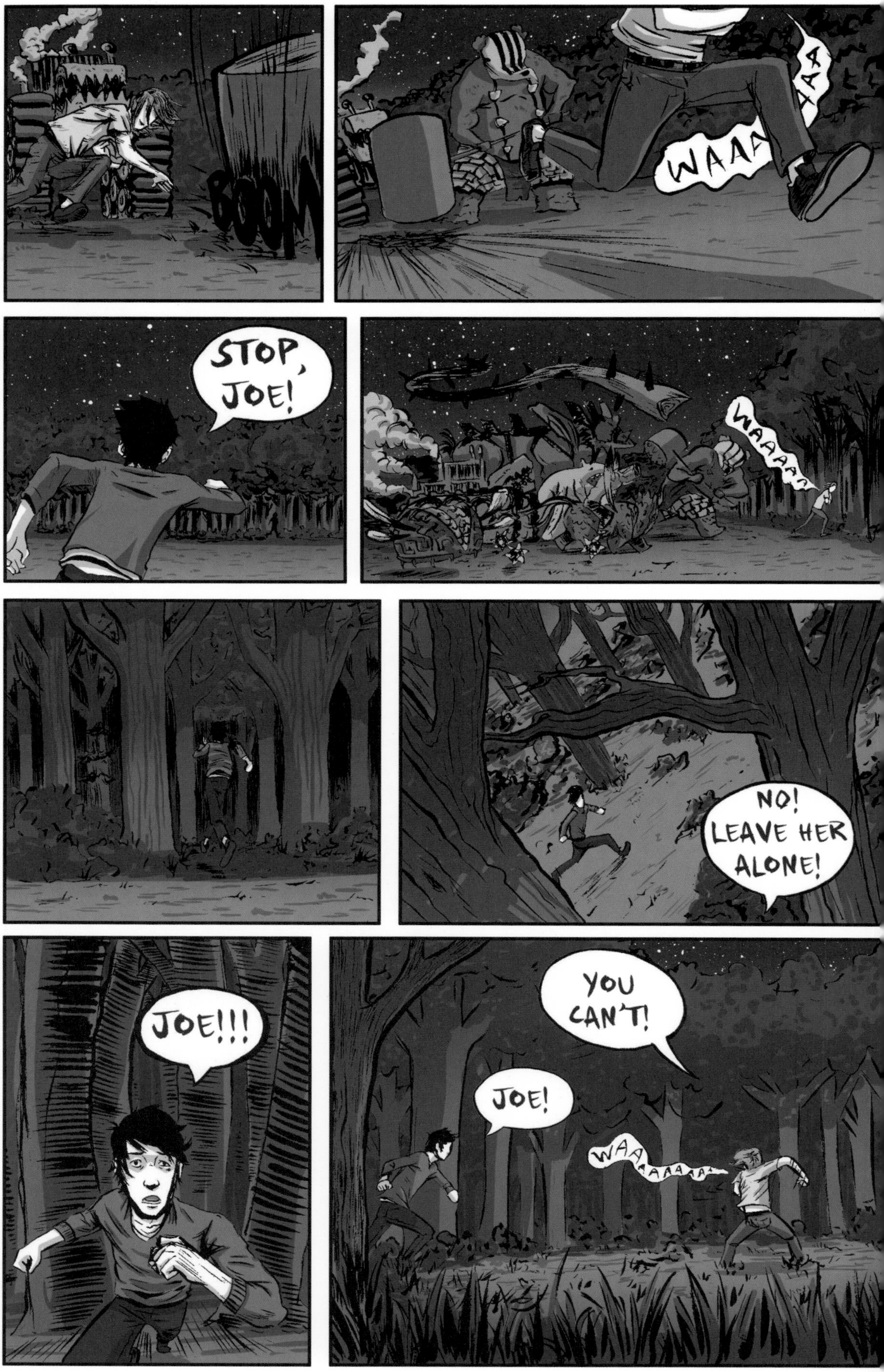
BOOM
WAAAAAAA
STOP, JOE!
WAAAAAA
NO! LEAVE HER ALONE!
JOE!!!
YOU CAN'T!
JOE!
WAAAAAAAA

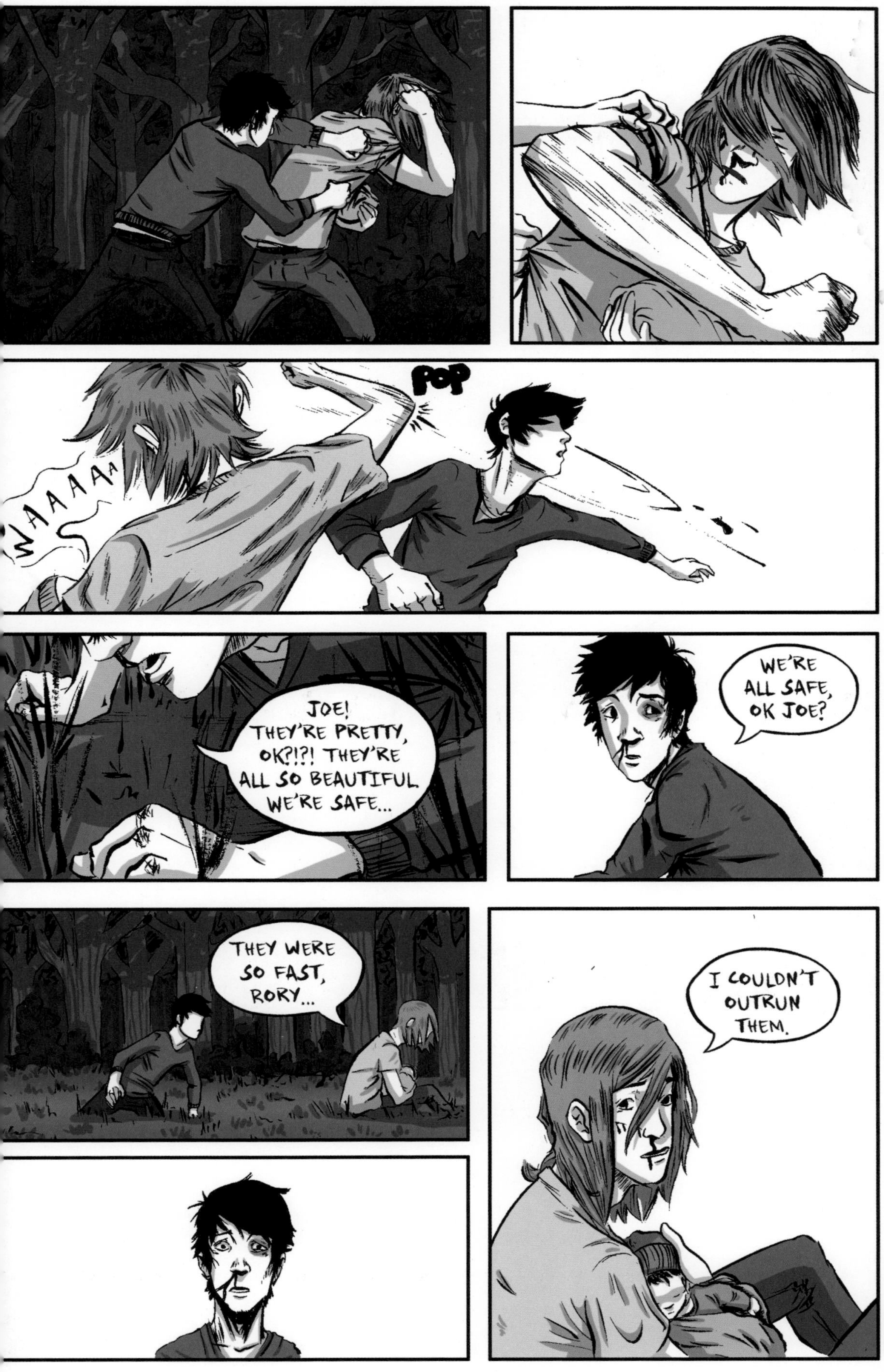
POP
WAAAAAA
JOE! THEY'RE PRETTY, OK?!?! THEY'RE ALL SO BEAUTIFUL WE'RE SAFE...
WE'RE ALL SAFE, OK JOE?
THEY WERE SO FAST, RORY...
I COULDN'T OUTRUN THEM.

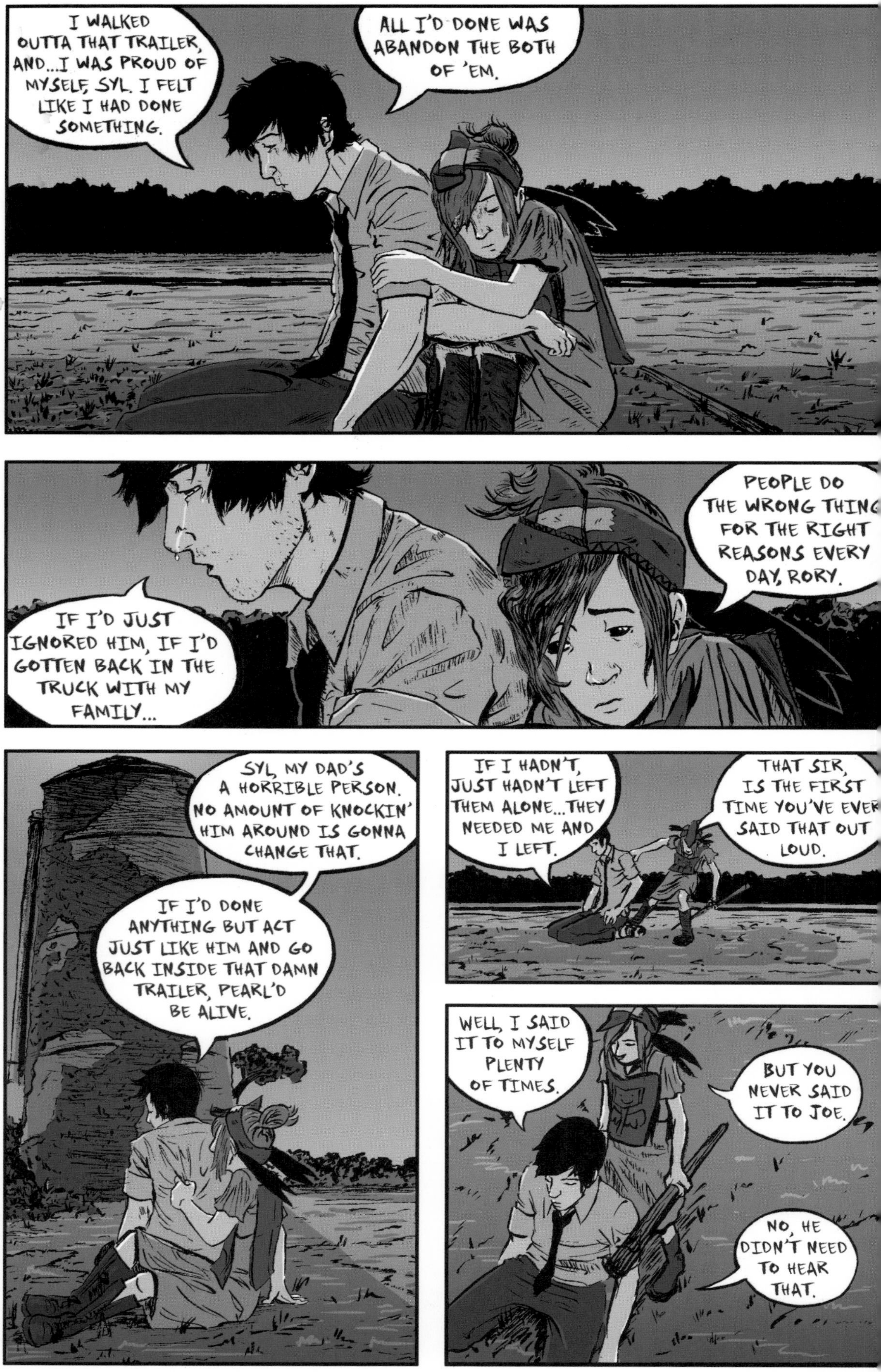
I WALKED OUTTA THAT TRAILER, AND...I WAS PROUD OF MYSELF, SYL. I FELT LIKE I HAD DONE SOMETHING.
ALL I'D DONE WAS ABANDON THE BOTH OF 'EM.
PEOPLE DO THE WRONG THING FOR THE RIGHT REASONS EVERY DAY, RORY.
IF I'D JUST IGNORED HIM, IF I'D GOTTEN BACK IN THE TRUCK WITH MY FAMILY...
SYL, MY DAD'S A HORRIBLE PERSON. NO AMOUNT OF KNOCKIN' HIM AROUND IS GONNA CHANGE THAT.
IF I'D DONE ANYTHING BUT ACT JUST LIKE HIM AND GO BACK INSIDE THAT DAMN TRAILER, PEARL'D BE ALIVE.
IF I HADN'T, JUST HADN'T LEFT THEM ALONE...THEY NEEDED ME AND I LEFT.
THAT SIR, IS THE FIRST TIME YOU'VE EVER SAID THAT OUT LOUD.
WELL, I SAID IT TO MYSELF PLENTY OF TIMES.
BUT YOU NEVER SAID IT TO JOE.
NO, HE DIDN'T NEED TO HEAR THAT.

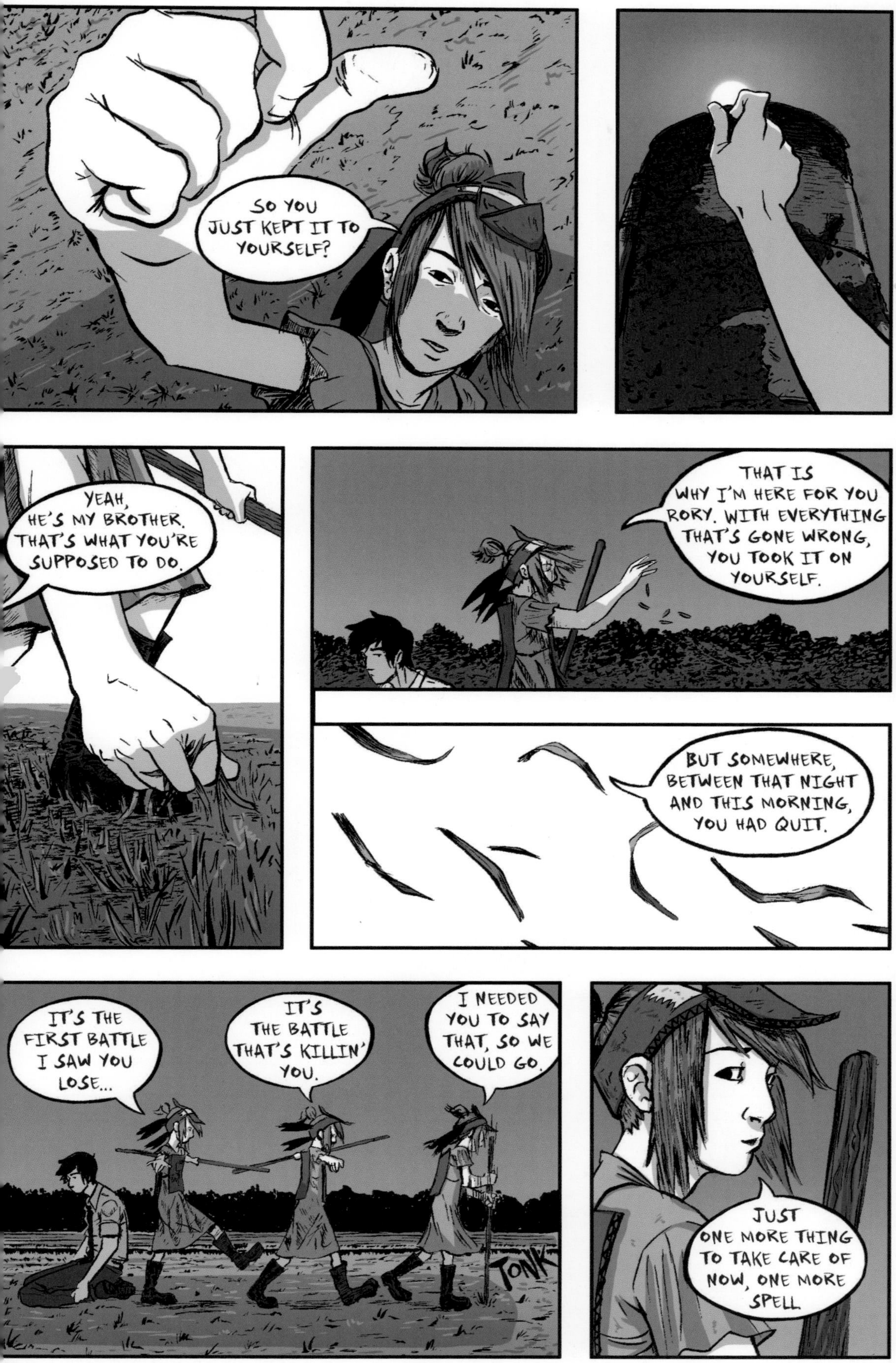
SO YOU JUST KEPT IT TO YOURSELF?
YEAH, HE'S MY BROTHER. THAT'S WHAT YOU'RE SUPPOSED TO DO.
THAT IS WHY I'M HERE FOR YOU RORY. WITH EVERYTHING THAT'S GONE WRONG, YOU TOOK IT ON YOURSELF.
BUT SOMEWHERE, BETWEEN THAT NIGHT AND THIS MORNING, YOU HAD QUIT.
IT'S THE FIRST BATTLE I SAW YOU LOSE...
IT'S THE BATTLE THAT'S KILLIN' YOU.
I NEEDED YOU TO SAY THAT, SO WE COULD GO.
TONK
JUST ONE MORE THING TO TAKE CARE OF NOW, ONE MORE SPELL

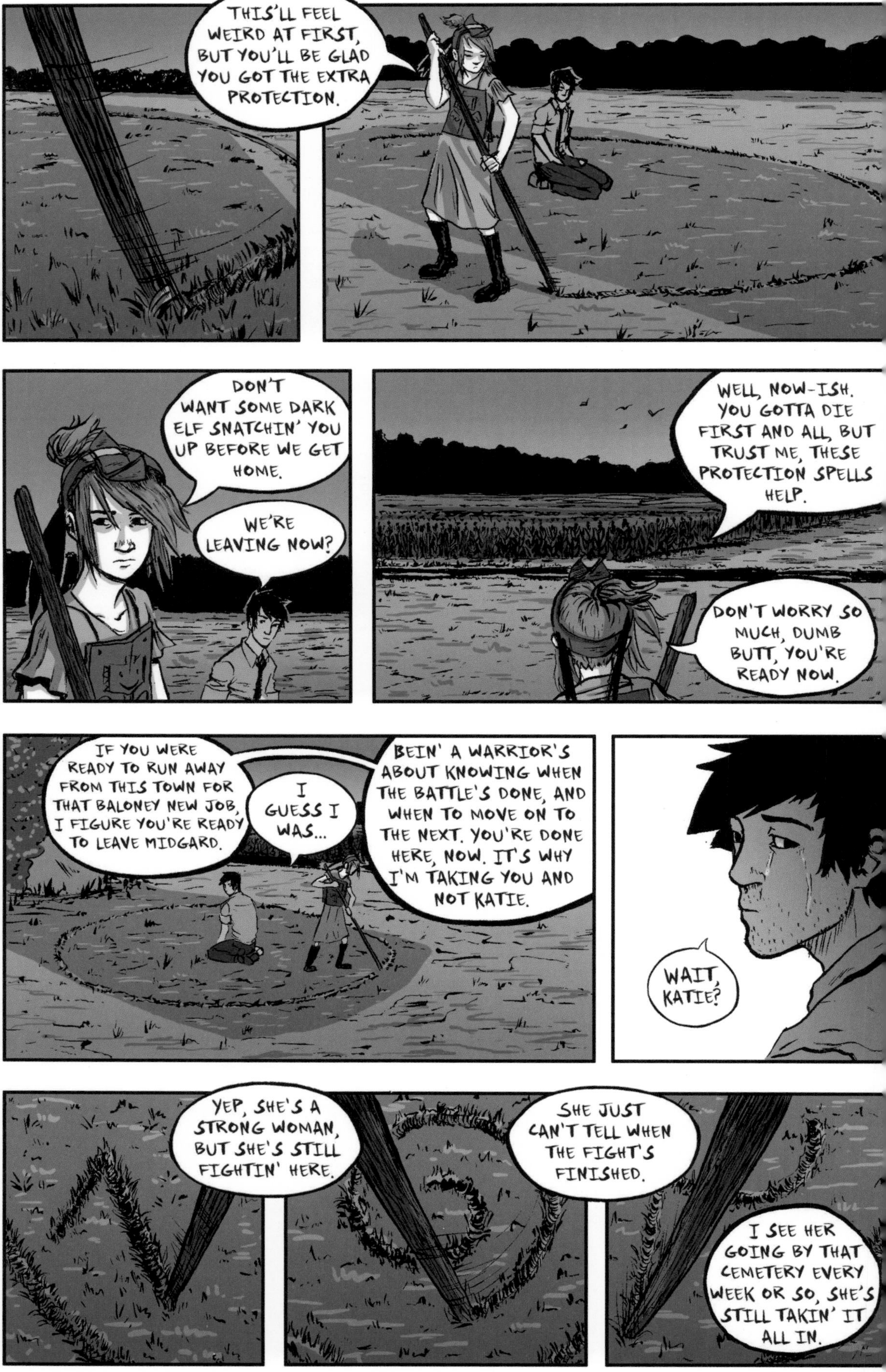
THIS'LL FEEL WEIRD AT FIRST, BUT YOU'LL BE GLAD YOU GOT THE EXTRA PROTECTION.
DON'T WANT SOME DARK ELF SNATCHIN' YOU UP BEFORE WE GET HOME.
WE'RE LEAVING NOW?
WELL, NOW-ISH. YOU GOTTA DIE FIRST AND ALL, BUT TRUST ME, THESE PROTECTION SPELLS HELP.
DON'T WORRY SO MUCH, DUMB BUTT, YOU'RE READY NOW.
IF YOU WERE READY TO RUN AWAY FROM THIS TOWN FOR THAT BALONEY NEW JOB, I FIGURE YOU'RE READY TO LEAVE MIDGARD.
I GUESS I WAS...
BEIN' A WARRIOR'S ABOUT KNOWING WHEN THE BATTLE'S DONE, AND WHEN TO MOVE ON TO THE NEXT. YOU'RE DONE HERE, NOW. IT'S WHY I'M TAKING YOU AND NOT KATIE.
WAIT, KATIE?
YEP, SHE'S A STRONG WOMAN, BUT SHE'S STILL FIGHTIN' HERE.
SHE JUST CAN'T TELL WHEN THE FIGHT'S FINISHED.
I SEE HER GOING BY THAT CEMETERY EVERY WEEK OR SO, SHE'S STILL TAKIN' IT ALL IN.

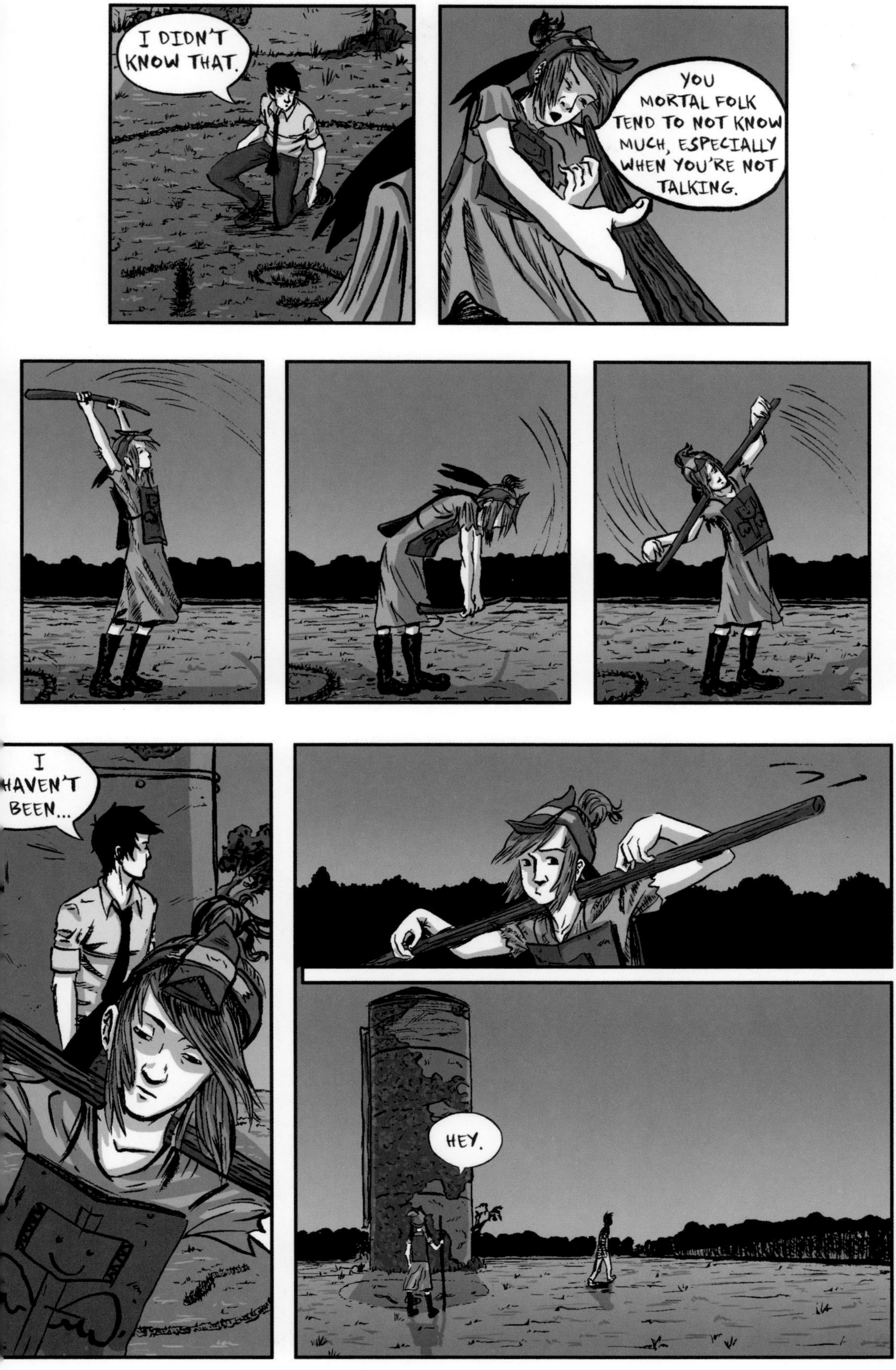
I DIDN'T KNOW THAT.
YOU MORTAL FOLK TEND TO NOT KNOW MUCH, ESPECIALLY WHEN YOU'RE NOT TALKING.
I HAVEN'T BEEN...
HEY.

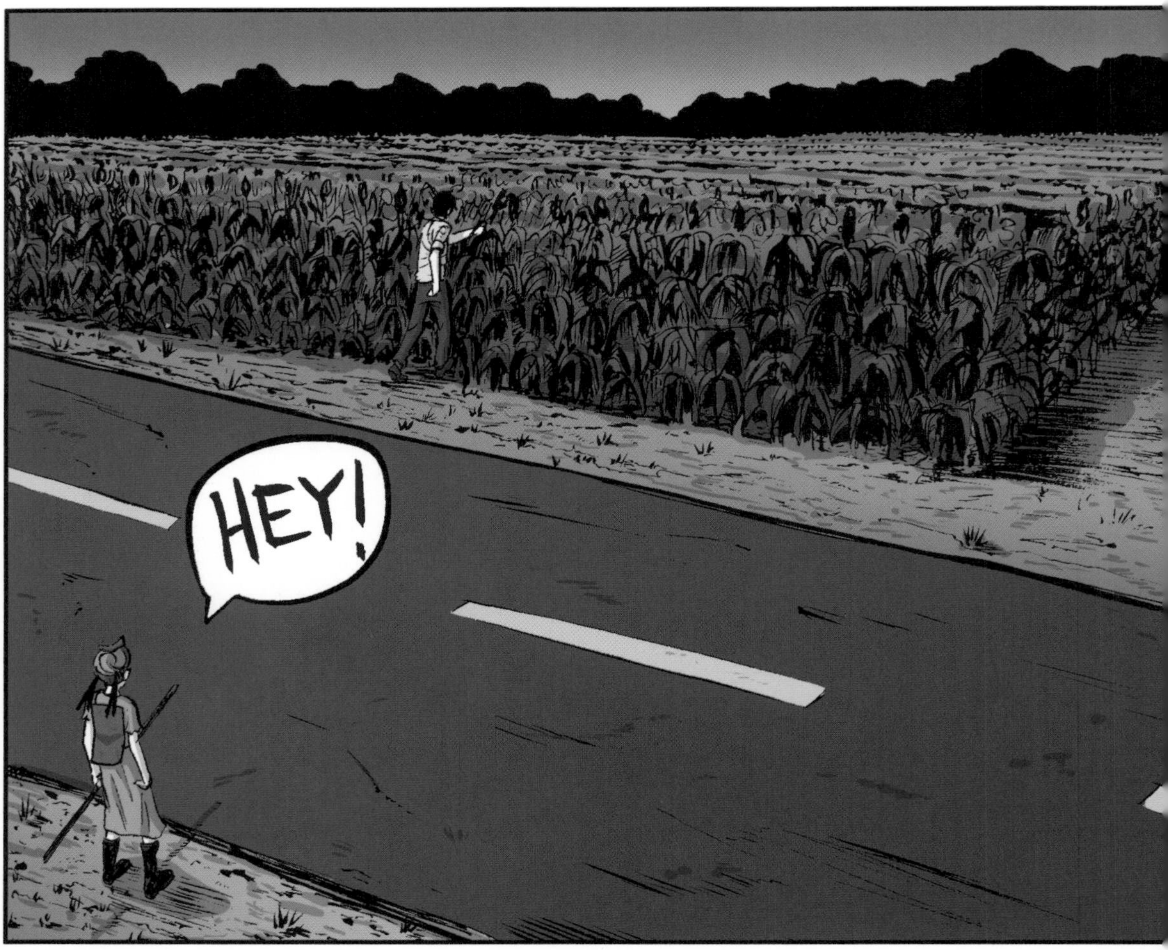
HEY!

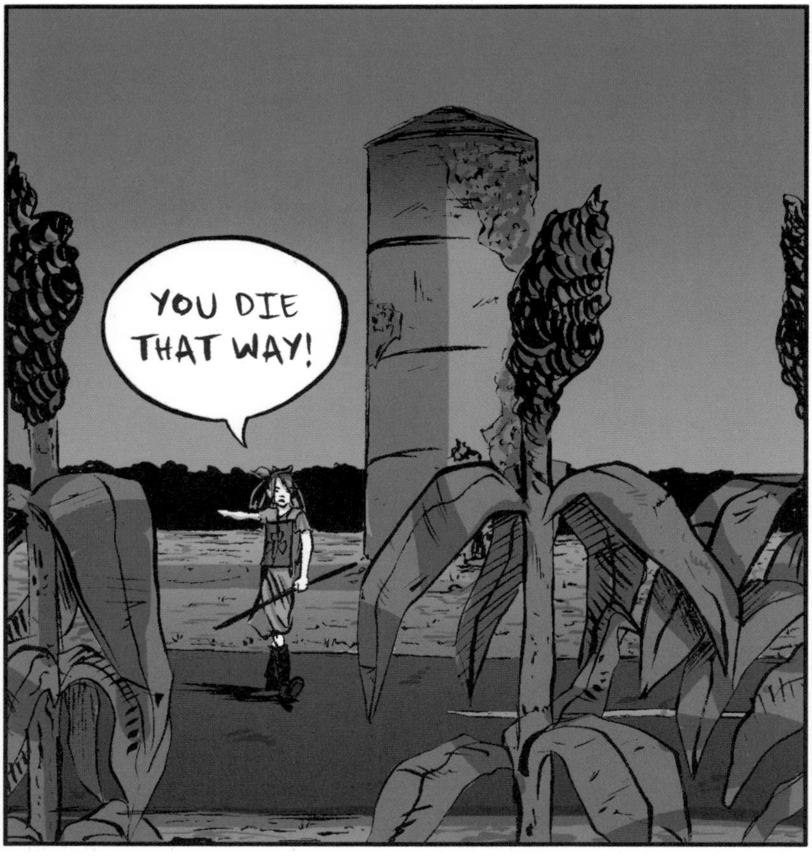
YOU DIE
THAT WAY!

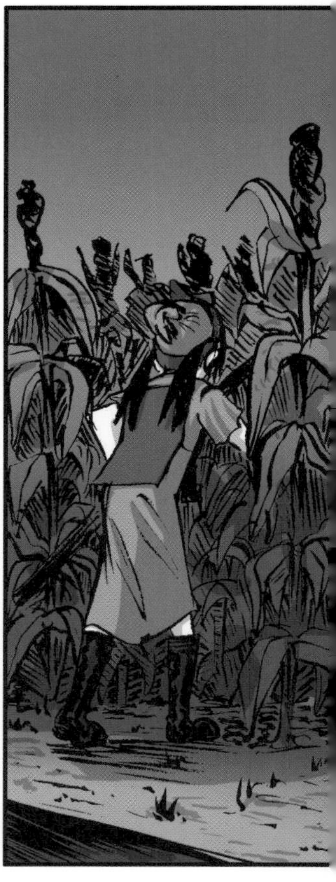

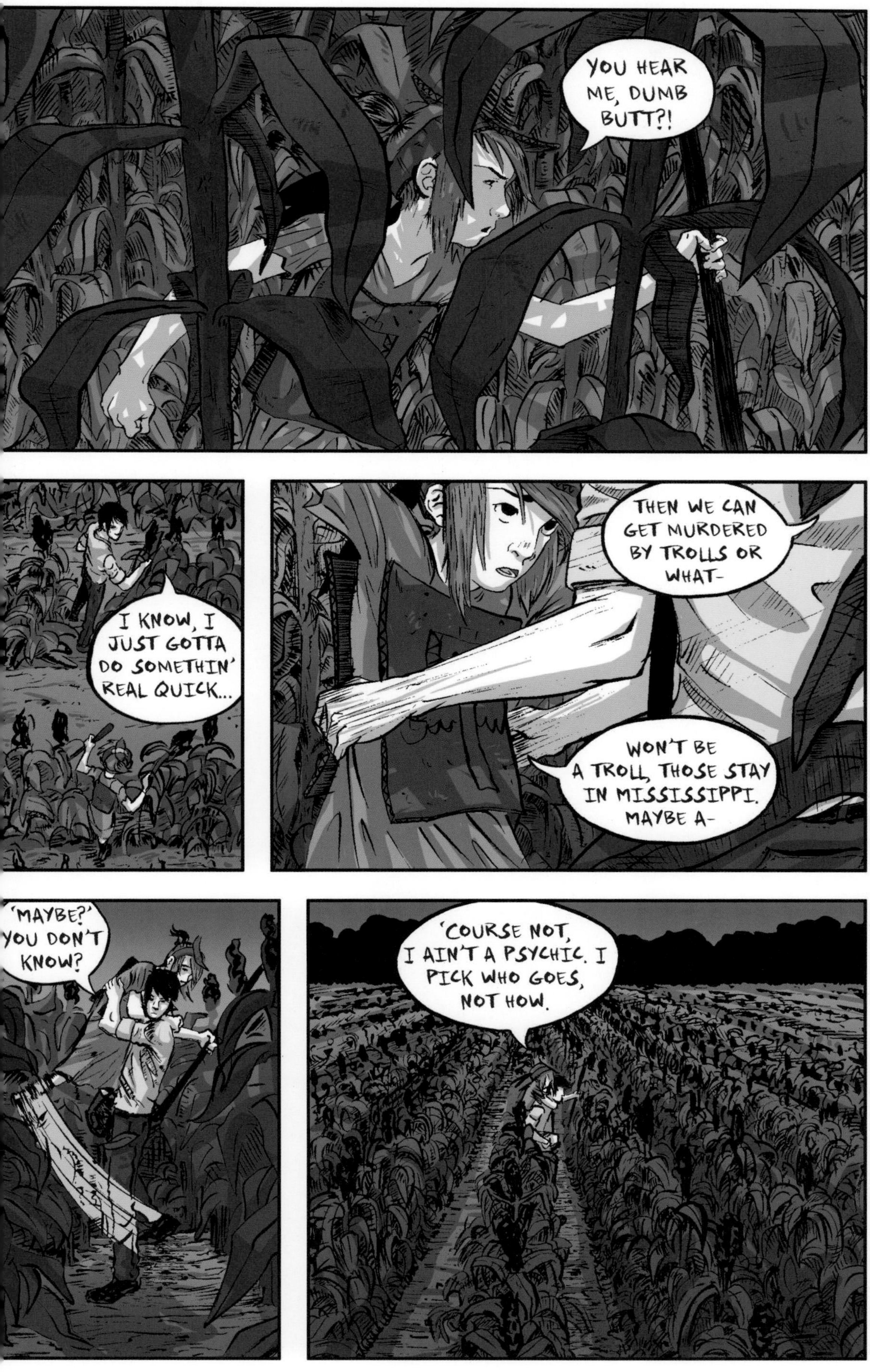
YOU HEAR ME, DUMB BUTT?!
THEN WE CAN GET MURDERED BY TROLLS OR WHAT-
I KNOW, I JUST GOTTA DO SOMETHIN' REAL QUICK...
WON'T BE A TROLL, THOSE STAY IN MISSISSIPPI. MAYBE A-
'MAYBE?' YOU DON'T KNOW?
'COURSE NOT, I AIN'T A PSYCHIC. I PICK WHO GOES, NOT HOW.

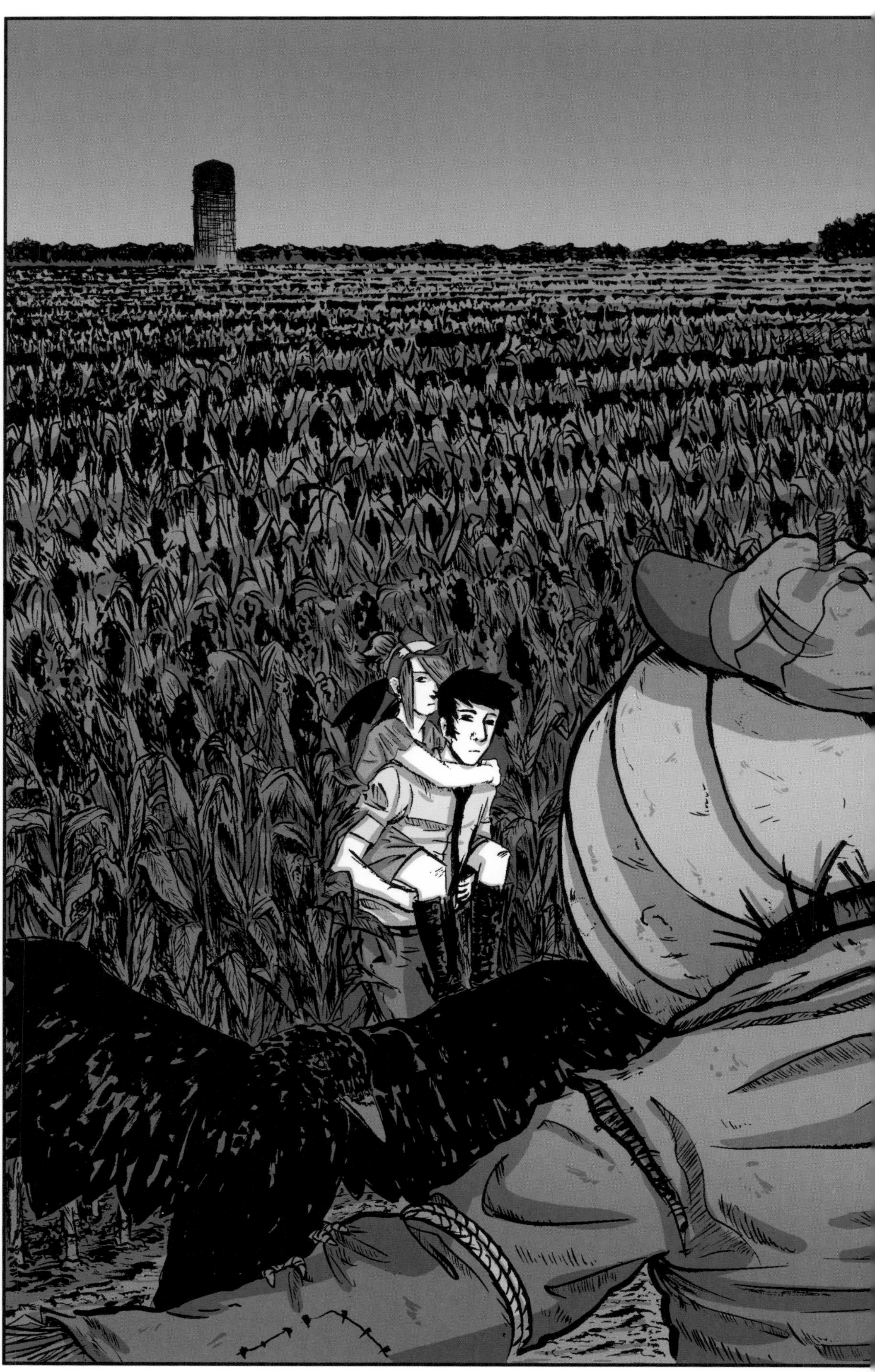

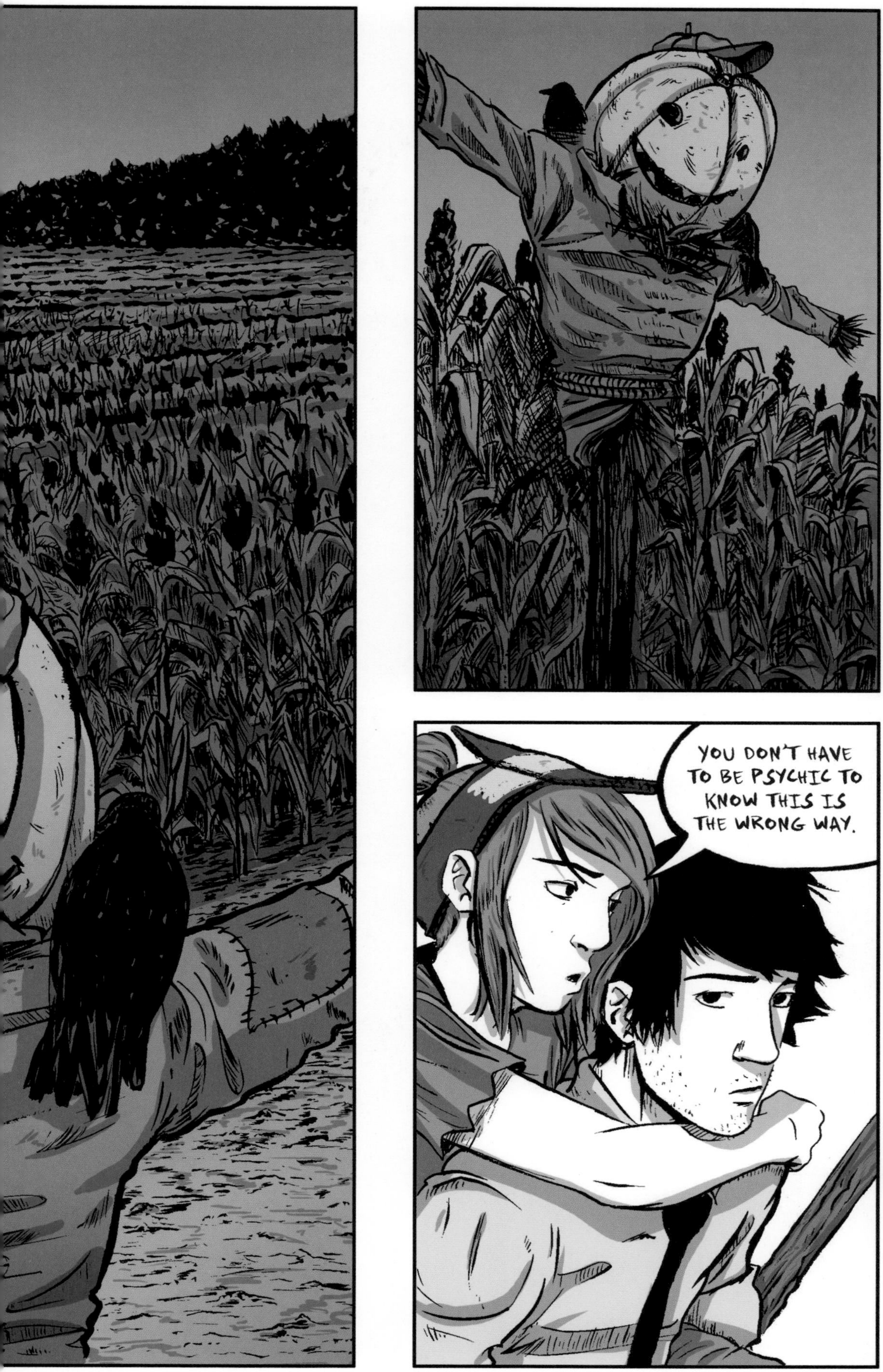
YOU DON'T HAVE TO BE PSYCHIC TO KNOW THIS IS THE WRONG WAY.

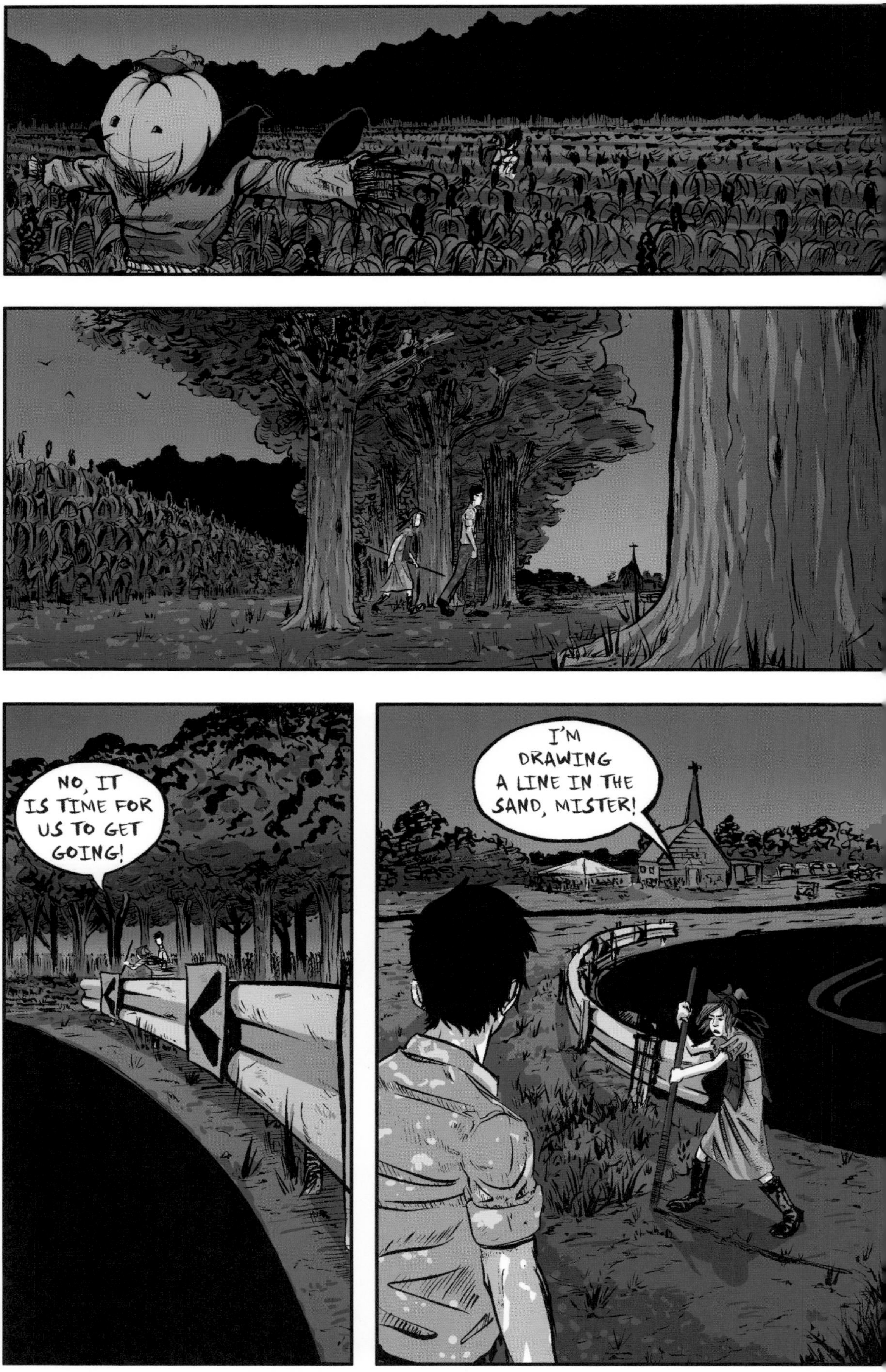
NO, IT IS TIME FOR US TO GET GOING!
I'M DRAWING A LINE IN THE SAND, MISTER!

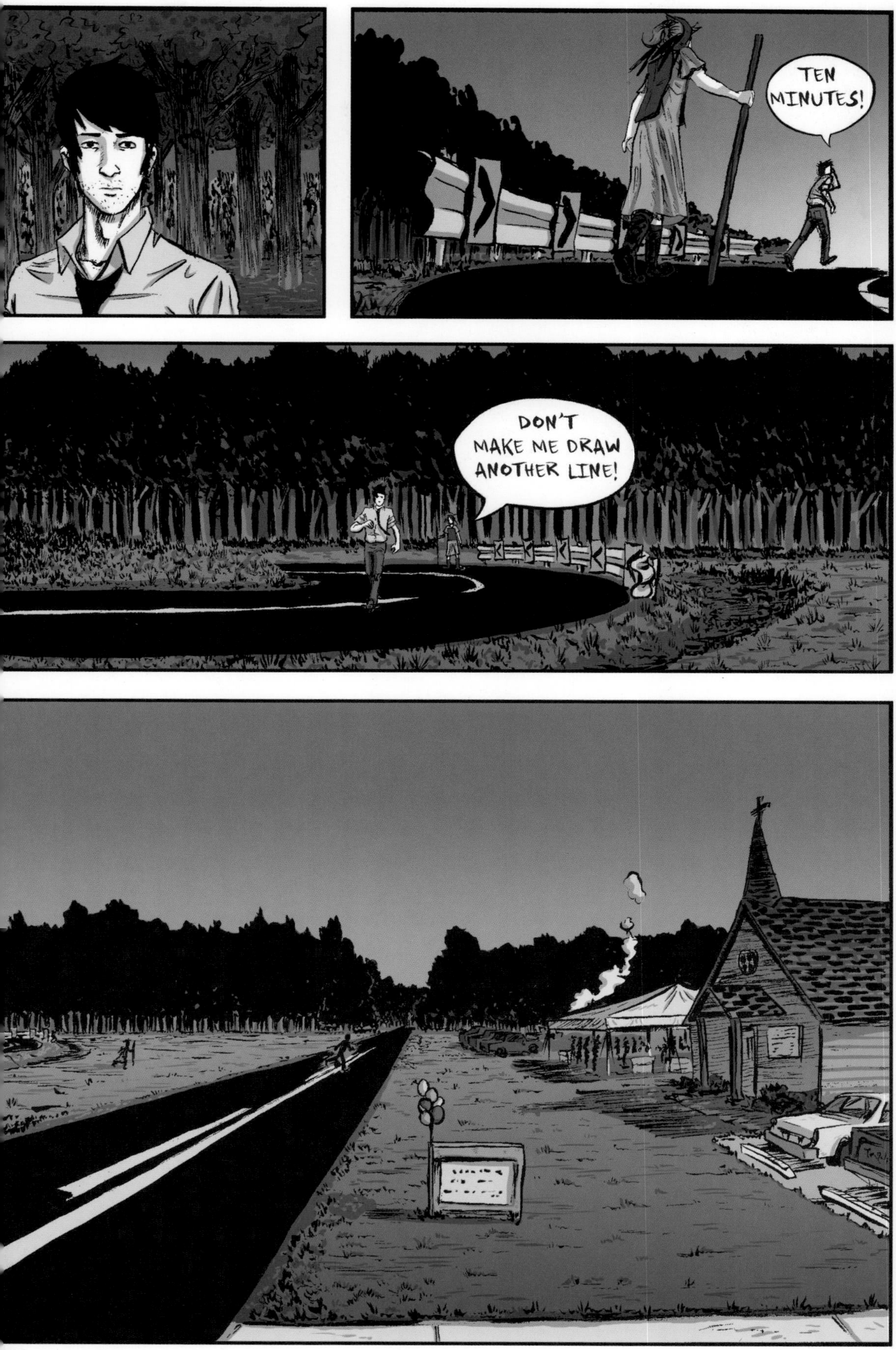
TEN MINUTES!
DON'T MAKE ME DRAW ANOTHER LINE!

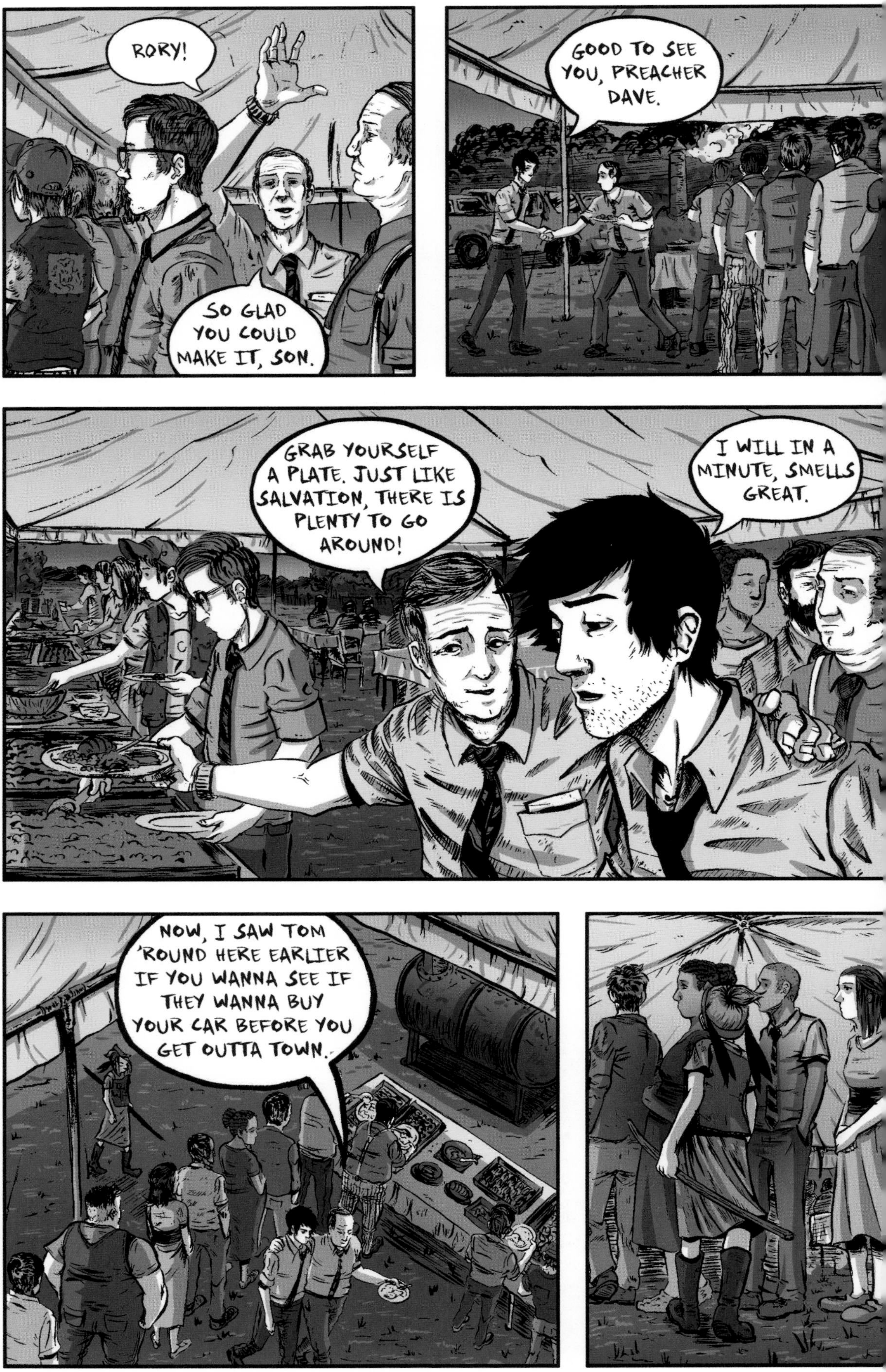
RORY!
SO GLAD YOU COULD MAKE IT, SON.
GOOD TO SEE YOU, PREACHER DAVE.
GRAB YOURSELF A PLATE. JUST LIKE SALVATION, THERE IS PLENTY TO GO AROUND!
I WILL IN A MINUTE, SMELLS GREAT.
NOW, I SAW TOM 'ROUND HERE EARLIER IF YOU WANNA SEE IF THEY WANNA BUY YOUR CAR BEFORE YOU GET OUTTA TOWN.

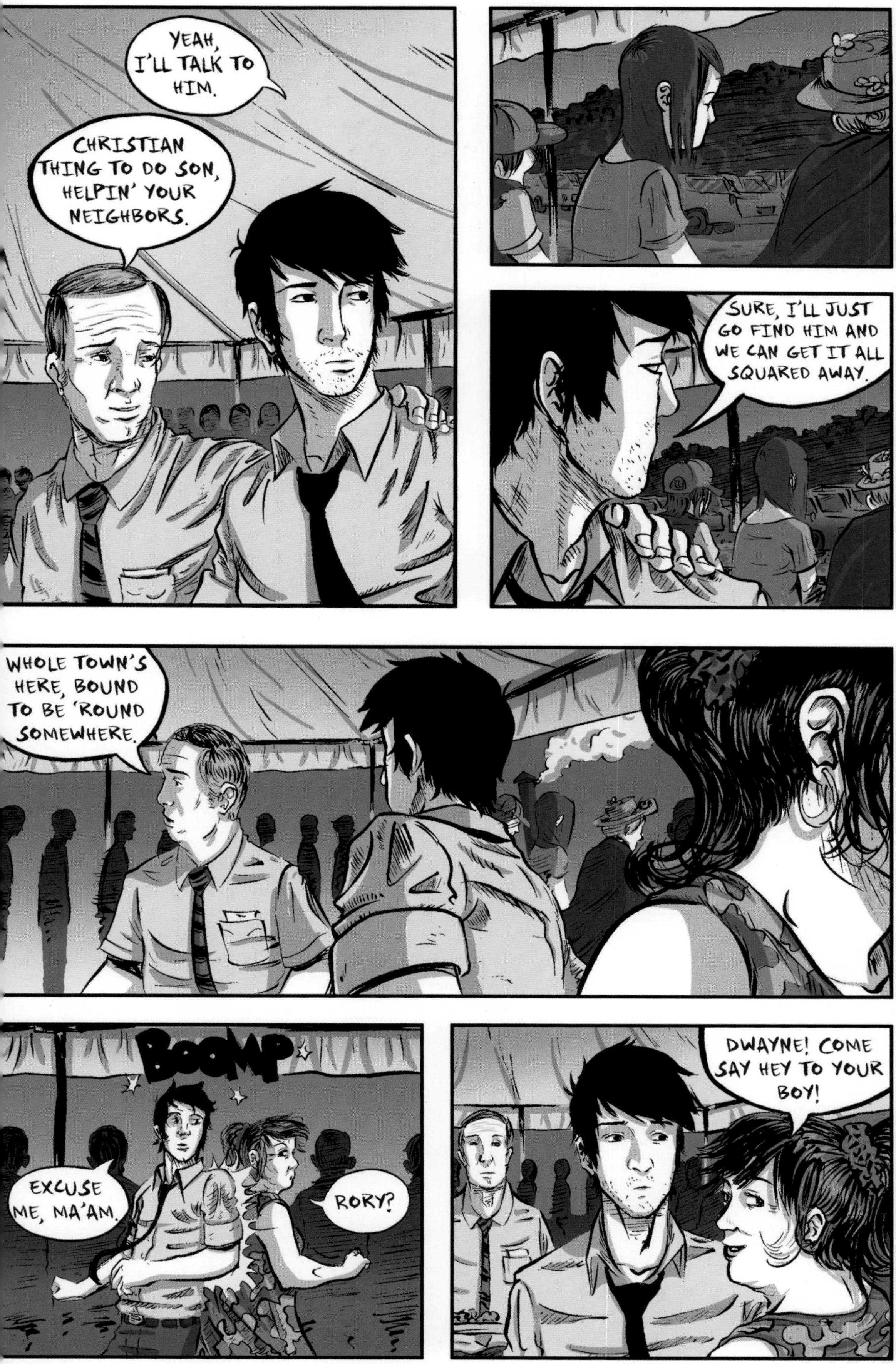
YEAH, I'LL TALK TO HIM.
CHRISTIAN THING TO DO SON, HELPIN' YOUR NEIGHBORS.
SURE, I'LL JUST GO FIND HIM AND WE CAN GET IT ALL SQUARED AWAY.
WHOLE TOWN'S HERE, BOUND TO BE 'ROUND SOMEWHERE.
BOOMP
EXCUSE ME, MA'AM.
RORY?
DWAYNE! COME SAY HEY TO YOUR BOY!

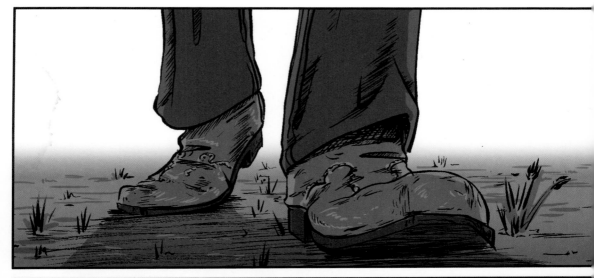

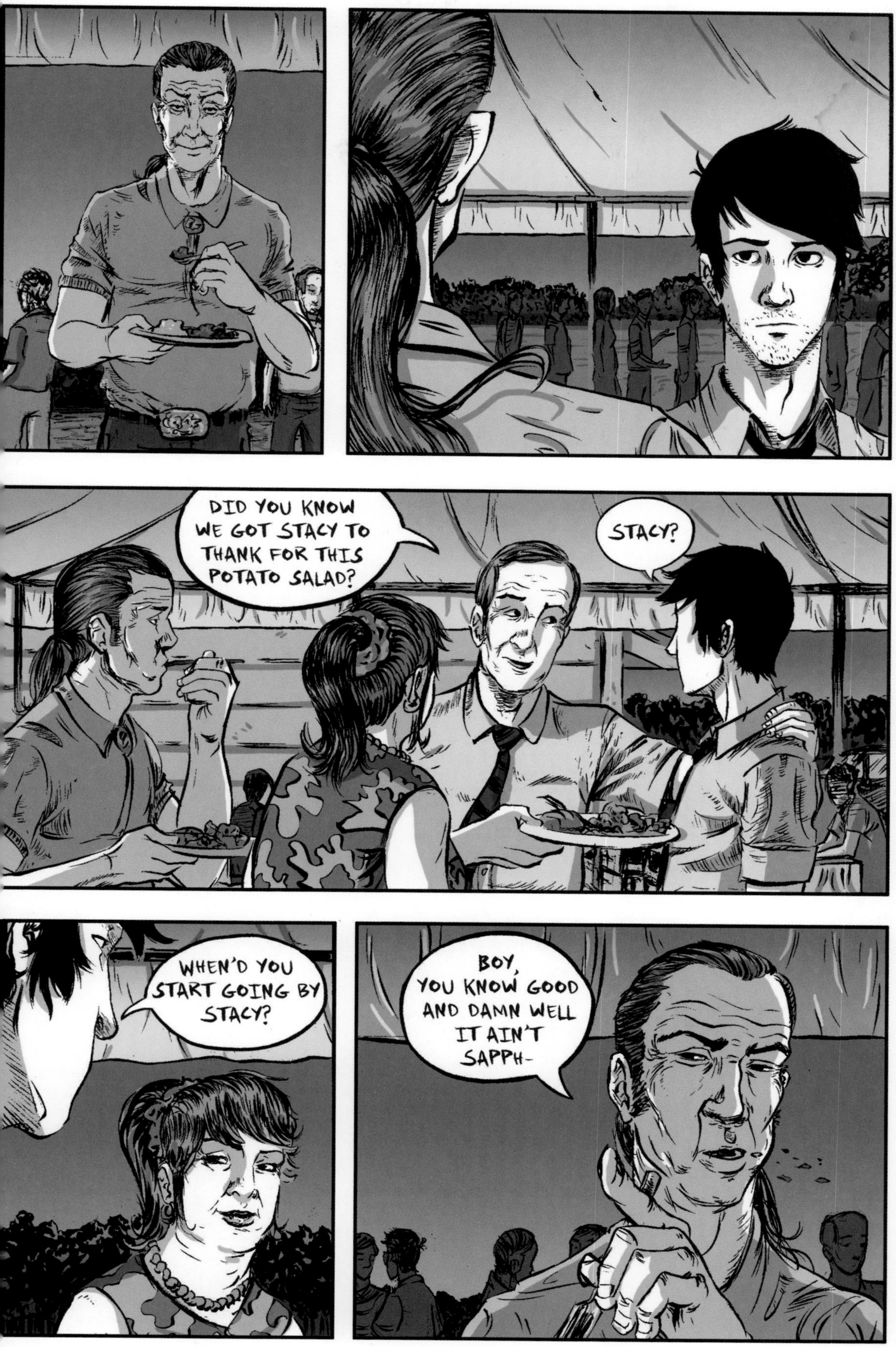
DID YOU KNOW WE GOT STACY TO THANK FOR THIS POTATO SALAD?
STACY?
WHEN'D YOU START GOING BY STACY?
BOY, YOU KNOW GOOD AND DAMN WELL IT AIN'T SAPPH-

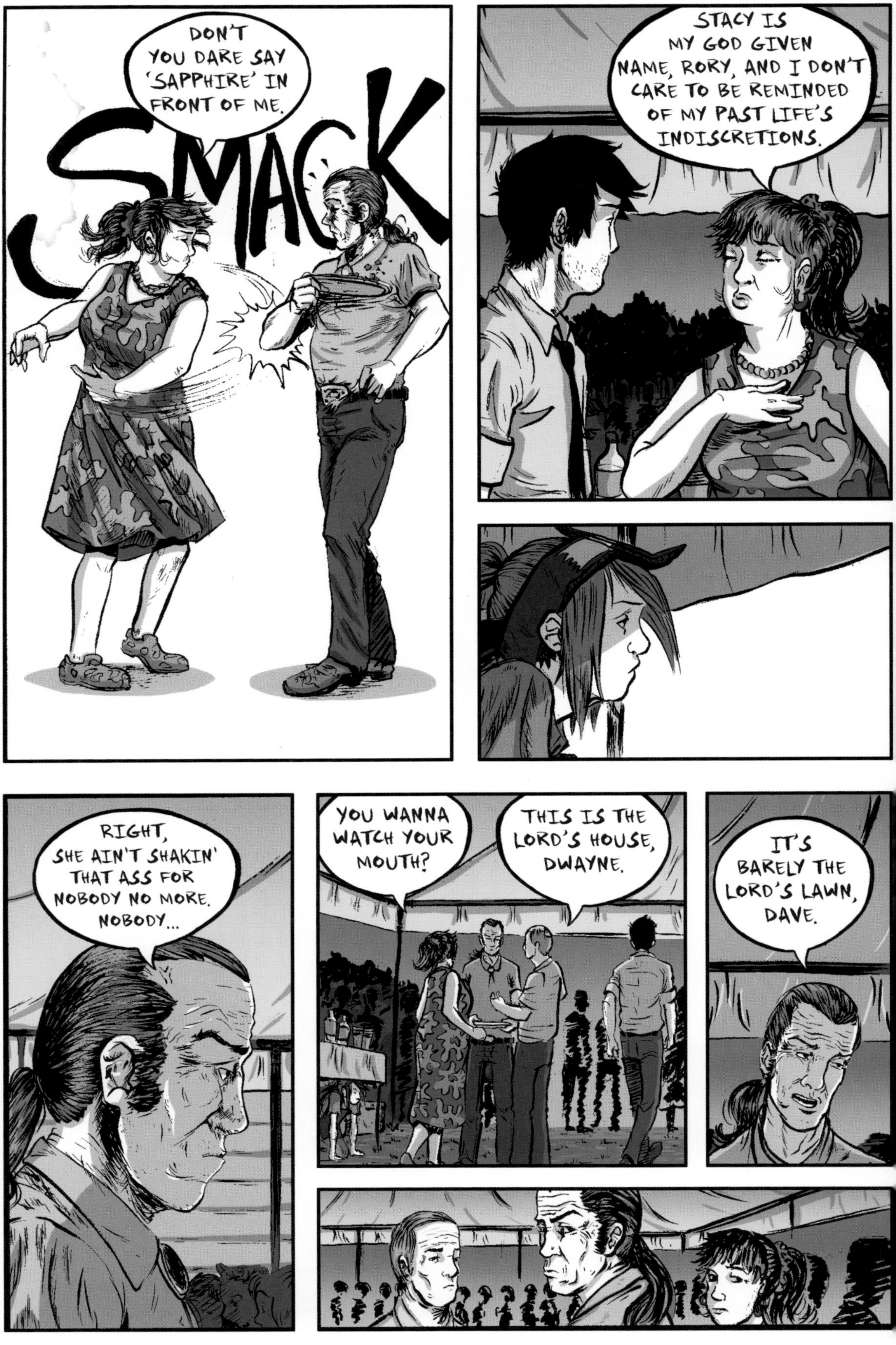
DON'T YOU DARE SAY 'SAPPHIRE' IN FRONT OF ME.
SMACK
STACY IS MY GOD GIVEN NAME, RORY, AND I DON'T CARE TO BE REMINDED OF MY PAST LIFE'S INDISCRETIONS.
RIGHT, SHE AIN'T SHAKIN' THAT ASS FOR NOBODY NO MORE. NOBODY...
YOU WANNA WATCH YOUR MOUTH?
THIS IS THE LORD'S HOUSE, DWAYNE.
IT'S BARELY THE LORD'S LAWN, DAVE.

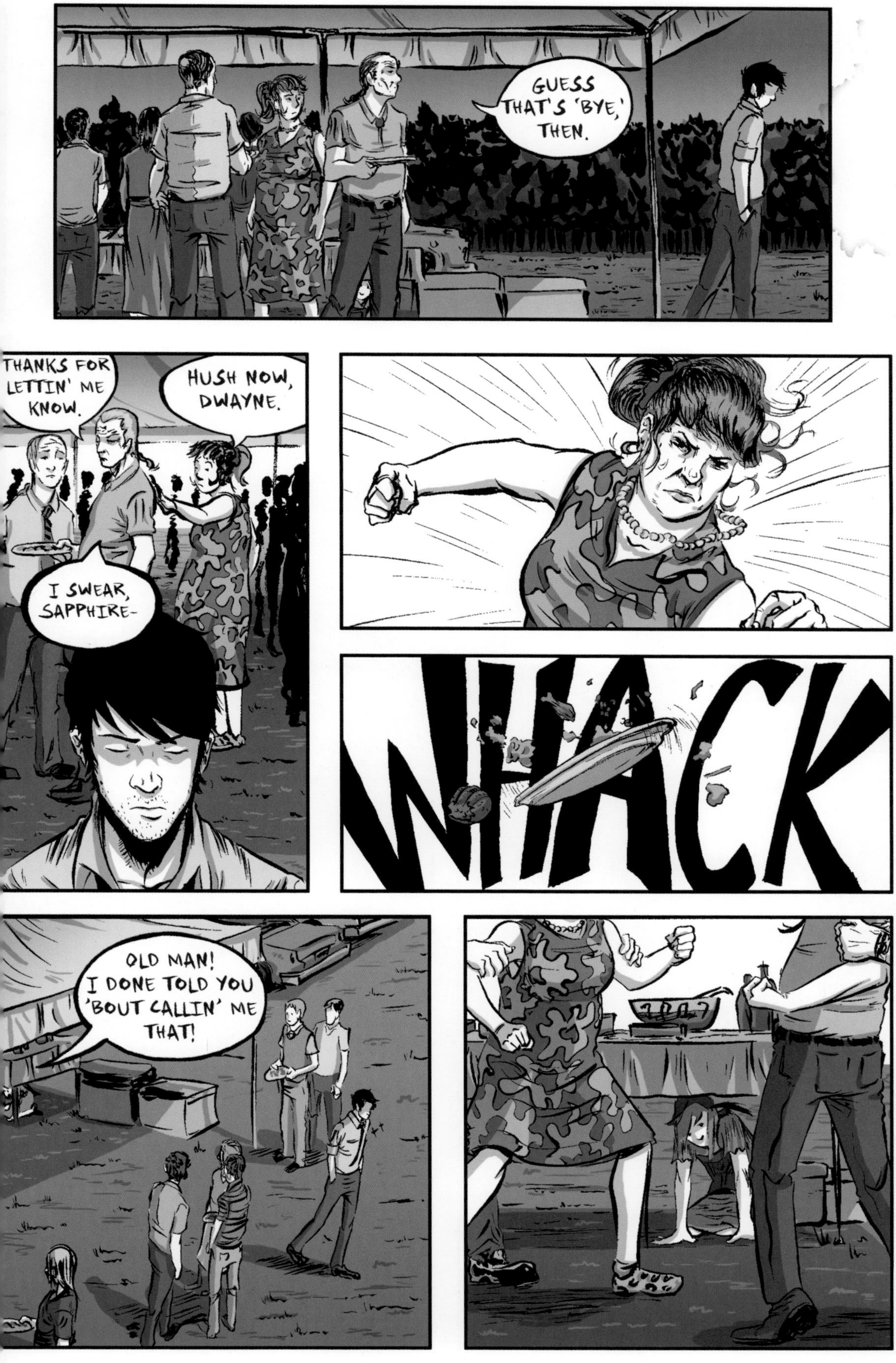
GUESS THAT'S 'BYE,' THEN.
THANKS FOR LETTIN' ME KNOW.
HUSH NOW, DWAYNE.
I SWEAR, SAPPHIRE-
WHACK
OLD MAN! I DONE TOLD YOU 'BOUT CALLIN' ME THAT!

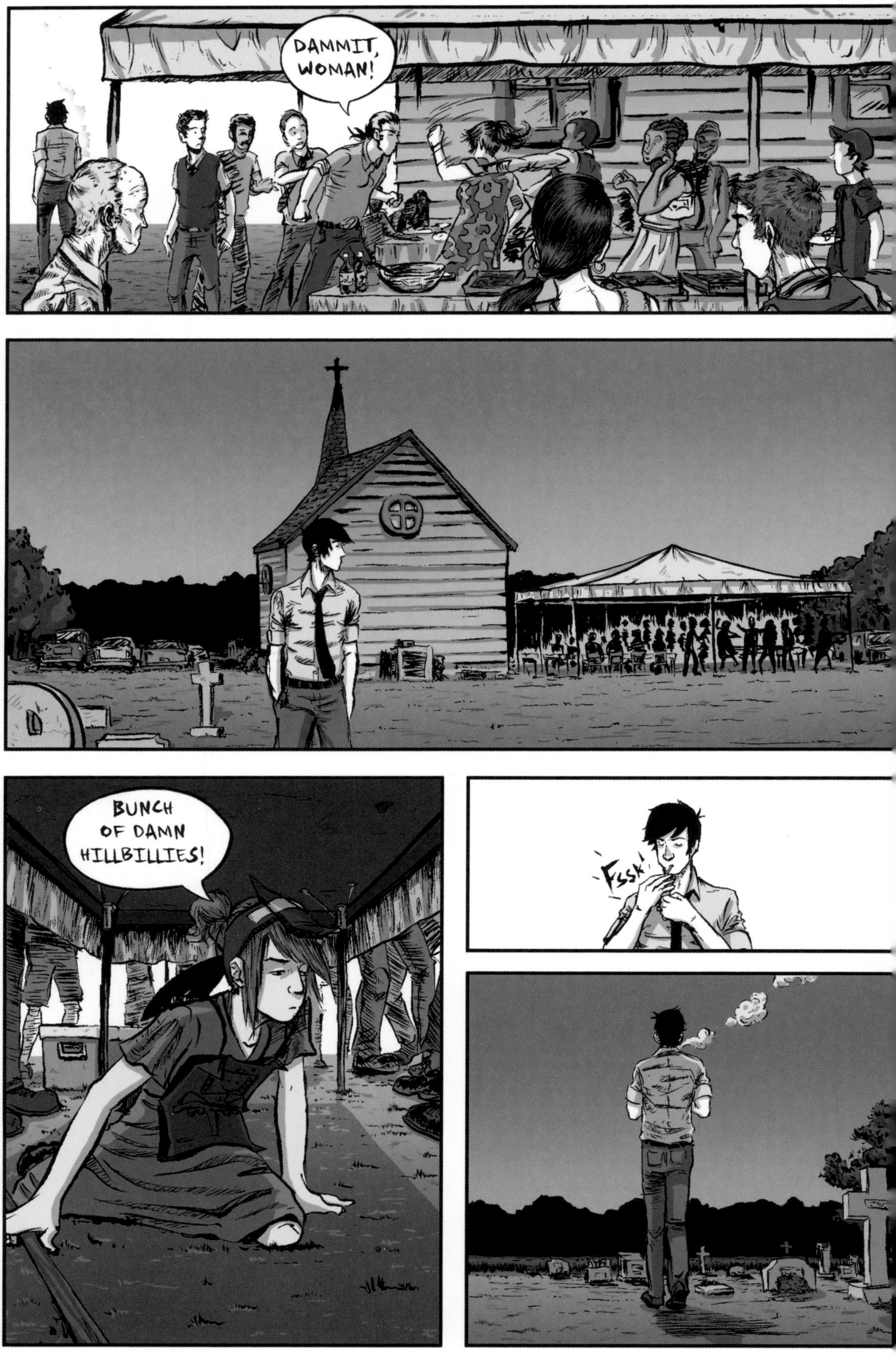
DAMMIT, WOMAN!
BUNCH OF DAMN HILLBILLIES!
FSSK

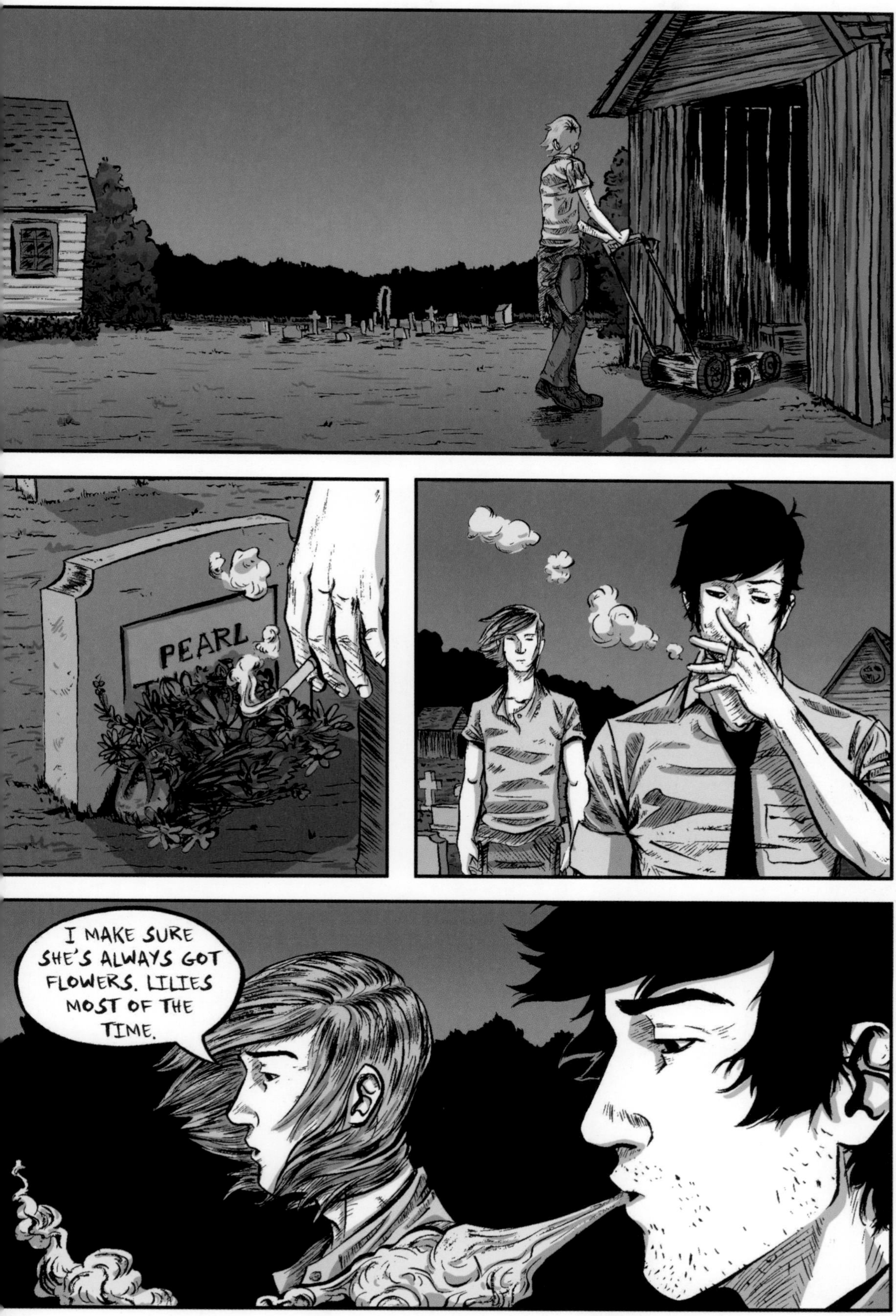
PEARL
I MAKE SURE SHE'S ALWAYS GOT FLOWERS. LILIES MOST OF THE TIME.

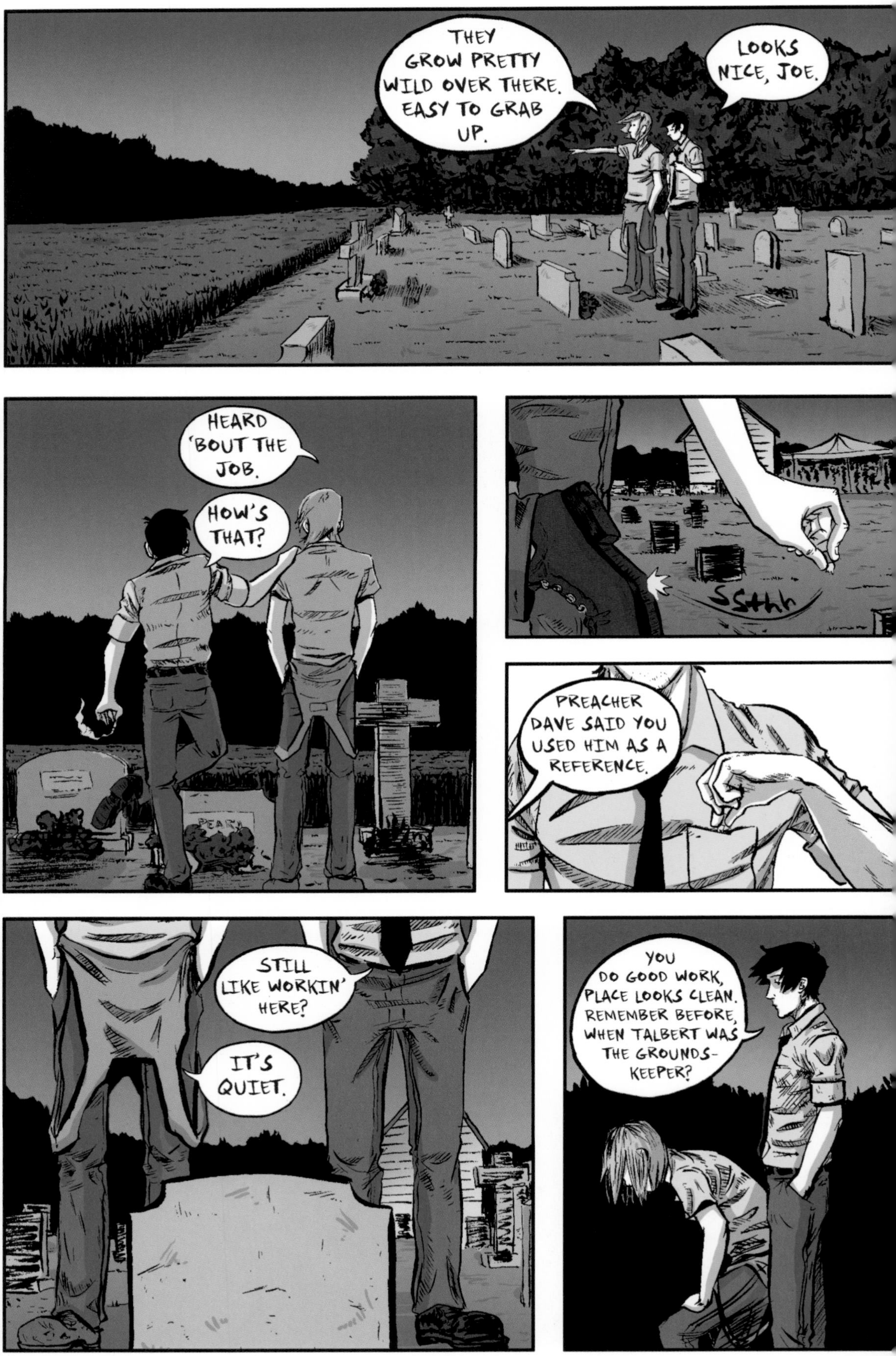
THEY GROW PRETTY WILD OVER THERE. EASY TO GRAB UP.
LOOKS NICE, JOE.
HEARD 'BOUT THE JOB.
HOW'S THAT?
SSthh
PREACHER DAVE SAID YOU USED HIM AS A REFERENCE.
STILL LIKE WORKIN' HERE?
IT'S QUIET.
YOU DO GOOD WORK, PLACE LOOKS CLEAN. REMEMBER BEFORE, WHEN TALBERT WAS THE GROUNDS-KEEPER?

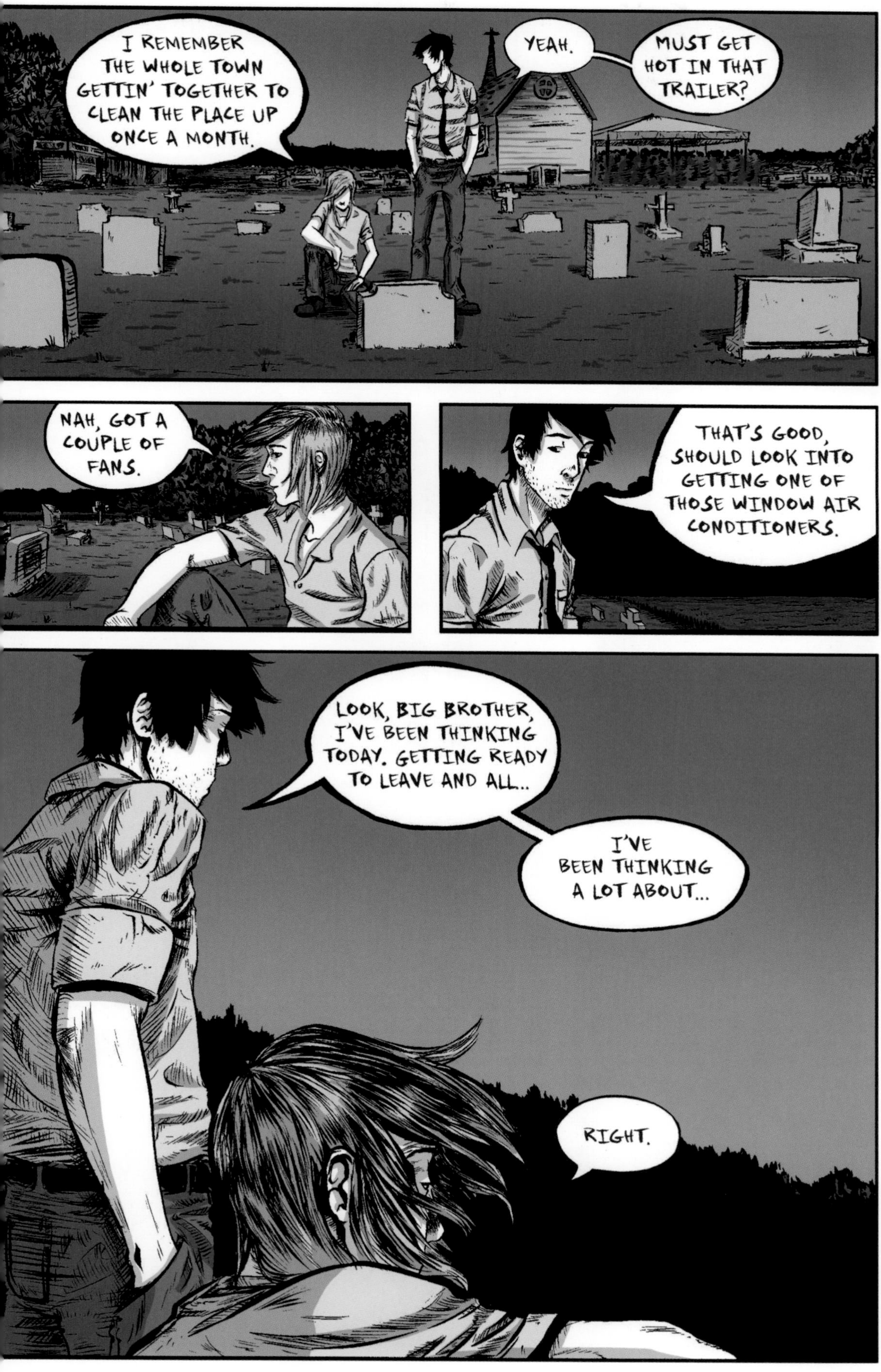
I REMEMBER THE WHOLE TOWN GETTIN' TOGETHER TO CLEAN THE PLACE UP ONCE A MONTH.
YEAH.
MUST GET HOT IN THAT TRAILER?
NAH, GOT A COUPLE OF FANS.
THAT'S GOOD, SHOULD LOOK INTO GETTING ONE OF THOSE WINDOW AIR CONDITIONERS.
LOOK, BIG BROTHER, I'VE BEEN THINKING TODAY. GETTING READY TO LEAVE AND ALL...
I'VE BEEN THINKING A LOT ABOUT...
RIGHT.

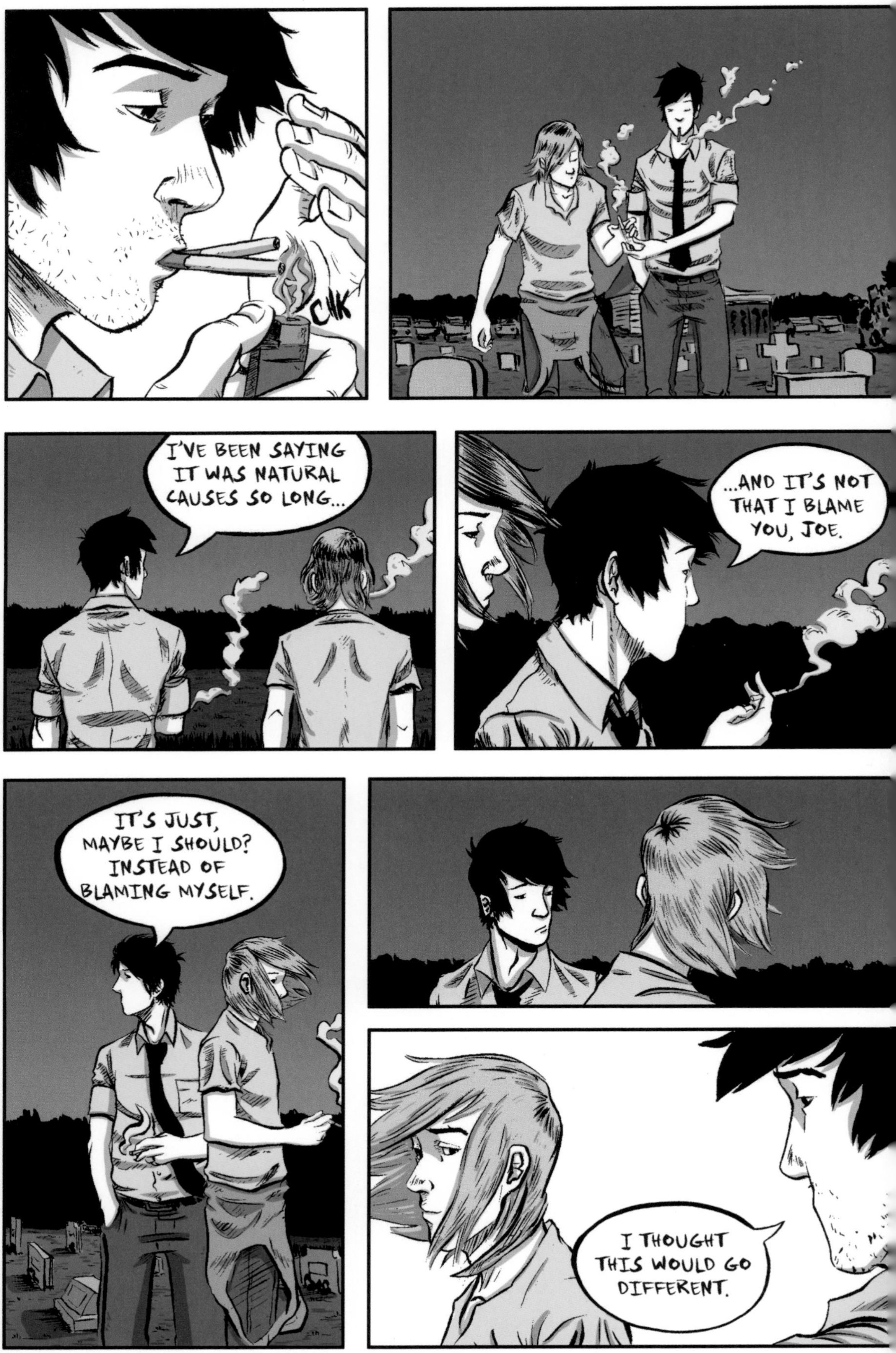
CHK
I'VE BEEN SAYING IT WAS NATURAL CAUSES SO LONG...
...AND IT'S NOT THAT I BLAME YOU, JOE.
IT'S JUST, MAYBE I SHOULD? INSTEAD OF BLAMING MYSELF.
I THOUGHT THIS WOULD GO DIFFERENT.

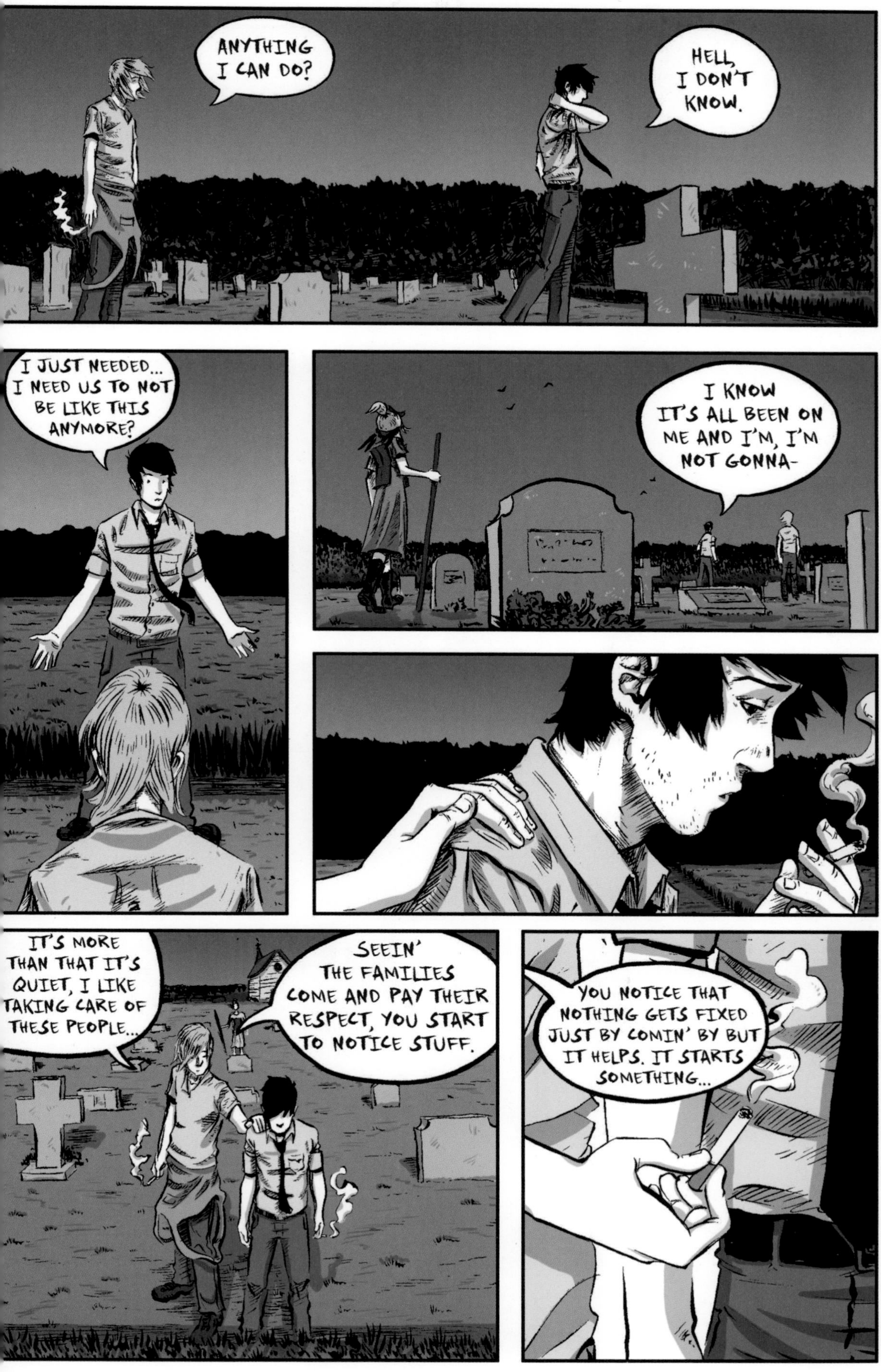
ANYTHING I CAN DO?
HELL, I DON'T KNOW.
I JUST NEEDED... I NEED US TO NOT BE LIKE THIS ANYMORE?
I KNOW IT'S ALL BEEN ON ME AND I'M, I'M NOT GONNA-
IT'S MORE THAN THAT IT'S QUIET, I LIKE TAKING CARE OF THESE PEOPLE...
SEEIN' THE FAMILIES COME AND PAY THEIR RESPECT, YOU START TO NOTICE STUFF.
YOU NOTICE THAT NOTHING GETS FIXED JUST BY COMIN' BY BUT IT HELPS. IT STARTS SOMETHING...

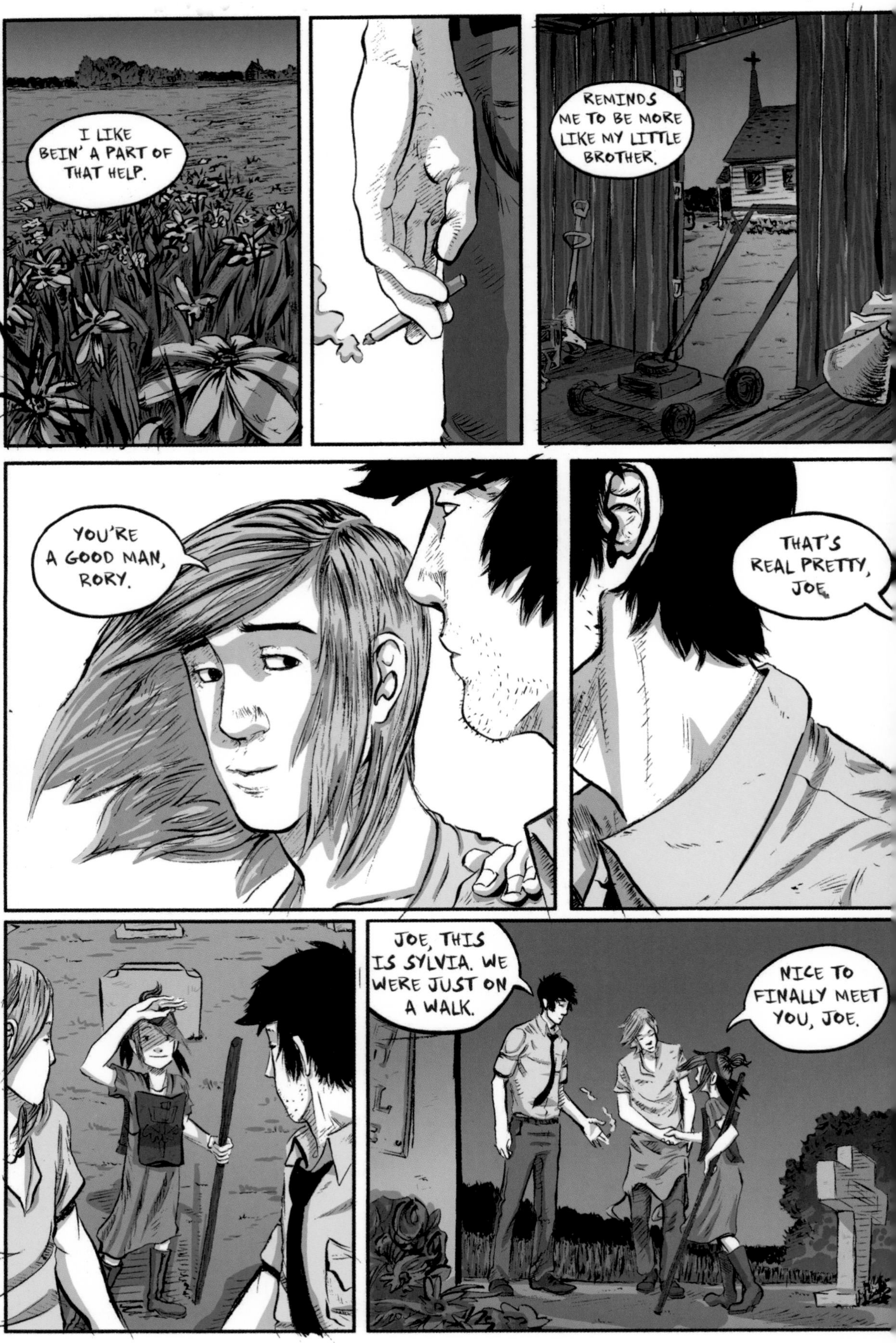
I LIKE BEIN' A PART OF THAT HELP.
REMINDS ME TO BE MORE LIKE MY LITTLE BROTHER.
YOU'RE A GOOD MAN, RORY.
THAT'S REAL PRETTY, JOE.
JOE, THIS IS SYLVIA. WE WERE JUST ON A WALK.
NICE TO FINALLY MEET YOU, JOE.

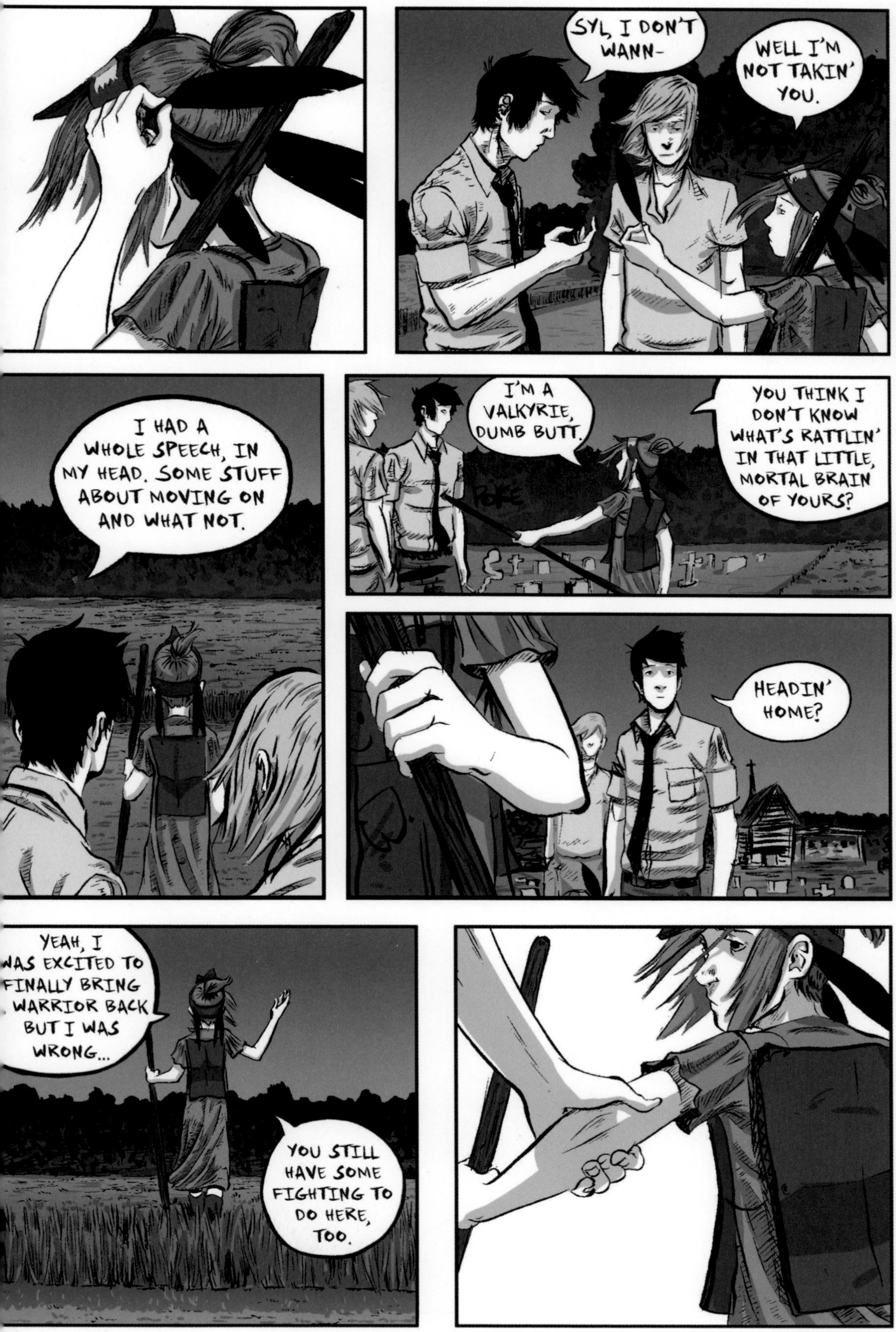

SYL, I DON'T WANN-
WELL I'M NOT TAKIN' YOU.
I HAD A WHOLE SPEECH, IN MY HEAD. SOME STUFF ABOUT MOVING ON AND WHAT NOT.
I'M A VALKYRIE, DUMB BUTT.
POKE
YOU THINK I DON'T KNOW WHAT'S RATTLIN' IN THAT LITTLE, MORTAL BRAIN OF YOURS?
HEADIN' HOME?
YEAH, I WAS EXCITED TO FINALLY BRING WARRIOR BACK BUT I WAS WRONG...
YOU STILL HAVE SOME FIGHTING TO DO HERE, TOO.

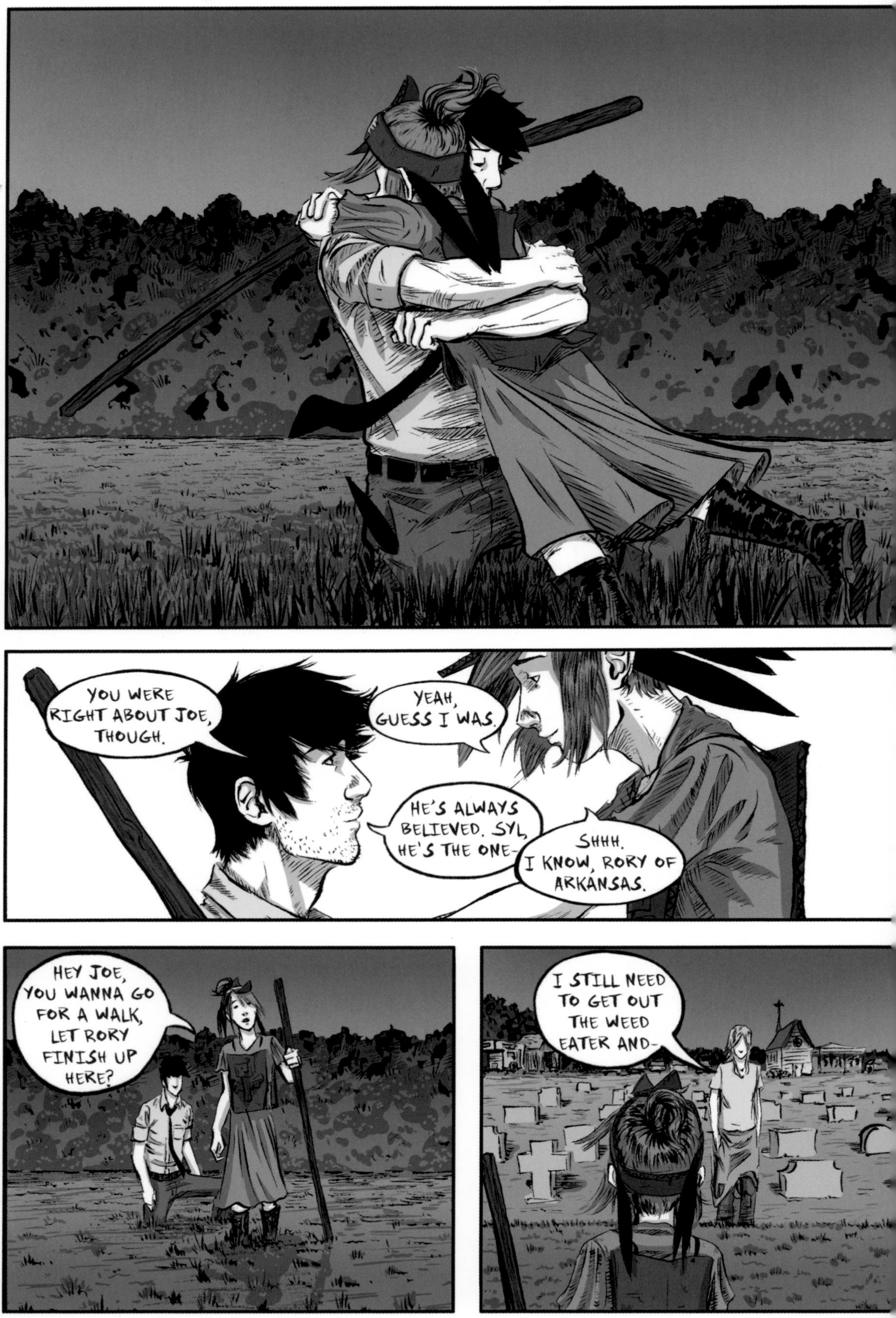

YOU WERE RIGHT ABOUT JOE, THOUGH.
YEAH, GUESS I WAS.
HE'S ALWAYS BELIEVED. SYL, HE'S THE ONE-
SHHH. I KNOW, RORY OF ARKANSAS.
HEY JOE, YOU WANNA GO FOR A WALK, LET RORY FINISH UP HERE?
I STILL NEED TO GET OUT THE WEED EATER AND-

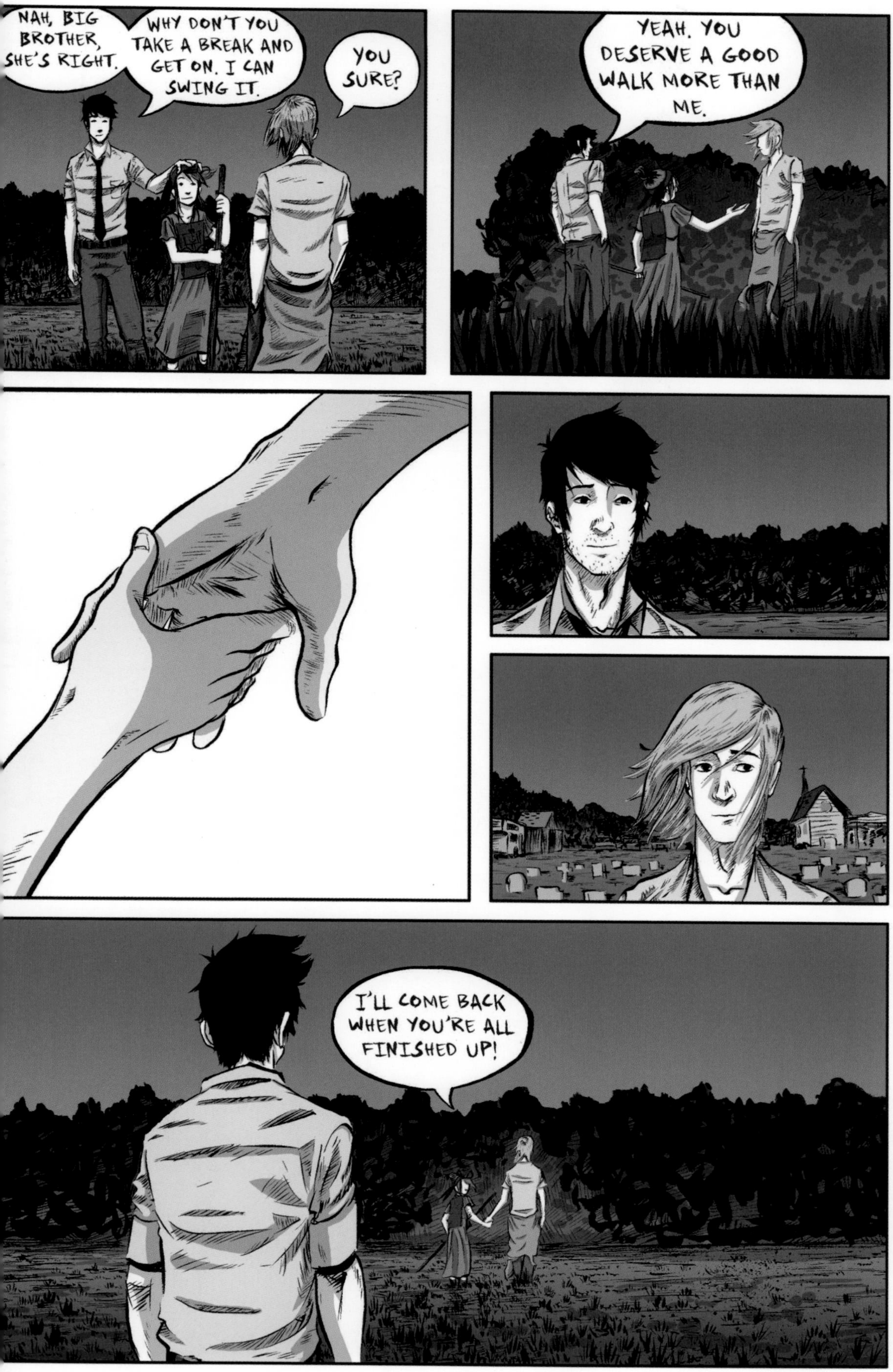
NAH, BIG BROTHER, SHE'S RIGHT.
WHY DON'T YOU TAKE A BREAK AND GET ON. I CAN SWING IT.
YOU SURE?
YEAH. YOU DESERVE A GOOD WALK MORE THAN ME.
I'LL COME BACK WHEN YOU'RE ALL FINISHED UP!

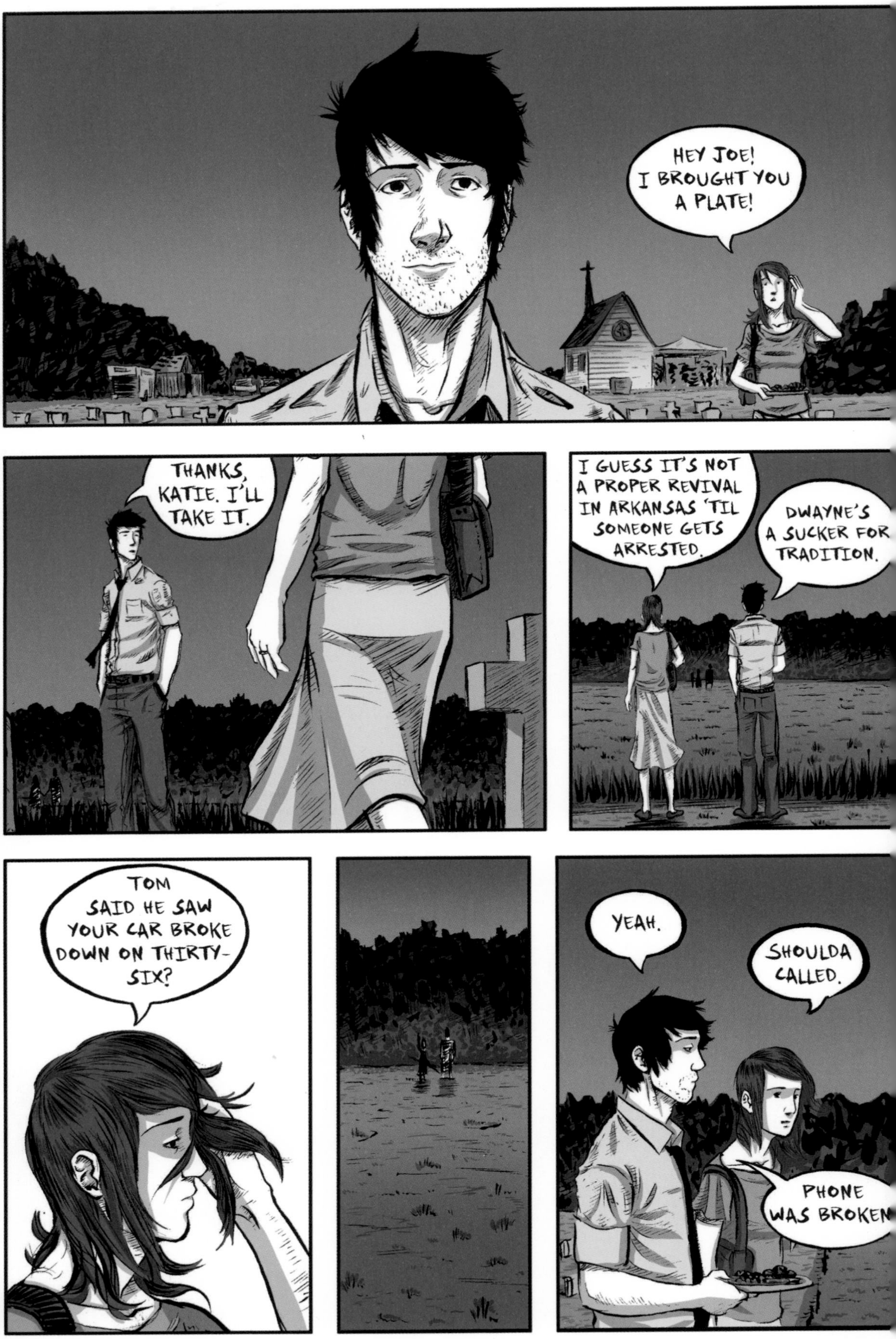
HEY JOE! I BROUGHT YOU A PLATE!
THANKS, KATIE. I'LL TAKE IT.
I GUESS IT'S NOT A PROPER REVIVAL IN ARKANSAS 'TIL SOMEONE GETS ARRESTED.
DWAYNE'S A SUCKER FOR TRADITION.
TOM SAID HE SAW YOUR CAR BROKE DOWN ON THIRTY-SIX?
YEAH.
SHOULDA CALLED.
PHONE WAS BROKEN

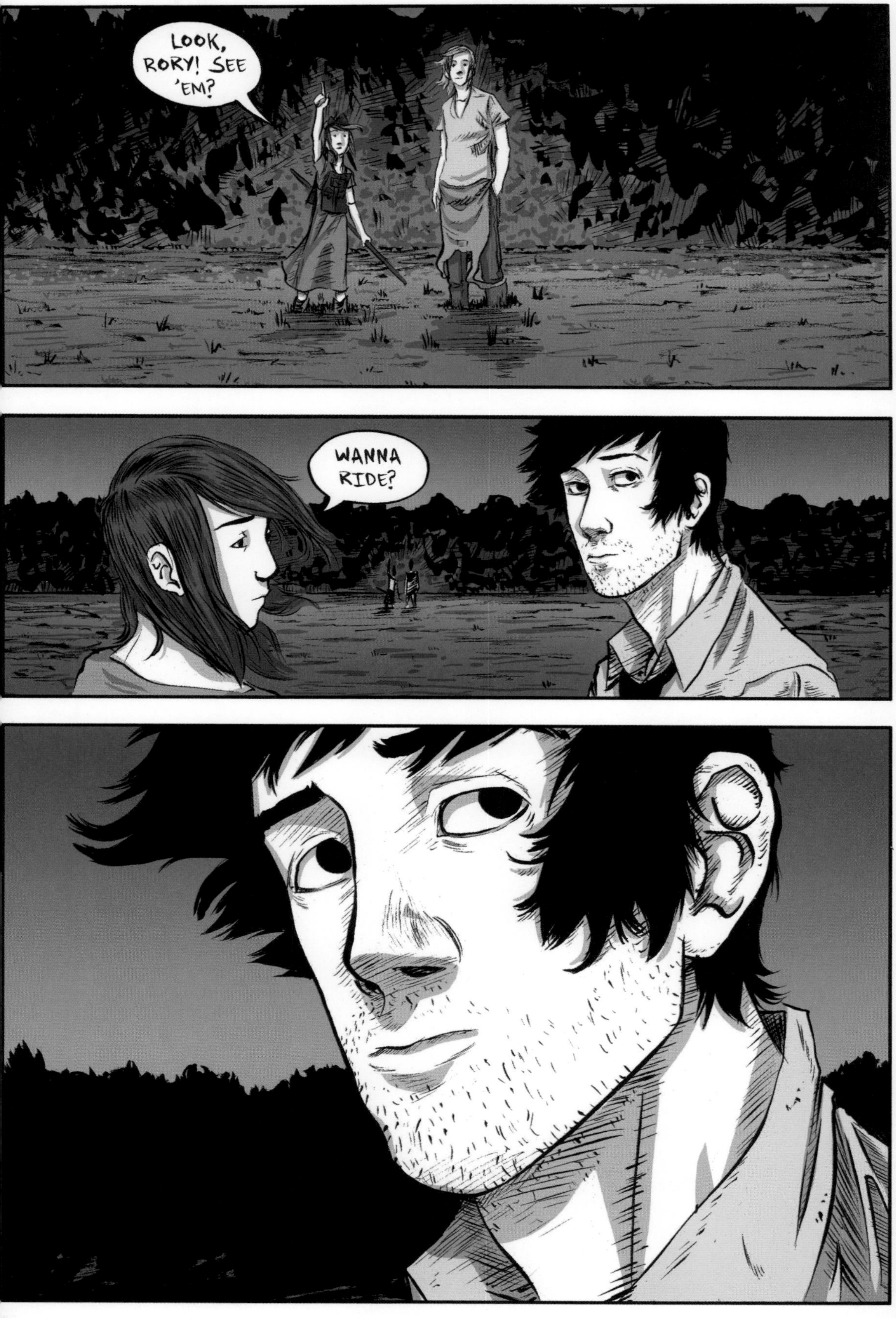
LOOK, RORY! SEE 'EM?
WANNA RIDE?

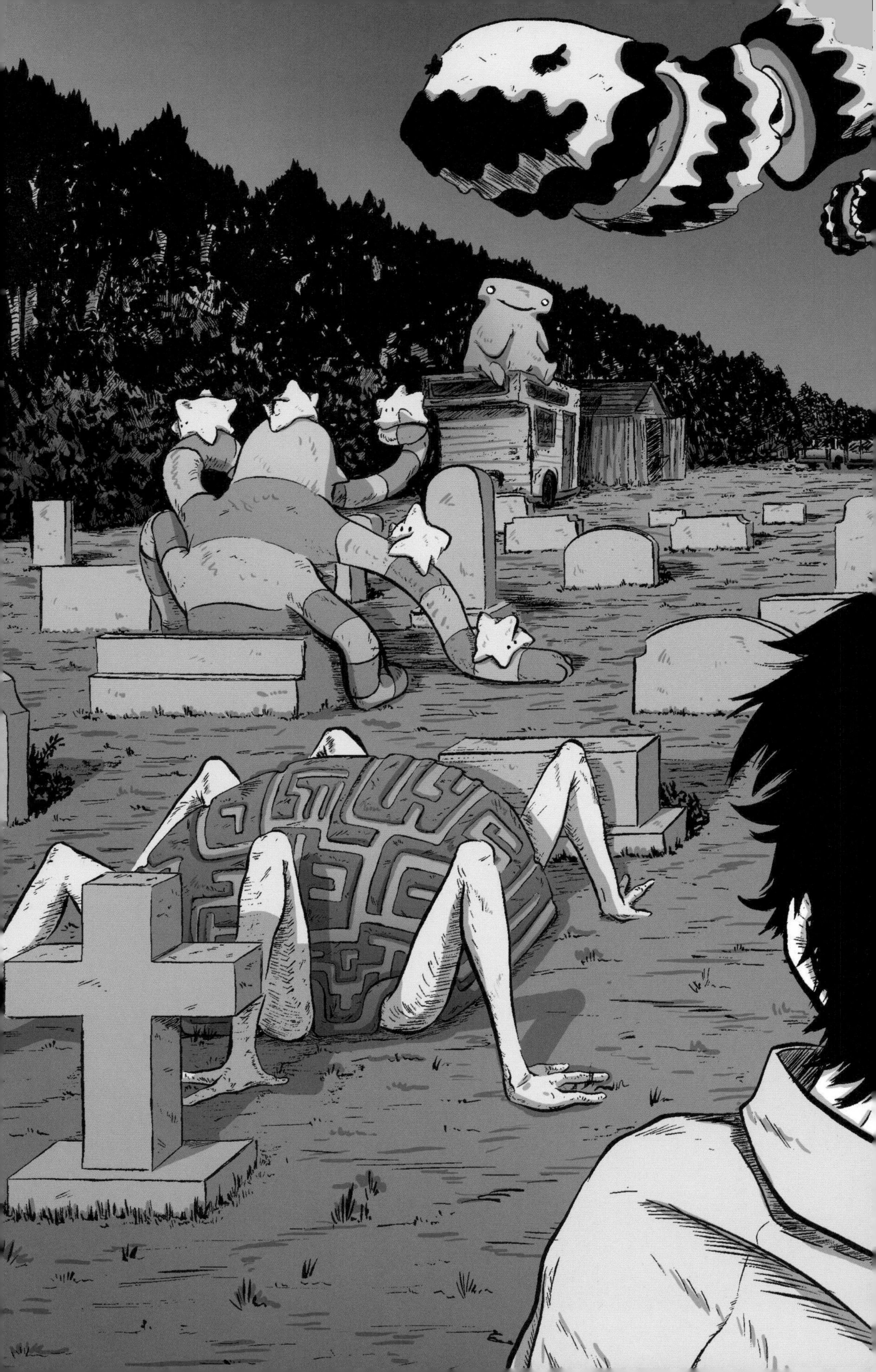

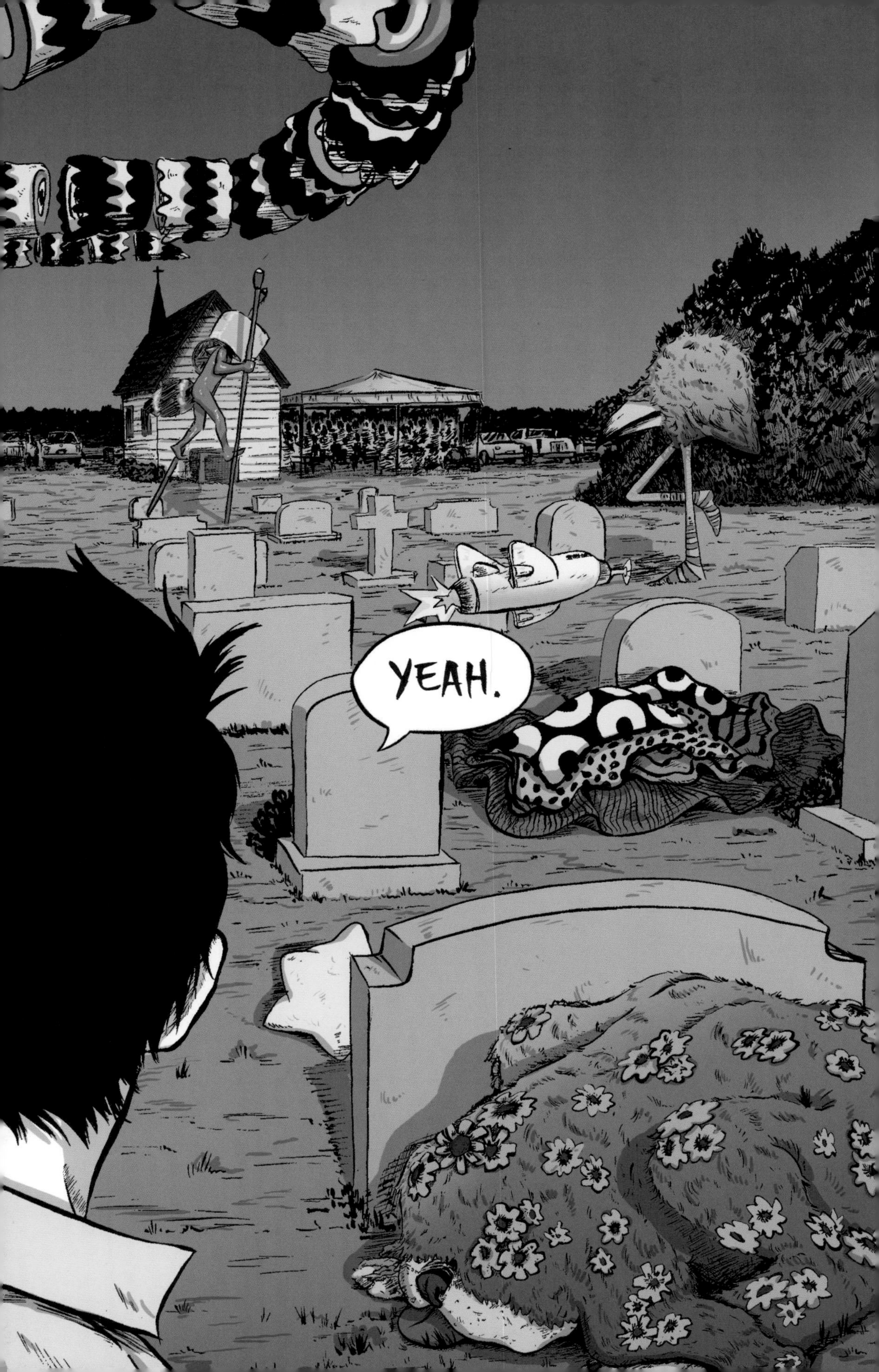
YEAH.

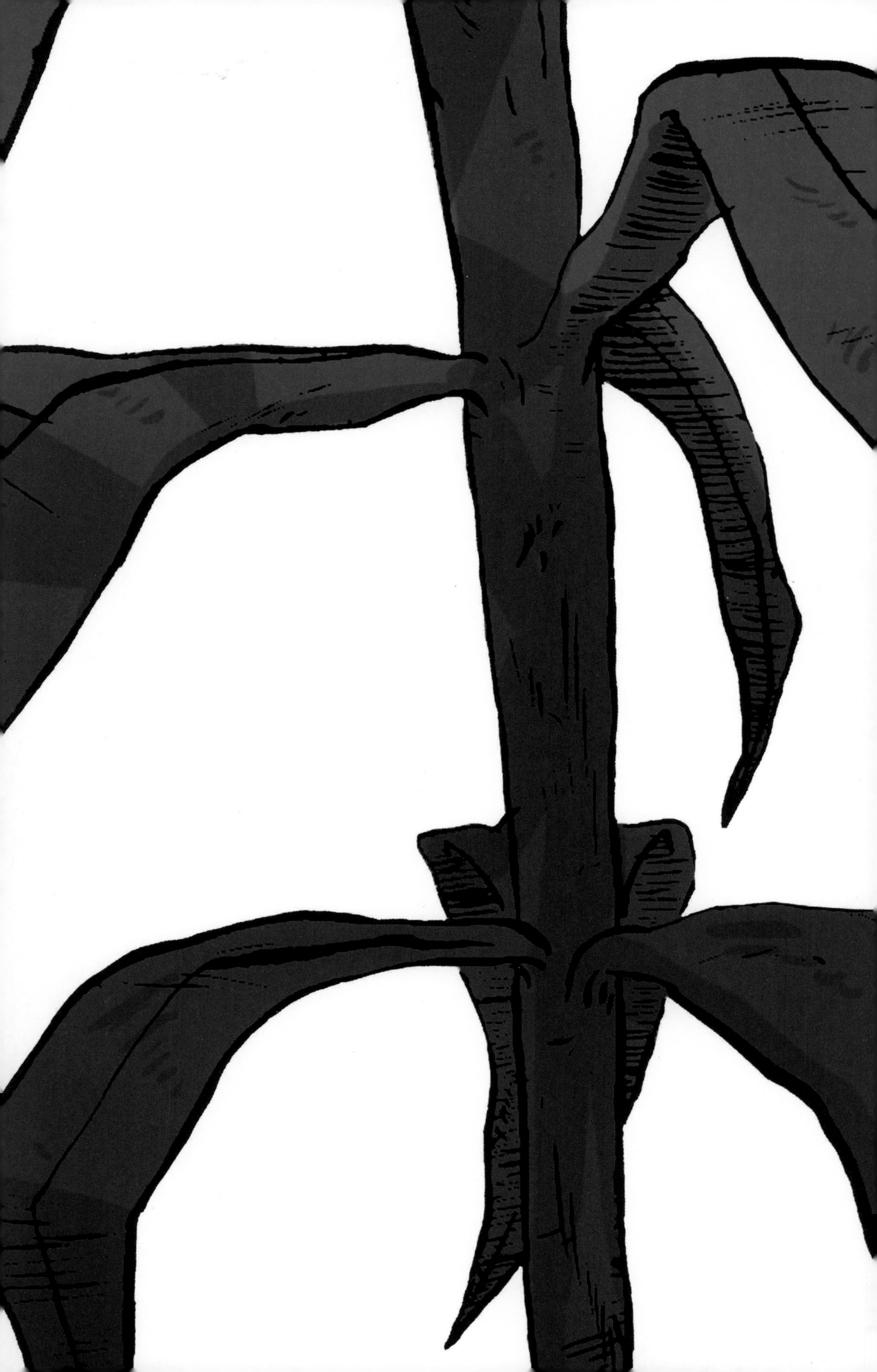

ABOUT THE AUTHORS

ADAM SMITH started self-publishing comix and zines in Arkansas while still in high school. He lives and writes in Kansas City, Missouri now. *Long Walk To Valhalla* with Matthew Fox is his first full length graphic novel.

MATTHEW FOX was born in Connecticut and raised in Jacksonville, Arkansas. After school he moved to Little Rock and started drawing local band flyers, album art, and shirt designs. He started self-publishing comics with Adam Smith in 2010. *Long Walk to Valhalla* is his first published comic.

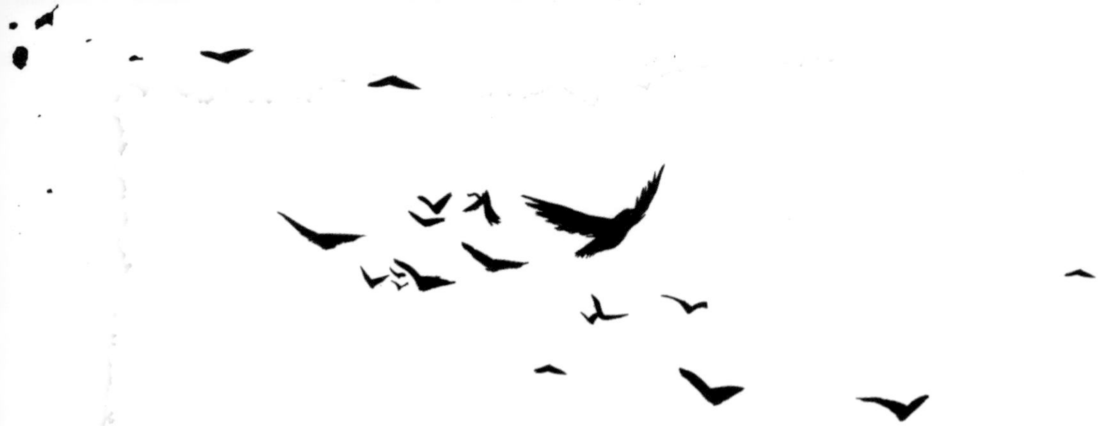

Art by
DUSTY HIGGINS

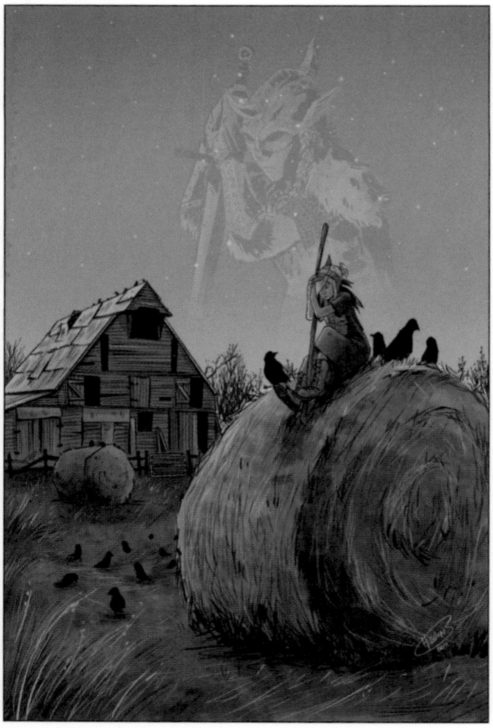

Art by
RACHEL WEISS

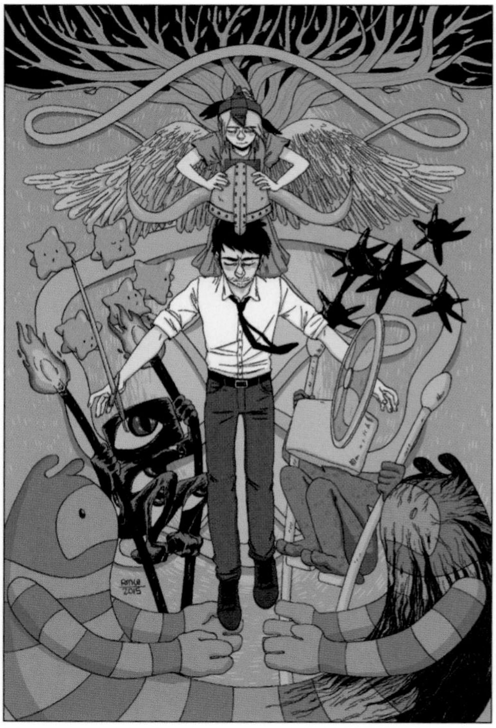

Art by

BUSTER MOODY

Art by

KELSEY WROTEN